JN437209

국제통상영어

International Trade English

유하상 저

불법복사는 지적재산을 훔치는 범죄행위입니다

저작권법 제97조의 5(권리의 침해죄)에 따라 위반자는 5년 이하의 징역 또는 5천만원 이하의 벌금에 처하거나 이를 병과할 수 있습니다.

머리말

국제무역은 서로 다른 언어를 사용하는 국가들 사이에 이루어지기 때문에 의사소통을 위한 공통의 언어가 필요하게 된다. 오늘날 국제무역에서는 대부분 영어를 사용하고 있어 국제통상 영어의 정확한 이해가 국제무역 수행에 필수적인 과제가 되고 있다. 국제통상 영어는 무역에 관한 전문용어가 사용되고 있으며, 국제무역의 오랜 역사를 통해서 관용적으로 사용되어온 문구도 포함하고 있다.

무역서신은 무역 분쟁이 발생할 때 법률적 책임을 판단하는 근거서류가 되기 때문에 잘못 작성될 경우 불리한 입장에 처하게 될 수도 있다. 따라서 무역실무에 관한 지식이 없이 단순한 영어실력으로만 무역서신을 작성할 경우 무역거래에 있어 오해와 분쟁의 여지를 제공하게 될 위험이 있다.

본 교재는 영어실력 또는 무역실무지식이 부족하더라도 쉽게 국제통상 영어를 접할 수 있도록 저술되었다.

첫째, 본 교재에 사용된 예문은 되도록 쉬운 문장을 엄선하여 수록하였다. 무역서신에서는 과도하게 어려운 단어나 문장을 구사함으로써 오히려 당사자 사이에 오해와 분쟁의 여지를 남기기보다는 전달하고자 하는 메시지를 정확하게 표현하는 것이 더 중요하기 때문이다.

둘째, 무역거래의 절차에 따라 편집함으로써 실무에 도움이 되도록 하였으며, 각각의 절차를 이해하는데 필요한 무역실무에 관한 해설을 추가하였다.

셋째, 본 교재에서 사용된 모든 예문 아래에 해당 예문을 이해하는데 필요한 단어 및 주요 구문에 대한 해석을 부기함으로써 일일이 영어사전을 찾는 불편을 최소화하였다.

넷째, 무역서신에서 자주 사용되고 있는 관용구 등을 여러 예문에서 반복하여 인용함으로써 자동적으로 습득되도록 하였다.

다섯째, 단원이 끝날 때마다 간단한 영작문을 익히도록 하여 실제 무역통신문 작성에 도움이 되게 하였다.

본 교재의 예문과 해설 중 상당수는 여러 선배 및 동료 교수들의 저서와 자료를 인용하여 사용하였다. 일일이 주석을 두는 것이 마땅하지만, 작업의 번거로움을 피하고자 부득이 본서의 끝에 참고문헌을 제시하는 것으로 대신하였다. 이점 양해 있기를 바란다. 또한, 매번 본 저자의 졸고를 기꺼이 출판해주신 도서출판 두남의 전두표 사장님, 그리고 출판 때마다 협조를 아끼지 않으신 이 승구 상무님과 본서를 깔끔하게 편집하여 주신 황 자애 씨에게 감사의 말씀을 드린다.

끝으로 저자가 맹하지절의 무더위를 무릅쓰고 본서를 간단없이 집필할 수 있었던 것은 의지할 사람 하나 없는 고립무원 이국땅에서 혈혈단신으로 자신의 인생을 개척해 나가면서도 아빠에게 힘찬 박수를 보내준 사랑하는 나의 딸 혜련이의 격려에 힘입은 바도 크다. 결혼을 축하하며, 엘칸과 함께하게 될 너희의 앞날이 늘 행복하길 바라는 아빠의 마음을 여기에 적어 남겨 둔다.

2013년 8월

저자 씀

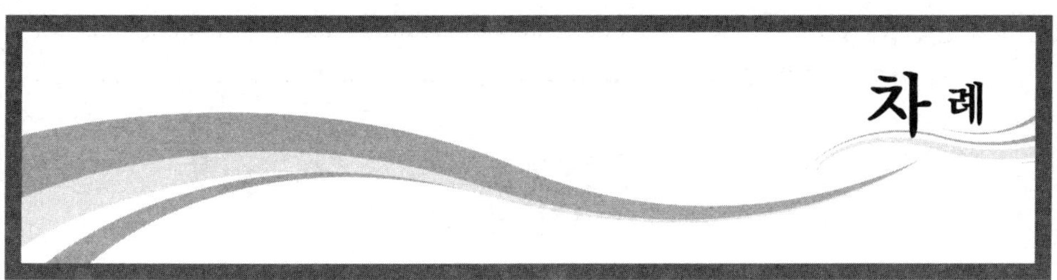

제1장 국제통상 영어의 기초

제2장 거래관계의 개설

제3장 조 회

제4장 청약과 승낙

제5장 주문과 수락

제6장 대리점

제7장 무역계약의 체결

제8장 대금결제와 신용장

제9장 해상적하 보험

제10장 선적과 결제서류

제11장 환어음 및 대금회수

제12장 무역클레임

제1장

국제통상 영어의 기초

I 국제통상영어의 구성

1 국제통상영어의 의의

국제통상영어란 국제무역 거래에 필요한 의사를 전달하기 위한 수단으로 사용되는 영어를 말하며, 무역영어라고도 한다. Business english for international trade, Trade english, Business english, 또는 Commercial english로 표현되고 있다. 무역영어는 일상적으로 사용되는 영어에 무역거래에서 사용되는 전문용어(technical terms)와 상업적 표현(commercial expression) 그리고 관습적으로 사용되어온 표현들이 추가된 영어라는 점에서 차이가 있다.

따라서 국제무역 실무자들은 ① 무역에서 사용되는 전문적 및 관용적 용어에 대한 개념을 이해하기 위한 국제통상 관련 전문적인 지식, ② 교역상대국의 상관습과 법령 및 국제규범에 대한 전문적인 지식, ③ 국제통상 실무에서 이용되는 각종 서식에 관한 지식 등을 갖추어야 한다.

국제통상 통신문에는 무역거래에서 사용되는 상업통신문이나 서신은 물론이고 운송계약, 보험계약, 대리점계약, 특허나 기술제휴 계약, 합작투자 계약 등 무역거래와 관련된 계약서, 각종 무역서류 및 광고물 그리고 통상과 관련된 여러 국제규범이 포함된다.

2 국제통상 통신문의 구성요소

국제통상 통신문은 반드시 기재하여야 할 기본요소 (basic parts)와 필요에 따라 기재하는 보조요소(supplementary parts)로 구성된다.

기본요소(basic parts)

① 서두(letterhead)

② 발신 일자(date)

③ 내부 수신인 주소(inside address)

④ 서두 인사(salutation)

⑤ 본문(body of the letter)

⑥ 결미 인사(complimentary close)

⑦ 서명(signature)

보조요소(supplementary parts)

⑧ 참조인 표시(attention line, particular address, special address)

⑨ 참조 번호(reference number, file number)

⑩ 제목(letter subject)

⑪ 관련자 약호(identification marks, initial, direction initials)

⑫ 우편물 종별표시(mailing direction)

⑬ 동봉물 표시(enclosure notation, enclosure)

⑭ 사본 배부처(carbon copy notation)

⑮ 추신(postscript)

⑯ 추가면(additional sheet, continuation sheet)

[예시] The Parts of a Business Letter

① Letterhead

② Date

③ Inside Address

⑨ Reference Number

⑧ Attention Line

④ Salutation

⑩ Subject

⑤ Body of the Letter

⑥ Complimentary Close

⑦ Signature

⑪ Identification Marks

⑫ Mailing Direction

⑬ Enclosure Notation

⑭ Carbon Copy Notation

⑮ Postscript

⑯ Additional Sheet(P.T.O)

[예시] Business Letter 의 작성사례

① UNITED EXPORTERS COMPANY

IMPORTERS & EXPORTERS

IMPORTERS & EXPORTERS
550 MARKET STREET SANFRANCISCO IICALF. U.S.A
C.P.O. BOX 4958

CABLE ADD : "KOREASA SEOUL"
TELEPHONE : 063-850-6278
TELEX NO. : KISMCL 387508

② March 15, 20XX

⑨ Your Ref. 5X20-3

③ Messrs. HS Mulsan Co., Ltd,
Sinrongdong Iksan, Korea

⑧ Attention : Trade Promotion Department

④ Gentleman,

⑩ Iron Steel Products

⑤ Your name and address have been given us by the Chamber of Commerce of your city as large importers of Iron & Steel Products, and we are writing you with a keen desire of opening an account with you.

We are long-established, leading manufacturers and exporters of the above products with ....

⑥ Sincerely yours,

⑦ UNITED EXPORTS COMPANY
hASNAG yOU
H. S. YOU
PRESIDENT

⑪ CNC/YK
⑫ Registered Mail
⑬ Encl. Price List 2 copies
⑭ C.C. The Empire Trading Company in New York
⑮ P.S. 10% discount can be made for a large order

⑯ 1/2(to be continued)

(1) 기본요소(Basic parts)

① Letterhead (서두)

대부분의 경우 회사의 전용서신용지(stationary of letter sheet)의 상단에 인쇄되어 있다. 회사명(firm name), 지점망(branch network), 주소(address), 우편사서함(C.P.O. box), 전신약호(cable address), 텔렉스 번호(telex number), 팩시밀리 번호(fax number), 전화번호(telephone number), 인터넷 및 전자우편 주소(IP address, e-mail address), 취급영업 종목(line of business), 상표(trade mark), 회사 창설 연도 등이 기재된다.

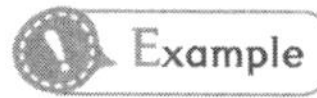

Wonkwang Trading & CO., LTD.

MAIL : CPO. BOX 45
CABLE : WILCO
http//www.wilco.com

GENERAL EXPORTER & IMPORTER
460 Iksan Bivd.,
Sinrong-dong Iksan, 570-749, Korea

TEL : 850-6278
FAX : 850-7303

② Date (발신 일자)

서신을 발행한 일자를 말하며, 기재방법에는 미국식과 영국식이 있다. 미국식(American style)은 월, 일, 년의 순서로 배열하며 일자(day)는 기수(cardinal number)로 표기한다. 영국식(British style)은 일, 월, 년의 순서로 배열하되 일자는 1st, 2nd, 3rd, 4th와 같이 서수(ordinal number)로 기재한다.

그리고 서신 본문에서 일자가 월보다 앞에 표기될 때는 "on the 21st of March"와 같이 서수로 표기한다. 국제표준화기구(ISO)는 컴퓨터에서 사용하기 편리하도록 20XX-03-15 또는 20XX0315 등으로 기재할 것을 권유하고 있다.

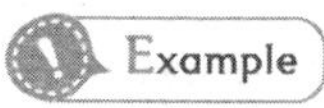

- 미국식 : January 10, 20XX　　October 13, 20XX
- 영국식 : 1st April, 20XX　　18th September, 20XX

다만 4.8.20XX 또는 4/18/20XX와 같이 표기한다든지, 월을 Apr., Mar.와 같이 약어로 표시하거나 생략해서는 안 되며, 연도를 줄여서 April 18, '14와 같이 표현하는 것은 피하는 것이 좋다.

③ Inside address(내부 수신인 성명 및 주소)

Inside Address는 경칭, 성명, 직책, 회사명, 주소 등으로 구성된다. 겉봉투에 기재된 주소가 훼손되거나 서신과 봉투가 엇갈렸을 때 쉽게 구별할 수 있도록 해주며 또한, 주소란이 투명창으로 되어 있는 봉투(window envelope)를 이용할 때는 Inside address가 투명창을 통해 보이도록 서신을 접어서 사용함으로써 겉봉투의 주소로 이용하기도 한다.

[수신인 주소에 사용되는 약어]

Ass.	Association	협회(協會)	Pl.	Place, Plaza	광장
Ave.	Avenue	가(街)	P.O. Box	Post Office Box	우체국사서함
Bivd.	Boulevard	대로(大路)	Prov.	Province	도, 주, 성
Bldg.	Building	건물	Rd.	Road	로(路)
c/o	(in) care of	~댁	Sect.	Section	과, 부
Dept.	Department	부(部)	Sq.	Square	광장
Div.	Division	사업부(국)	St.	Street	가(街)
Dr,	Drive	자동차로	Ter.	Terrace	대지로
Hwy.	Highway	고속도로	Ter.	Territory	속령, 영토
Mfg.	Manufacturing	제조	Co.	Company	회사
Pty.	Proprietary	개인회사	Inc.	Incorporated	주식회사(미)
Corp.	Corporation	법인회사	Ltd.	Limited	주식회사(영)

Inside Address는 첫째 줄에 수신인의 성명과 직책, 둘째 줄에는 회사명, 셋째 줄에는 주소, 넷째 줄에는 도시명, 주명, Zip code, 국명을 기재한다. 그러나 국명은 줄을 바꾸어 마지막 줄에 둘 수도 있으며 첫째 줄의 직책을 둘째 줄에 배열할 수도 있다.

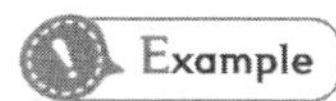

Mr. Author O. Brown, President
Wallace Motor Corporation
300 West 43D Street
New York, N.Y. 10036
U.S.A.

직책명이 너무 길 때는 두 줄로 하여 사선으로 배열하여 표기할 수도 있다.

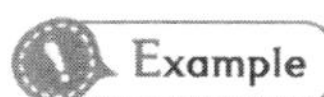

Mr. John P. Hemphill, Jr.
Vice President and Director
of Research and Development

수신자명에는 적절한 존칭을 같이 사용하는 것이 예의이다. 존칭은 수신인의 성별(sex), 학위(degree), 직위(status), 직업(profession) 등에 따라 적절히 사용하여야 한다.

개인에 대한 존칭으로 남자 단수일 때는 "Mr.(Mister)", 복수일 때는 "Messrs (Messieurs)"로 표기한다. 미혼인 여자 단수일 때는 "Miss", 복수일 때는 "Messrs"로 표기하며, 기혼 여자, 미망인 단수일 때는 "Mrs.(Mistress)", 복수일 때는 "Mmes. (Mesdames)"로 표기한다.

④ Salutation(서두 인사)

Salutation은 본문을 시작하기 전에 쓰는 간단한 인사말로 영어의 "How do you do?", "How are you?"나 우리말의 "근계(謹啓)"[1]에 해당하는 말이다. Inside address의 아래에 배열한다.

수신인이 단수이면 Salutation도 단수로 일치시켜야 한다. 다만 "Gentlemen :" 을 사용할 경우에는 복수형으로만 사용하여야 한다. 서두 인사의 구두점은 영국식은 comma(,), 미국식은 colon(:)이 많이 사용된다.

---

1) 근계란 '삼가 아뢰니다.'라는 뜻으로 편지의 서두에 '근계 시하 성하지절에...'의 형태로 사용된다.

[무역회사에서 사용되는 주요 직책명]

구분	직책	영문
회 장		Chairman of the Board, Chairman of the Directors
이사장		Chief Director, Director General
사 장		President, Director of President
부사장		Vice President, Deputy President, Executive Deputy President
이 사	대표이사	Representative Director (Executive, Senior) Managing
	전무이사	Director, Senior Executive Director
	상무이사	Standing (Executive, Managing) Director, Managing Director
	상임이사	Standing Director
	이 사	Director
(상임)감사		(Standing) Auditor, Comptroller
부 장	본 부 장	General Manager
	수출부장	Export Manager
	수입부장	Import Manager
	경리(회계)부장	Finance (Accounting) Manager
	총무부장	Administration (General Affairs) Manager
	인사(노무)부장	Personal (Labor) Manager
	생산부장	Production Manager
	구매부장	Purchasing Manager
	영업(판매)부장	Sales Manager, Business Manager
장	공 장 장	Factory (Plant) Manager
	기 능 장	Chief Engineer
	지 점 장	Branch (office) Manager
	부 장	Manager of the Division (department)
	차 장	Assistant Manager, Sub-Manager
	과 장	Section Chief, Section Manager
대 리	부장대리	Acting Division Manager
	대 리	Pro. Manager, Deputy (Acting) Manager
	계장, 주임	Chief, Chief Clerk, Supervisor

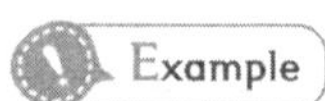

- 미국식 : Gentlemen :
  Mesdames :
  Dear Mr. Mitchell :
- 영국식 : Dear Sirs,
  Gentlemen,
  Dear Mesdames,
  Dear Mr. Mitchell,

[서두 인사에 사용되는 주요 표현]

구 분		미국식	영국식
회 사		Gentlemen :	Dear Sirs,
이름을 모르는	남자	Dear Sir :	Dear Sir,
	여자	Dear Madam :	Dear Madam,
이름/성별을 모르는 사람		Dear Sir or Madam :	Dear Sir or Madam,
아는	남 자	Dear Mr. Kim :	Dear Mr. Kim,
	기혼 여자	Dear Mrs. Kim :	Dear Mrs. Kim,
	미혼 여자	Dear Miss Kim :	Dear Miss Kim,
결혼 여부를 모르는 여성		Dear Ms. Kim :	Dear Mrs. Kim,
아는	부 부	Dear Mr. and Mrs. Kim :	Dear Mr. and Mrs. Kim,
	미혼남녀	Dear Mr. and Miss Kim :	Dear Mr. and Miss Kim,
친구 또는 친지		Dear Yongsu :	Dear Yongsu,

⑤ Body of the letter(본문)

서두 인사 아래에 배치한다. 서신은 가능한 한 한 장으로 작성하는 것이 좋지만, 내용이 길 때는 여러 장으로 작성되어도 무방하다. 본문은 대체로 다음과 같이 구성된다.

- Opening : 서한문을 작성하는 이유
- Purpose : 서한문의 구체적인 내용
- Action : 어떤 상황에 대한 조치, 행동 또는 결과 설명
- Polite Expression : 감사의 표현

⑥ Complimentary close(결미 인사)

Closing이라고도 하며 무역통신문을 끝맺음하는 인사로 우리말의 "여불비례(餘不備禮)"[2)]에 해당한다. 본문의 아래에 배치하며, 첫 자는 대문자로 하고 끝에는 Comma를 붙인다. 결미 인사에는 아래와 같은 것들이 있으며, 최근에는 서신, Fax, e-mal 등에서 "Best Regards"가 사용되기도 한다.

---

2) 여불비례(餘不備禮)란 편지를 마치면서 쓰는 관용적인 표현으로 '이하에서는 예를 갖추지 못하였으니 이해해 주십시오.'라는 뜻이다.

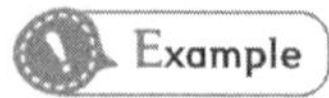

• 미국식

Yours truly,
Truly yours,
Yours very truly,
Very truly yours,

• 영국식

Yours faithfully,
Faithfully yours,
Yours very faithfully,
Very faithfully yours,

⑦ Signature

Signature는 서신에 신뢰성을 부여하고 효력을 발생시키는 중요한 요소이므로 서명자가 친필로 서명하는 것이 좋다. Signature는 Complimentary Close 한 줄 아래에 배치하되 회사명, 서명자의 서명, 성명 및 직책 등을 3~4행으로 구성한다.

Signature에서는 다음과 같은 사항을 유의하여야 한다.

첫째, 서명의 글씨체는 항상 일정하여야 한다.

둘째, 다른 사람이 판독하기 쉬워야 한다.

셋째, 다른 사람이 위조할 수 없어야 한다.

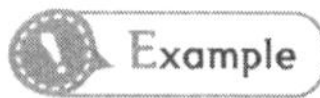

Hudson Publications, Inc.
Paul Thomas(Signed)
Paul Thomas(Typed)
President

만약에 위임장(power of attorney) 등에 의해서 법률적으로 대리 서명권한을 위임받은 사람이 서명권자를 대리하여 서명하는 때에는 회사명 앞에 라틴어인 "Per Procuration"(~의 대리로)의 약자인 "p.p."나 "p. pro." 또는 "per pro."를 붙이고 서명하여야 한다.

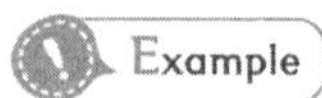

p.p. Hudson Publications, Inc.
Diana Green(Signed)
Diana Green, Manager(Typed)

서명권자 또는 대리 서명권자가 서명할 수 없어 서명권한이 없는 사람이 대신 서명을 하게 될 때는 회사명 앞에 "by", "per", "for" 등을 붙이고 직책은 명시하지 않는 것이 좋다.

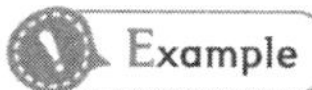

by Hudson Publications, Inc.
Claire Odom
Claire Odom

(2) 보조요소 (supplementary parts)

보조요소는 서신의 작성자가 필요에 따라 가감할 수 있다. 보조요소에는 다음과 같은 것들이 있다.

⑧ Attention line(참조인)

서신을 받는 회사 내의 특정부서나 특정인 앞으로 발송하기 위해 기재하며, 특정수신인(Particular address)이라고도 한다. "Attention" : 또는 "Attention of ..." 등으로 표기하며, "Att.", 또는 "Attn.", "ATTN.",과 같이 약어로 표시하기도 한다.

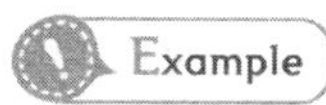

- Attention : Mr. Michael Smith

⑨ Reference number(참조번호)

문서의 보관이나 후일 업무의 편의를 위해 Date 또는 Inside Address 사이에 문서번호를 붙이는 것을 말한다. 서두 아래에 "Your Ref. No."(귀사의 참조번호), "File No.", "In replying", "Please refer to No.", 또는 "Our Ref. No."(당사의 참조번호)와 같이 표기한다.

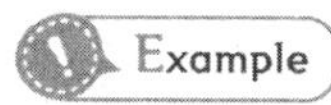

- Your Ref. No. 159
- Our Ref. No. 206

⑩ Letter subject(서신의 제목)

수신자가 서신내용을 읽기 전에 그 서신의 내용을 쉽게 파악할 수 있도록 서신의 내용을 요약하여 표시한다. 제목 앞에 "Re : " 또는 "Subject : "를 붙이기도 한다.

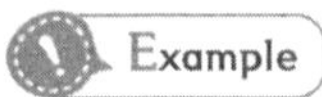

- Subject : Order No. 132
- Re : Shipping Advice

⑪ Identification Marks(발신 관계자 식별부호)

Initials 또는 Direction initials라고도 하며 서신작성과 관련하여 그 책임소재를 분명히 하기 위하여 서신의 작성자, 서명자와 타자수의 머리글자(initial)를 따서 기재하는 것이다. 동일한 이름을 가진 타자수가 한 회사 내에 여러 명인 경우 일련번호를 기재하기도 한다. 이는 보통 Signature의 2행 아래 왼쪽에 배치한다.

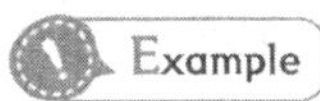

- KDJ : sj
- KJP/sa
- PTJ : 3

⑫ Mailing direction(우편종별 표시)

서신 작성자가 발송 담당자에게 우편 발송 방법을 지시하기 위한 것으로, Identification marks 아래의 왼쪽이나 봉투 전면의 좌측 상부 또는 중앙에 "Express (Special) Delivery"(속달), "Registered Mail"(등기), "Airmail"(항공우편) 등으로 표시한다. 그러나 이러한 지시는 대부분 구두로 이루어지므로 최근에는 별로 사용하지 아니한다.

⑬ Enclosure Notation(동봉물 표시)

무역통신문에는 서신 이외에 주문서나 수표 등을 동봉하는 경우가 있다. 서신을 취급하는 사람이나 수신자에게 동봉물이 있다는 것을 표시하여 주의를 환기하고자 할 때 사용된다.

동봉물 내용을 기재하지 않고 단순히 동봉물 숫자만을 표시할 경우는 "enclosure 2" (또는 Encl.2)로 표시하고 동봉물 내용을 밝힐 경우는 "Encl. : Offer No.55192 and Debit Note" 등으로 표시한다.

⑭ Carbon Copy Notation(사본 배부처 표시)

Carbon Copy Notation(c.c)은 서신의 사본이 수신자 이외의 자에게도 보내졌음을 표시하는 것으로 Identification Marks의 2행 아래 배치되며 "c.c" 또는 "copy to"로 표시한다.

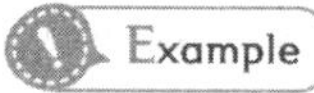

- c.c. : Our branch in L.A.
- copy to Mr. Judith Smith

⑮ Postscript(추신)

종전에는 본문을 작성할 때 누락된 내용을 추가할 목적으로 사용되었지만, 최근에는 주로 의도적으로 본문의 요점을 강조하거나 본문의 용건과 다른 사항을 간단하게 덧붙일 경우에 사용한다. P.S.는 라틴어 "Postscriptum"의 약어이며, 만약에 추신이 2개인 경우 2번째 추신은 "P.P.S(Post Post-Scriptum)"로 표시한다.

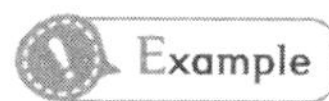

- P.S. Do not forget to send us samples before March 15.

⑯ Additional sheet(추가면)

무역통신문의 내용이 많아 용지의 한 면에서 다 끝나지 못할 경우에는 부득이 Continuation sheet를 사용하게 된다. 첫 면과 같은 크기, 색깔 및 지질의 용지를 사용하여야 하며, Letter-head가 없거나 있더라도 회사명만 간략하게 인쇄된 용지를 사용하여 수신인의 성명이나 약자, 페이지 수 및 날짜를 쓰고 그 아래에 내용을 기재하게 된다.

둘째 면은 적어도 본문이 세 줄 이상이 추가 면에 쓰일 수 있는 경우에만 사용되어야 한다. 따라서 본문이 없이 결미어(結尾語)나 서명만 둘째 면으로 넘기는 것은 좋지 않으므로 본문의 장단을 적절히 조정해야 한다. 1면 끝에 "P.T.O.(please turn over)"란 표시를 하고 뒷면에 계속 쓰는 경우도 있다.

Ⅱ 무역통신문의 형식

1 무역 통신문형식과 관련된 구두점(punctuation)

(1) Open punctuation(개방구두점)

무역통신문의 본문을 제외한 나머지 구성요소의 끝에 구두점을 생략하는 형식으로 매우 편리하여 최근 들어 많이 사용되고 있다. 이 형태는 Full block style이나 Simplified style에 쓰이는 경우가 많다.

(2) Closed punctuation(폐쇄 구두점)

모든 구성요소의 각 행 끝마다 comma를 붙이고 구성요소가 2행 이상으로 되어 있는 때는 마지막 줄에는 Period를 찍는다. Indented style에 주로 많이 사용된다.

(3) Mixed punctuation(절충식 구두점)

Open punctuation과 Closed punctuation의 혼합 형태로 본문과 서두 인사 및 결미 인사 뒤에만 구두점을 찍는 형태이다. 서두 인사는 미국식은 Colon 또는 Semicolon을 영국식은 Comma를 찍는다. 그러나 결미 인사는 미국식이나 영국식 모두 Comma를 사용한다.

2 무역통신문의 배열형태

(1) Indented Style with Closed Punctuation(사선식 폐쇄 구두점)

보수적이고 오랜 관습에 대한 존경을 표시하는 형식으로 영국에서 자주 사용한다. Inside address는 첫 행은 좌측 여백에 맞추나 둘째 행부터는 사선식(indented)으로 들어 쓰기(indenting)를 하여 배열하며, 본문은 매 Paragraph 첫 행은 띄어서 쓰고 나머지 행은 좌측 여백에 맞춘다. Complimentary clause와 Signature group은 중앙에서 시작하되, Signature group은 사선식으로 작성한다. 각 행의 끝마다 구두점(comma)을 찍고 마지막 행에는 마침표(period)를 찍는 Closing punctuation과 모든 구두점을 생략하는 Open punctuation의 두 가지 유형이 있다. 이 형식은 작성이 까다로워 시간이 많이 필요하다는 단점이 있다.

(2) Block Style with Mixed Punctuation(수직식 절충형 구두점)

미국에서 많이 사용하는 형식으로 각 구성요소를 Left margin에 일직선 수직으로 배열하고, Inside Address와 Salutation, Salutation과 Body of letter 그리고 Body of letter의 각 절(paragraph) 사이는 Double Space로 한다.

이 형식은 Salutation 뒤에는 Colon(:)이나 Comma(,)를 찍고, Complimentary close 뒤에 Comma(,)를 찍으며, 본문 이외의 모든 구성요소에는 구두점을 생략하는 형태로 많이 사용된다.

Indented style
(with closed punctuation)

Letterhead

① ________,
② ________ ,
… ________ ,
….. ________ ,
③ ________ :
④ …..________________
____
________________ .
…..________________
________________ .
⑤ ________ ,
⑥ ________
…________
…..________
⑦ ________

Block style
(with mixed punctuation)

Letterhead

① ________
② ________
____
____
③ :
④ ________________
________ .
____
____
________ .
⑤ ________ .
⑥ ________
____
____
⑦ ________

Notes
① Date Line
② Inside Address
③ Salutation
④ Body of the Letter
⑤ Closing
⑥ Signature
⑦ 보조요소

(3) Full block style with Open Punctuation(전수직식 개방형 구두점)

Letter-head를 제외한 모든 구성요소를 전부 좌측 여백(left margin)에 일직선으로 맞추어 배열하는 방식으로 Complete block style이라고도 한다. 이 형태는 Block style의 변형으로 최근 들어 시간을 절약할 목적으로 사용이 증가하고 있지만, 모든 요소가 좌측에 몰려 있으므로 서신 전체가 균형을 이루지 못하여 보기에 답답한 느낌이 든다는 단점이 있다. 본문 이외의 모든 구성요소의 행 끝에 구두점을 생략하는 Open Punctuation의 형태로 작성되는 경우가 많다.

(4) Modified block style with Open Punctuation(준수직식 개방형 구두점)

Full block style 서신의 구성요소 중 Inside address와 Body or letter의 각 행을 모두 좌측 끝에서 시작하여 수직이 되도록 일치시키고, Date, Compliment close와 Signature Group은 서신용지의 중간 지점에 수직으로 일치하여 시작되도록 배열하는 형태이다. 보통 Open punctuation으로 사용되며, 가장 많이 이용되는 형태이다.

Full block style
(with open punctuation)

Letterhead

① ______
② ______
③ ______
④ ______ .
______ .
⑤ ______
⑥ ______
⑦ ______

Modified block style
(with mixed punctuation)

Letterhead

① ______
② ______
③ ______ :
④ ______ .
______ .
⑤ ______ ,
⑥ ______
⑦ ______

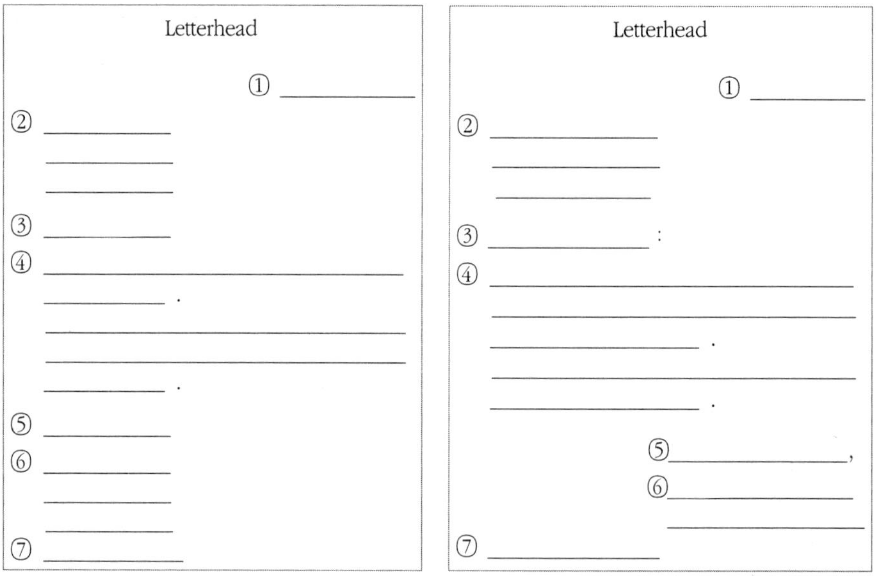

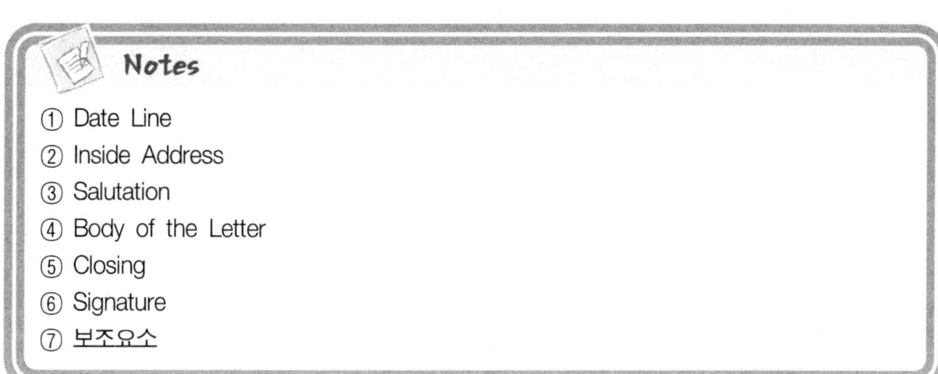
Notes

① Date Line
② Inside Address
③ Salutation
④ Body of the Letter
⑤ Closing
⑥ Signature
⑦ 보조요소

(5) Semi block style with Mixed punctuation(반수직식 절충형 구두점)

Block style과 Indented style의 절충형이다. Modified block style과 동일하나 본문의 Paragraph를 시작할 때 첫 행만 좌측 여백에서 5자 정도 띄어서 문장을 시작하며 둘째 줄부터는 좌측여백에 맞추어 배열하는 형태이다.

(6) Hanging style(현수 경사식)

Hanging indented style이라고도 하며 구성요소의 배열방식은 Block style과 동일하나 본문의 각 Paragraph에서 첫째 행은 좌측 여백에 맞추어 시작되나 둘째 행부터는 3~4자 띄어서 배열한다. 그다지 많이 사용되는 형태는 아니다.

Semi block style
(with mixed punctuation)

Letterhead
① ______
② ______
______
______
③ ______ :
④ ______
______
______ .
______
______
______ .
⑤ ______ ,
⑥ ______
______
⑦ ______

Hanging style
(with mixed punctuation)

Letterhead
① ______
② ______
______
③ ______ :
④ ______
______
______ .
______
______
______ .
⑤ ______ ,
⑥ ______
______
⑦ ______

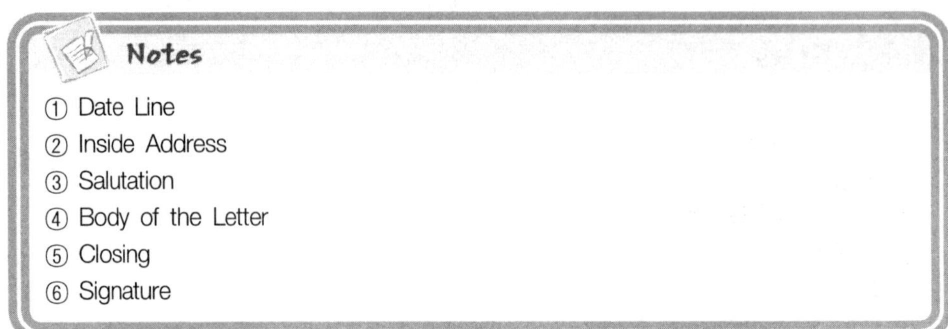
Notes

① Date Line
② Inside Address
③ Salutation
④ Body of the Letter
⑤ Closing
⑥ Signature

(7) Simplified style(간이식)

Full block style과 같으나 Salutation과 Complimentary와 같은 형식적인 인사문은 생략하는 형식으로 배열하는 것을 말한다. Typing시간의 단축으로 신속하고 간편하다는 장점이 있다. Salutation 대신에 Subject line은 모두 대문자로 표기된다.

Simplified style
(with open punctuation)

Letterhead

① ____________
② ____________
____
③ ____________
④ ______________________________
____
__________________________ .
____
____
__________________ .

⑤ ____________________ ,
⑥ ____________________
____

3 봉투(Envelope)

(1) 봉투의 종류

봉투는 크기에 따라 소형(Business-size)인 $6\frac{3}{4}$호 봉투(가로 : $6\frac{1}{2}$, 세로 : $3\frac{5}{8}$인치)와 대형(Large-size or Official size)인 10호 봉투(가로 : $9\frac{1}{2}$, 세로 $4\frac{1}{2}$인치)가 있는데 요즘은 대부분의 회사가 대형 봉투를 이용하는 경향이 있다.

(2) 봉투기재방식

봉투의 주소(outside address)는 Inside address와 똑 같아야 하며 그 형식도 같아야 한다. 즉 Inside address가 Block style이면 Block style로 Indented style이면 Indented style로 일치시켜 기재해야 한다.

[Block Style]

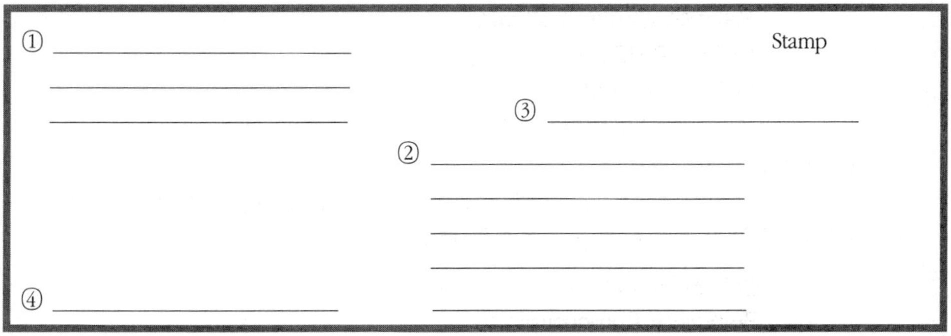

① ________________　　　　　　　　Stamp
____
________________　　③ ________________
　　　　　　　　② ________________
　　　　　　　　________________
　　　　　　　　________________
　　　　　　　　________________
④ ________________　________________

[Indented Style]

① ________________　　　　　　　　Stamp
　________________
　　________________　③ ________________
　　　　　　　　② ________________
　　　　　　　　　________________
　　　　　　　　　　________________
　　　　　　　　　　　________________
④ ________________　　　　________________

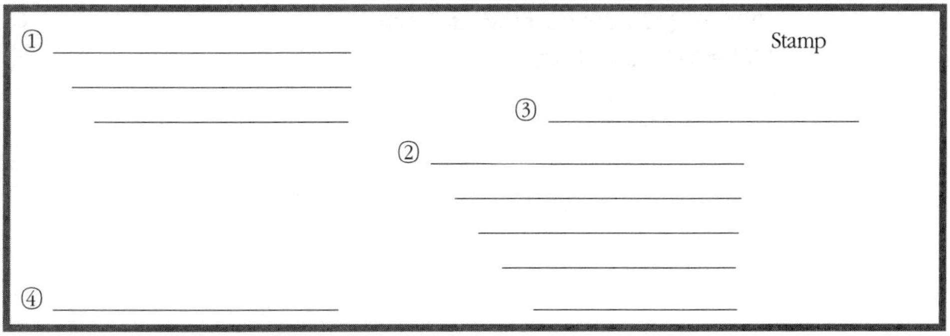

Notes

① **발신인 주소**(return address or sender's address)
서신이 배달 불능인 때 반송되는 주소로서 봉투전면의 왼편상단으로부터 2행 밑에 기재되며 Zip code(우편번호)까지 써주는 것이 좋다. 국명은 기계가 빨리 읽어낼 수 있도록 모든 활자를 대문자로 Typing하는 것이 좋다.

② **수신인 주소** (receiver's address)
수신인 주소로 서신이 배달되므로 정확히 써야 한다. 다만 Window Envelope를 사용할 때는 Inside Address가 그대로 Envelope Address가 되도록 서신을 접으면 된다. 봉투의 가로 중심선에서 1~2행 밑에서 시작하는 것이 좋다.

③ **우송지시**(mailing directions)
우송편을 지시하는 표시로 오른쪽 상단 부분에서 6~7행 아래, 즉 우표 바로 아래쪽에 표시되며 지시문언은 다음과 같다.

항공우편(Via Air Mail, By Air Mail, Par Avion, Air Mail)
인쇄물(Printed Matter)
사진재중(Photo Only)
등기우편(Registered Mail, Registered)
일반우편(By Surface Mail)
속달(Special/Express Delivery)
아리랑호 편으로(by s/s "Arirang")
Via Panama(파나마 경유)
Fifth Class Mail(제5종 우편)

④ **주의사항** (special remarks)
수신인이나 우송과정에서 특별히 취급 주의해야 할 사항으로 보통 봉투 왼편 끝에서 위쪽으로 2행쯤 올라가서 다음과 같이 표시한다.

인비, 친전(Private, Personal, Confidential)
극비(Strictly Confidential)
지급(Urgent, Immediate)
리차드 씨에게 부탁함(Kindness of Mr. Richard)
무료 견본(Sample of No Commercial Value)
미첼 씨 참조(Attention of Mr. Mitchell)
계좌번호(Account Number)

Ⅲ 무역통신문의 작성요령

1 무역통신문작성의 기본원칙

효과적인 무역통신문을 작성하기 위한 원칙으로 G.B. Hotchkiss는 "Handbook or Business English"에서 Correctness, Clearness, Conciseness, Courtesy, Character 등의 5C's를 제시하고 있다.

(1) Correctness(정확성)

무역통신문은 통신문의 내용, 형식 그리고 문법과 문장의 구조가 정확해야 한다. 특히 철자, 구두점, 대문자의 사용에 틀림이 없어야 한다.

Example

- Wrong : April 18th 200_
- Right : April 18, 200_
- Wrong : My Dear Sir,
- Right : My dear Sir,
- Wrong : He enjoys skiing and to swim.
- Right : He enjoys skiing and swimming.

(2) Clearness(명료성)

무역통신문 내용이 명료하지 못하면 상대방은 필자의 의도를 바로 이해하지 못하거나 잘못 이해하여 분쟁이 발생할 수도 있고 뜻밖의 손실을 볼 수도 있다. 따라서 애매한 표현을 피하고 의미가 분명한 표현을 골라서 사용해야 하며 약어와 기호를 남용하지 않아야 한다.

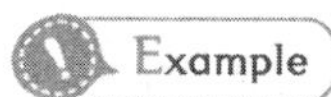

- Obscure : Thank you for your recent order.
- Clear : Thank you for your order No. 100 of May 5.
- Obscure : He had a picture in his house which he was proud of
  (Was he proud of his house?)

- Clear : He was proud of the picture in his house.
  (Or In his house he had a picture which he was proud of.)

(3) Conciseness(간결성)

무역통신문이 상대방에 지루한 느낌을 주지 않도록 하기 위해서는 장황하게 늘어놓거나 반복하지 않고 간결하여야 한다. 또 너무 상투적이고 낡은 인사어구는 피하여야 한다. 그렇다고 하여 지나치게 간결하게 함으로써 문장이 완전하지 못하거나 예의에 어긋나서는 안 된다.

Example

- Wordy : We would like to thank you for your cooperation in this difficult claim matter, GH-17491.
- Concise : Thank you for your cooperation in this claim matter, GH-17491.
- Wordy : You asked us when the new model of the PCs came on the market. It is now available.
- Concise : The new model of the PCs is now available.

(4) Courtesy(예의)

무역거래에서 너무 자신만의 이익을 추구한 나머지 상대방을 배려하지 않으면 오히려 손해를 볼 수도 있다. 특히 상대방을 의심하는 표현은 가급적 피해야 하며 상대방의 요구를 거절할 때에도 완곡히 거절하는 표현방법을 택하여야 한다. 또한, 서신을 작성할 때 자기 본위(We, Our)가 아니고 상대방의 입장(You- attitude)에서 작성하는 것(You, Yours)이 더 예의 바른 표현이 된다.

Example

- Impolite : If you are dissatisfied ~
- Polite : If you are not completely satisfied ~
- Impolite : You are requested to open an L/C in our favor immediately.
- Polite : Your prompt L/C in our favor would be much appreciated.

(5) Character(개성)

타인의 서신을 맹목적으로 모방하게 되면 서신내용이 형식적이고 상투적인 표현이 될 염려가 있다. 따라서 독창적인 표현을 써서 품위 있고 개성 있게 작성해야 한다. 하지만 과도한 독창적 표현은 해석상의 오해가 발생할 수 있으므로 삼가야 한다.

Example

- Poor : We beg to acknowledge receipt of your esteemed favor of 20th inst.
- Better : Thank you for your letter of October 20.
- Poor : It is our understanding that ~
- Better : We understand that ~

2 자주 사용되는 표현들

(1) 상대방의 통지를 받고 회신하는 경우

- Thank you for your letter ~
- We are duly in receipt of your letter ~
- We are obliged for your Fax of June 10
- Your cable of September 26 would be obliged
- It is our great pleasure in receiving your letter dated ~
- We acknowledge with thanks your inquiry about ~

(2) 신규거래를 제의하는 경우

- Though the courtesy of ~, we acquired your name ~
- We owe your name and address to ~
- We haverned from ~ that your are ~
- We are indebted for the ~ for the name of your firm
- Your name and address was given by ~
- Reference is made to your advertisement in ~
- We have found your name in the directory
- Your esteemed organization has been recommended to us by ~ as one of the ~

(3) 일반적인 소실을 통지하는 경우

- We are pleased to (inform) you that ~
- We have the pleasure to (inform) you that ~
- It is our great pleasure to (inform) you that ~
- This is to (inform) you that ~
- We advise (or announce) you that ~
- The purpose of this letter is to inform you that ~
- Please note that ~

(4) 상대방에게 나쁜 소식을 통지하는 경우

- We regret to (inform) you that ~
- We are very sorry to have to draw your attention to ~
- To our greatest regret that we must inform you that ~

(5) 상대방에게 요청할 때

- We shall much appreciate it if you will send us ~
- Please let us know `
- we shall(would) be much obliged if you inform us ~
- We would like (receive) your (offer)
- Your kind cooperation in this matter would be appreciated.
- You are requested to send(know) some samples ~

제2장

거래관계의 개설

I 거래처 소개 의뢰서

1 거래처 소개의뢰의 의의

해외시장조사 결과에 따라 무역상대국을 결정한 후에는 그 국가 내의 거래처를 선정하는 절차에 들어간다. 적절하고 신용이 있는 거래처를 선정하는 것은 무역업의 성패를 좌우할 정도로 매우 중요하다. 거래처는 직접 수출국에 방문하거나 무역박람회 등에 참여하여 물색할 수도 있지만, 국내의 상공회의소, 한국무역협회, 대한무역투자진흥공사, 외국은행, 외국 공사관, 해당 업종의 협회나 조합, 유명 상업흥신소에 비치하고 있는 상공인명부나 이들 기관에서 발행하는 각종 간행물을 이용하여 직접 거래처와 서신을 교환함으로써 물색할 수도 있다. 최근 들어서는 인터넷을 통해 비용 및 시간을 절약하면서 거래처를 물색하는 방법도 많이 활용되고 있다.

무역 관계기관에 해당국 내의 믿을만한 거래처를 소개해주도록 의뢰하는 서신을 거래처 소개의뢰서라고 하는데, 자기회사의 간략한 소개와 취급상품, 신용조회처, 거래처에 대한 희망 사항 등을 내용으로 하여 작성한다.

2 거래처 소개의뢰 관련 통신문

Model letter 1 면직물 수입업자 소개의뢰

March 5, 20--

The New York Chamber of Commerce
1244 East St. Forty Second

New York, N. Y. 10017
U. S. A.

Gentlemen :

We are long-established exporters of all kinds of cotton goods and have wide and closed connections with the leading manufacture hear.

As we are now desirous of extending our business to your market, we shall be much obliged if you will introduce us to some reliable firms in your city who are interested in this line of business.

As to our credit standing, Korea Exchange Bank. Seoul will supply necessary information.

We thank you for your trouble in advance, and earnestly await your reply.

Very truly yours,

Notes

- Chamber of Commerce 상업회의소
  cf. Korea Chamber of Commerce and Industry(KCCI), 대한상공회의소
- long-established 설립한 지가 오래된, 전통 있는, 명망 있는(well established, old established, well-founded)
- leading 일류의, 굴지의, 주요한
- are desirous of +동명사 ~을 열망하다.(= are desirous to + 동사)
- extend to A to B A를 B까지 확장하다. A를 B에게 베풀다, A를 B까지 연장하다.
- oblige 고맙게 여기게 하다. 부득이 ~하게 하다
- introduce A to B A를 B에게 소개하다. A가 길 때는 introduce to B A로 도치된다.
- firm 회사(= concerns, houses, companies, corporations, limited)
  cf. 확고한(firm offer : 확정청약)
- this line of business 이 영업 종목
  cf. line of credit(신용한도)
- as to ~에 대하여, ~에 관한(= as for, regarding, concerning)
- in advance 미리, 먼저, 앞서서

단어 및 어휘연구

1. ~에 관하여, ~에 대하여

- on, of, about

  * on이 of보다 더 상세한 의미가 있으며, about는 더 자세하게 말할 때 사용

- concerning, regarding, respecting, referring to

  * concerning(일반적인 단어), regarding(무역에서 많이 사용되는 단어), respecting(회사, 은행 등의 기관에 대한 경우에 많이 사용), referring to(서신의 서두에 많이 사용)

- with (in) reference to, referring to, with regard(regarding), with respect to(respecting), as to, as for, concerning, regarding, as regards, with regard to, in regard to, with respect to

  * as to : as regards, with regard to 보다는 간단한 표현
  * as for : = speaking of, as far as ~ concerned, 즉 ~에 대하여 말한다면
  * I didn't know as to that man.
  * As for that man, I don't want to meet him again.

2. 매도인(seller)과 매수인(buyer)에 대한 표현

	수입상(importer)		수출상(exporter)	
매매관계	buyer	매수인	seller	매도인
운송	shipper consignor	송화인 송화인	consignee notify party	수화인 착화통지처
신용장	applicant opener customer	개설의뢰인 개설자 고객	beneficiary user addressee	수익자 신용장 사용인 신용장 수령인
환어음	drawee payer	피발행인 지급인	drawer payee	발행인 대금수취인
계정	accountee	대금결제인	accounter	대금수령인

3. A를 B에게 소개/추천해 주십시오.

- Please introduce A to B

  * Please introduce some reliable houses to us. 당사에 몇몇 믿을만한 회사를 소개해 주십시오.
  * We shall be obliged if you will introduce some firms to us.
  * We should be obliged if you would introduce to us some exporters of sporting goods.

  ~께서 귀사를 A라고 소개해 주다(~ have given us your name as A)

  * They have given us your name as importers of dolls. 동 상사는 귀사가 인형을 취급하는 수입업자라고 당사에 소개해 주었다.
  * Your name has been introduced to us by your Chamber of Commerce as manufacturers of garments. 귀 시의 상업회의소에서 의류품 제조업체로서 귀사를 당사에 알려주었다.
  * Through The Medium Industrial Bank in your area, we learn that you are exporters of socks. 귀사가 속한 지역의 중소기업은행을 통해서 당사는 귀사께서 양말류 수출업체라는 것을 알게 되다.
  * Your name has been given us by the Korea Chamber of Commerce and Industry in Seoul as exporters of garments. 서울 소재 대한상공회의소에서 의류수출업자로서의 귀사의 명을 알려주었다.

- give A B as
- introduce B to A
  * Your name have been given us by the Chamber of Commerce,
  * Through the Chamber of Commerce, We acquired your name.

4. ~를 알게 되다
- We learn(see, understand, know) that

5. 재정(신용) 상태 : credit standing(status, position, condition, state)
- 당사의 신용상태에 관해서는(As to our credit standing)
  * As to credit and financial standing of our firms, Korea Exchange Bank will supply necessary information. 당사의 신용과 금융상태에 대해서는 한국외환은행이 필요한 정보를 제공해 드릴 것입니다.
  * Concerning our credit standing, the Korean Consulate in New York will supply you with necessary information. 당사의 신용상태에 관해서는 뉴욕주재 한국영사관이 귀사에 필요한 정보를 제공해 드릴 것입니다.
  * Regarding our financial standing and reputation, The Korea Exchange Bank will provide you with necessary information. 당사의 신용상태와 평판에 관해서는 한국외환은행이 필요한 정보를 제공해 드릴 것입니다.
  * As to credit standing, Kangnam Trading Co., Ltd. Seoul, will supply you with necessary information. 동 상사의 신용상태에 관해서는 서울에 있는 강남무역회사가 필요한 정보를 제공해 드릴 것입니다.

Model letter 2 면직물 수입업자 소개(회신)

March 12, 20--

Seoul Trading Co., Ltd.
C.P.O. Box 777
Seoul, Korea

Dear Sirs,

In replying to your letter of March 26, we are please to recommend you the following firm :

Tom & John Co., Ltd.
43 South St., New York,
NY 10005, U. S. A.

This firm has been long established and enjoys a good reputation as one of the leading importers of cotton goods.

We are happy to recommend this firm and shall be please to supply further information should it be required.

Yours truly,

Notes

- in reply to ~에 대한 회신으로(= in answer to, in response to, answering, replying, replying to, as you mentioned in)
- be pleased to 기꺼이, 기쁘게 ~하다. ~하게 되어 기쁘다.(= have the pleasure in(of) ~ing, be glad to)
- recommend 추천하다. 권하다.
- recommend A B A에게 B를 추천하다.
- reputation 평판, 명성, 호평
  enjoy a good reputation = 호평을 받다.(= enjoy popularity, be of good repute)
- We have enjoyed a good reputation for the past three decades. (당사는 지난 30년간 좋은 평판을 받아 왔습니다.)
- should it be required 필요하다면(= if it should be required)

단어 및 어휘연구 ··· ~하게 되어 기쁘다

- We are pleased(glad, delighted) to + root
- We have the pleased of ~ing ~하게 되어 기쁘다. 기꺼이 ~하다.
- It gives us pleasure to + root
  ① We are please to inform you that we have commenced the import business of silk goods.(당사기 비단제품의 수입거래를 개시하였다는 것을 귀사에 알리게 되어 기쁩니다.)
  ② We have the pleasure of sending you a copy of our latest illustrated catalog by airmail. (귀사에 항공우편으로 당사의 최근의 도해 카탈로그 1부를 발송하게 되어 기쁩니다.)

Model letter 3 전자계산기 수입업체 소개 의뢰

January 25, 20--

New York Chamber of Commerce
150 State st., New York
N.Y. 12207 U. S. A.

Gentlemen :

We have been exporting electronic calculators for more than ten years and have wide and close connections with the leading manufacturers here.

As we are now desirous of extending our business to your market, we shall be much obliged if you will introduce to us some reliable firms in your city who are interested in this line of business.

As to our credit standing, Korea Exchange Bank, Ltd., Head Office, Seoul, will supply necessary information.

We thank you for your trouble in advance and earnestly you reply.

Yours very truly,

Korea Trading Co., LTD.
H. S. You
Director, Trading Department

Notes

- wide and close connections 광범위하고도 밀접한 관계
- are desirous of ~ing ~을 열망하다.(= want to, are desirous to + 동사)
- oblige 고맙게 여기다. 부득이 ~하게 하다.(항상 수동태 형태로만 사용됨)
  We shall be obliged if you will ~

단어 및 어휘연구

1. 이상, 이하(금액, 수량 등)

① more than 30 sets, not less than 30 sets(31세트 이상)
more than 30 sets including(= inclusive of) 30 (30세트 이상)
30 of more(over, above) (30 이상)
US$ 30 or up(upward) (30달러 이상)

② less than 30 sets, not more than 30sets (29세트 이하, 30세트 미만)
less than 30 sets including(= inclusive of) 30 sets (3세트 이하)
30 or less(under below) (30 이하)
at or below US$ 30(30달러 이하)

2. ~에 감사하다

- thank(주로 서신의 처음에 사용)
  * Thank you ver much for your letter. We thank you very much for ... (Many thanks (to you) for ..., We are very thankful for ...
- thank A for B + 동(명)사 (A에게 B에 대해 감사하다.)(=be obliged(grateful) to A for B
  * We are very much obliged to you for your trouble. (귀사의 노고에 감사드립니다.)
- appreciate(서신의 끝 부분에 사용)
  * We would appreciate your favorable reply(능동태)
  * We would greatly appreciated (of) your sending a favorable reply to us.
  * We shall be highly appreciative of any reply.
  * We would be appreciated with your favorably reply.
  * Your favorable reply would be highly appreciated,(수동태)
  * It would be greatly appreciated if you would send us a favorable reply.
- grateful, obliged(서신의 중간에 많이 사용)
  * We shall grateful(obliged) if you would send us a favorable reply.

Model letter 4 전자계산기 수입업체의 소개(회신)

February 3, 20--

KOREA TRADING CO., LTD.
250-10, Samsung-dong, Kangnam-ku,
Seoul, 100-200. KOREA

Gentlemen :

In reply to your letter of January 15. we are grad to recommend you the following firms :

Name : General Electronics Co., Inc.
Address : 50 Church St., New York, NY 10007

Name : American. Electronic Service Inc.
Address : 1202 East 42nd St., New York, N.Y. 10017

While these firms are reliable and of good repute here, we, of course, are unable to make ourselves responsible for them.

For any information you may desire as to their credit standing, we advise you to write directly to them who will give you their references.

We hope our ready will be helpful and of service to you, and if there is anything more we can do for you, please do not hesitate to let us know.

Yours very truly,

New York Chamber of Commerce
Claire Eddings
Secretary

Notes

- follow firm 다음의 회사
- repute(= fame, renown, prestige) 평판, 명성, 호평, 덕망
  make ourselves responsible for(= be accountable for ~. take charge of ~, take responsibility for, assume any responsibility(liability) for, be in charge of, answer for ~) ~에 대해 (당사가) 책임을 지다.
- credit standing 신용상태(= credit status, credit position, credit condition)
- be of service to ~ ~에게 봉사하다. ~에게 도움이 되다
- do not hesitate to 망설이지 말고 ~하십시오.
- let us know 알려주십시오(= inform us of ~)

단어 및 어휘연구

1. let us의 문장 표현

let us know(= Please inform us of (that ~), Let us have, Please send us~) (당사로 하여금 알게 하여 주십시오.)

① Let us know your terms and conditions of business. (거래조건을 알려주십시오.)(= Please inform us of your terms and conditions of business.)

② Let us have your newest catalog. (최근 카탈로그를 보내주십시오.)(= Please sen us your newest catalog.)

③ Let us have your reply by April 20. (4.20까지 귀사의 응답을 보내주십시오.)

④ Let us have your bank(trade) reference. (동업자(은행) 신용조회처를 알려 주십시오.)

⑤ Please let us know (have) the names and address of firms in your place(city) which may need(requirc, be in need of) our products. (당신의 제품을 필요로 하는 귀 지역에 있는 회사들의 사명과 주소를 알려주십시오.)(= Please inform us of the names and address of the firms in your place(city) which may need(require, be in need of) our products.)

2. ~에 대해 책임을 지다

- make ourselves responsible for
- be accountable for~
- take charge of ~
- take responsibility for
- assume any responsibility(liability) for
- be in charge of
- answer for ~

Ⅱ 거래제의 서한과 권유장

1 거래제의의 의의

목적 시장과 거래처가 선정되면 거래제의서(letter of proposing business, inquiry) 또는 권유장(circular letter)을 작성하게 된다. 이 서신에는 대체로 다음과 같은 내용이 기재된다.

① 상대방의 회사명과 연락처를 알게 된 경로와 서신을 작성하는 목적(거래를 개시하고자 하는 희망 등)

② 자기회사에 대한 간단한 소개(업종, 취급상품, 기존의 거래시장, 자기회사의 자

국 업계에서의 지위, 경험, 생산규모 등)

③ 거래하고자 하는 상품의 명세(품목, 가격, 품질, 수량, 선적 및 지급조건, 주문에 응할 수 있는 수량 등)

④ 자기회사의 신용조회처 제시

⑤ 호의적인 회답을 희망하는 문구가 포함된 정중한 결미 인사.

때에 따라서는 취급상품의 목록(catalog 등), 가격표(price list) 또는 Offer sheet나 견본을 동봉함으로써 거래제의서의 효과를 높이기도 한다.

한편, 권유장이란 특정물품의 구매와 판매를 권유하는 서신을 말한다. 권유장에는 일반통지(general announcement)와 상품안내장(trade circular)이 있다.

일반통지는 회사의 신설 또는 해산, 지점, 대리점 등의 설치 및 폐지, 조직변경, 합병, 중요한 인사이동, 기타 영업상으로 상대방에게 알릴 필요가 있는 사항을 통지하는 서신을 말하며, 상품안내장은 이미 알고 있는 거래처나 아직 알지 못하고 있는 미래의 고객으로 하여금 구매의욕을 자극하는 서신을 말한다.

2 거래제의 관련 통신문

Model letter 1 여행용 가방 거래제의

July 15, 20--

Gentlemen :

Your name and address were given through the Chamber of Commerce of New York and one of the well-known importers handling various Travel Bags and we are writing you with a keen desire to open an account with you.

As you will see in the enclosed catalogue, we have been established here for more than thirty years as exporters of Travel Bags.

In this line of business we enjoy a specially advantageous position as we have wide and direct connections with the first class manufacturers in Korea, and you may be assured that any orders you may send us will be executed at the lowest market prices and on the best terms possible.

We do business on a Banker's Confirmed Letter of Credit, under which we may draw a draft at sight. Prices are based on FOB Busan in USD, but we can make up CIF prices or delivery price at any port of your country, if you so desire.

If you are interested in Travel Bags, Please write us conditions upon which you are able to transact with us.

We look forward to your trial order.

Yours very truly,

Notes

- with a keen desire to ~할 간절한 마음으로
- open an account with ~와 거래관계를 갖고자
  = enter into business relations with,
  = open business relations(connection) with
  = open an account with
  = establish an open account with
  = do business with
  = build up business connection with
- enjoy a specially advantageous position 특별히 유리한 고지를 점하고 있다.
  = occupy a specially advantageous position
- execute an order 주문을 이행하다(= fill an order, fulfill an order, perform, carry out an order)
- Banker's Confirmed Letter of Credit, under which we may draw a draft 확인신용장 하의 일람불환어음
- make up 계산하다.(= figure out, calculate)
- delivery price at any port of your country 귀국의 어떤 항구에서 인도하는 가격(도착지 인도조건 즉, D그룹 조건을 의미함)
- trial order 시험주문

~와 거래관계를 개설하다.

- Open an account with ~
- start business with
- establish a connections with
- come into contract with
- in business relations with
- enter into business relations with
- opening an account with
- do business with
- entering into business relations with
- build up business relations with
- a business relations with
- We want to enter into business connections with them. (당사는 동 상사와 거래관계를 개설하기를 바라고 있습니다.)
- We want to enter into business relations with traders of your market.

동봉하다, 발송하다

- 동봉하다 enclose, inclose
- 첨부하다 attach, append, annex, accompany
- 발송하다 forward, dispatch, send out, ship

① As we have enclosed a cheque for $1,000, please count and receive it. (1,000달러의 수표를 동봉하였으므로 그것을 검수하여 주십시오.)

② We have enclosed a cheque for $1,000 and hope you will accept it. (당사자가 1,000달러의 수표를 동봉하였고 귀사가 그것을 수락할 것으로 희망합니다.)

③ Enclosed please find a cheque for $1,000. (1,000달러의 수표를 동봉하였으니 받아보십시오.)

④ We have shipped your Order No. 753 on board s/s "Hanjin Oslo" leaving Busan today, which will, we trust, be found in (good) order. (당사는 오늘 부산을 출항한 "한진 오슬로"에 귀사의 주문 753를 선적하였고 그것이 좋은 상태라는 것을 알게 될 것으로 믿습니다.)

⑤ Attached are the official documents of ownership. (소유권에 관한 공식서류가 첨부되었습니다.)

⑥ We will forward the B/L to you the moment it is received. (당사는 선화증권이 수취 되는 즉시 귀사에 그것을 발송할 것입니다.)

귀사를 B를 통하여 알게 되다

- Your name has been given through B.
- We owe your name to B.
- We are indebt to B for your name.
- Through B, we have learned(god) your name.
- Your name and address were given through XXX
  = Your name and address have been recommended to us by XXX
  = From(Through) XXX, we have learned that
  = Through the courtesy of XXX, we have learned that
- Your name and address have been given through the Chamber of Commerce of New York as one of the well-known importers handling various travel bags.
- We owe your name and address to the Chamber of Commerce of New York as one of the well-known importers handling various travel bags.
- We are indebted to the Chamber of Commerce of New York as one of the well-known

importers handling various travel bags.
- Through the Chamber of Commerce of New York we have learned that you are one of the well-known importers handling travel bags.

가격과 관련된 표현

cost price	원가	face value	액면가격
buying price	구매가격	cash price	현금가격
quotation	견적, 시세	price list	가격표
list price	가격표상 가격	base price	기준가격
net price	공장도가격	market price	시장가격
current(ruling) price	시가	going price	현행가격
spot price	현장가격	wholesale price	도매가격
retail price	소매가격	customer price	소비자 가격
fixed(set) price	정가	price range	가격대
ceiling price	최고가격	gross price	총가격
all-around price all-inclusive price	총괄가격	floor price rock-bottom price	최저가격
price idea	가격이 어느 정도인지	remunerative price	이익이 남는 가격
advantage price	유리한 가격	cutting price	할인가격

- 잘못된 표현 : The price is cheap(inexpensive) 가격이 싸다?
- 올바른 표현 : The goods are cheap. cheap는 질 좋고 가격이 저렴하다는 의미도 있으나, 품질이 낮은 싸구려라는 의미도 있으므로, 이를 피하고자 inexpensive라는 표현이 자주 쓰임

물가변동

가격이 상승경향을 보여 주고 있습니다. (상승경향에 있습니다.)
- The prices show(= are in, are on the advance) an upward(= an advancing, a hardening, a rising) tendency.
  ① There has been decidedly a hardening tendency in the sugar market for some time past, which, we believe, will continue for some period. (지난 얼마 동안 설탕 시장에서 명백히 상승경향이 있었는데 이것이 당분간 지속할 것으로 당사는 믿습니다.)
  ② It is highly probable that cotton will even top the opening price of the last season. (면화가 지난 시즌의 개장가격을 능가할 것이 확실합니다.)
  ③ Under the present conditions, when the cost of labor and raw materials may go up any delay, it is impossible for us to guarantee the price for any definite period. (임금과 원재료가 언젠가 상승할 수 있는 현재 상황 하에서 당사가 어떤 특정기간에 대해 가격을 보증하는 것은 불가능합니다.)

Model letter 2 회신

Gentlemen :

We have received the circular letter of April 20 for Travel bags.

We are now considering the possibility of commencing business with you concerning purchase of Korean sundries, if your terms and conditions meet our requirements.

We should be pleased if you send us your catalogue with a price list, informing us of your full discount rates and the period of credit for a substantial amount of orders.

We are looking forward to receiving your reply at an early date.

Yours very truly,

Notes

- commencing business **거래를 개시하다**(= beginning business)
- terms and conditions terms와 conditions는 유의어로서 모두 '조건'으로 번역되지만 약간의 의미상의 차이가 있다. terms는 당사자들 사이에 청약과 승낙으로 합의된 조건을 말하며, conditions는 청약의 조건 이외의 조건 예컨대 정지조건이나 해제조건과 같은 부관이라고 할 수 있다. 일반적 의미에서의 '계약조건'을 표현할 때는 두 단어 중 어느 것도 사용할 수 있으나 '부관'의 경우에는 'conditional contract(조건부계약)'과 같이 반드시 'condition'을 사용해야 한다. 'terms and conditions'처럼 표현하는 것은 영미법계통 특유의 관행으로서 더 정확하고 엄격하게 표현하자는 데에 그 목적이 있다.
- sundry **잡화**(= miscellaneous goods, general merchandise)
- meet **충족시키다**(= satisfy)
- full discount rate **최고의 할인율**(maximum discount rate, allowance, reduction)
- substantial amount of order **대량주문**(= bulk of order, volume order, quantity order, bi) order, large(considerable) order, tolerable order)

Model letter 3 거래제의

March 15, 20--

Gentlemen :

Your name has been given by the New York Chamber of Commerce as one of the reputable importers of Leather Products in your city.

We are large manufacturers and exporters in Korea producing all kinds of leather products including Jackets and Vest.

Our products are highly reputed by the importers of U.K., Germany and France, etc.

In order to diversify our existing market, we are interested in supplying our quality products to you on favorable terms.

Upon receipt of your drawings or inquiries, we could submit our samples with competitive price to you.

As for our company, we have two ultra modern factories, one in Seoul and the other in Busan, with over 500 workers and our export record for last year was over Ten Million US Dollars and we are aiming to surpass Twenty Million US Dollars this year.

As to our credit standing, we refer you to the Korea Exchange Bank, Seoul or any of the commercial banks in Korea.

Your early reply would be appreciated.

Yours very truly

Seoul Trading Co., Ltd.
Min-ho Kang
General Manager

Notes

- quality products 우수한 품질
- upon receipt of ~을 받자마자
- credit(business/financial) standing(status/[position/condition/state] 신용상태
- competitive price 저렴한 가격(= favorable, reasonable, good, low, workable, utmost, rock bottom, keenest, best price)

단어 및 어휘연구

~하여 주시면 고맙겠습니다.

- We shall(should) be please(grateful, glad, happy) if you will(would) ~
- We shall appreciate your ~ing
- We shall appreciate it if you will ~
- It will be appreciate if you will ~
- We shall feel grateful if you will ~

귀사가 ~해 주시면 고맙겠습니다.

- We shall be pleased if you will let us know your market condition. (상태를 알려주면)
- We shall appreciate your trial order. (시험 주문해 주시면)
- We shall appreciate it if you will agree these terms. (조건에 동의해주시면)
- Your order will be appreciate. (주문하시면)
- We appreciate your order (주문에 감사드린다.)

Model letter 4 회신

March 21, 20--

Seoul Trading Co., Ltd.
C.P.O. Box 777
Seoul, Korea

Gentlemen :

We thank you very much for your letter of May 8, 20-- in which you expressed your willingness to open an account with us.

We are grad to learn that you are specially interested in shipping cotton shirts and in these we may say that we are specialists.

We should appreciate receiving your best CIF New York on men's cotton shirts as well as several sample by air.

If your prices are completive and merchandise is suitable for our trade, we will be able to place large orders.

We look forward to hearing from you soon.

Yours very truly,

Notes

- open an account with　~와 거래관계를 개설하다
- suitable for one's trade　~의 영업에 적합하다
- large order　대량주문

단어 및 어휘연구 … Sample and Catalogue

- sample(견본), illustrated catalog(도해, illustrations), patterns : 견품, 모형(직물), specimen : 표본(광물, 식물), cutting : 자른 것(보석)
- description(설명서), literature(인쇄물 광고), specification(명세서)
- pamphlet(booklet) : 소책자, brochure(소책자, 몇 페이지의), leaflet(한 장의 인쇄물)

Model letter 5 신형 컴퓨터의 거래제의

March 30, 20--

Gentlemen :

From the Chamber of Commerce of United States, we have learned that you are one of the largest wholesalers dealing in computers.

As a large manufacturer and exporter of electronic products, we have many years of experience in exporting computers all over the world.

We believe you will be interested to hear about latest lap-top computer, which we have just introduced to market. Our research engineers have finally come up with the answer to some of those problems you have with mini-type computers.

The present product is multi-purpose type with the highest technical development and very economical, and has passed tests run by our engineers.

If your engineers want to inspect these computers and see it in operation, please say any time when it is convenient and our representative there will be pleased to arrange a demonstration at your place.

As you see in the enclosed price list, our terms of dealing are superior to any other suppliers. And we can allow you additional discounts for the order not less than 3,000 sets.

With regard to our credit standing, we may refer you to our banker, The Bank of JeonBuk, Iksan and following firm :

Hana Trading Co., Ltd.
1215 Meongsung Bld.
509 Namnosong-Dong, Wansan-Ku
Jeonju, Korea

Sincerely yours,

Encl. 1 Specification No. 333
1 Price List

Notes

- dealing in **취급하다, 거래하다**(= who deal in), 복문을 단문으로 하기 위한 현재분사임
- many years of experience **다년간의 경험**
  cf. many experiences 여러 가지 다양한 경험(복수형)
  much experience 심도 있는 경험(단수형)
- come up with the answer to **~에 대한 해결방안을 내놓다(도달하다)**
  come up with **따라잡다, 찾아내다, 생각해 내다**
- in operation **작동상태**
- convenient **편리한, (상황, 시간, 물건 등)의 형편이 좋은. ~에 가까운**
- not less than **~이상**(= more than)
- with regard to **~에 관하여**(= regarding, concerning, referring to, with (in) reference to, as to(for), about
- refer **~에게 조회를 시키다. 조회하다, 인용하다**
- establish a business connection with **거래관계를 개설하다**(= enter into business relations with, open an account with)

단어 및 어휘연구 **가격할인 표현**

(1) 할인과 유사한 개념
- discount(할인), reduction(가격할인), deduction(공제), concession(가격할인), allowance(가격할인, 클레임의 경우), drawback(환급, 환불금), rebate(할인, 사례비)
- 할인을 수식하는 형용사
  liberal(substantial, large, great) discount(대량할인), small discount(소량할인), retail discount (소매할인), wholesale discount(도매할인), cash discount(현금할인), special discount(특별할인), usual discount(통상적 할인), prompt discount(직불할인), extra(additional) discount(추가할인), quantity discount(수량할인)

(2) 할인의 동사형
- make(allow, grant, accord)
- discount 1) 할인하다. 2) 할인을 견적하다.
- offer a discount(할인을 제공하다.
- get(obtain, secure) a discount(할인을 받다.)
- claim an allowance(할인을 요구하다.)
- raise(increase) the rate of discount(할인율을 인상하다.)
- lower(decrease) the rate of discount(할인율을 인하하다.)
- make an allowance(가격을 인하하다.)
- make a reduction in price(가격을 인하하다.)
- make a concession in price(가격을 인하하다.)

Model letter 6 회신

April 3, 20--

Gentlemen :

Thank you for your letter of March 30 in which you expressed your willingness to open an account with us.

We are glad to learn that you are searching for a reliable importer for lap top computers, and in these we dare to say that we are specialist.

Items we are handling are various from the personal computers for domestic use to workstations. We are especially interested in highly developed makes such as computers with CPU of Intel pentium or XP and Lap Top Computers with memory card.

With the rapid increase of demand for personal computers, we expect a successful sale depending on your prices. We would like to have your quotations on CIF New York. And if your prices are reasonable and delivery is punctual, we will be able to place considerably large orders with you.

We are looking forward to your favorable reply.

Sincerely yours,

Notes

- specialists 전문가, 항상 복수형으로 사용(= expert)
- for domestic use 가정용, 국내용
- workstation PC 사용자의 모든 욕구를 만족시키며 host 컴퓨터와 연결하여 다른 사용자들과 정보를 쉽게 교환할 수 있는 기능을 가진 단말장치(고성능 컴퓨터)
- memory card 기존 Ram(random access memory, 임시기억장치)이 가진 전원이 꺼지면 기억된 자료가 소실되어 버리는 단점을 개량한 대용량 기억장치
- depending on ~에 따라서는
- quotation 인용, 견적, 견적서
- reasonable prices 합리적인 가격(= (cheap, low, competitive, attractive, proper, moderate, good, inexpensive) price)

단어 및 어휘연구 ··· 주문하다

- A에게 B를 주문하다 (place order A with B)
- B에게 A를 주문하다 (place an order for A with B)
  = order A from B, give B an order for A)
- place regular order with A (정기적으로 주문하다.)
- He placed an order for ten pairs of shoes with the firm.
- We are pleased to place an initial order for your products with you.(with 사용)
  ※ initial order= first order, an opening order
- We are pleased to give(send) an initial order ... to you.(to 사용)
- We are please to an initial order the products from you(from 사용)
- Please favor us with your order.
- Please give us have a reorder(an additional order)
- Please let us have a reorder(a further order)
- We are pleased to place a trial order with you.
- We are pleased to place an order with you on a trial basis.
- We are pleased to place an order with you as a trial.

Model letter 7 회신(거래제의 거절)

Gentlemen :

We thank you for your letter of July 15, 2009, offering to open an account with us.

To our regret, we are not in a position to accept your kind proposal at present, as we have some regular sources of supply in your country, and moreover, the market here is somewhat dull.

However, we will keep your name in our file, and when times take a favorable turn, we will write to you again for your help.

Yours faithfully,

Notes

- open an account with ~ **~와 거래를 개시하다.**(= open connection with , do business with, open business with, establish connection with, enter into business relations with ~)
- to one's ~ (~ **하게도**)
  cf. to our regret(유감스럽게도), to my sorrow(슬프게도), to our disappointment(실망스럽게도)
- be in a position to **~할 처지가 되다. ~할 수 있다.**(be able to)
- the market here is somewhat dull **이곳 시황이 다소 침체국면에 있다.**
- when times take a favourable turn **시황이 호황국면으로 돌아서면**

단어 및 어휘연구

유감스럽다

- (Much) to our regret (당사가 매우 유감스럽게도)
- We regret to know that (that 이하를 알게 되어 유감이다.)
- We are sorry to hear that (that 이하를 듣게 되어 유감이다.)
- It is with great regret that (that 이하가 매우 유감이다.)
- It is to be regretted that (that 이하가 유감스럽다.)
- It is a matter for (of) regret that (that 이하가 유감스럽다.)

① We deeply regret to inform you that we have been unable to dispatch in full your order received on July 31. (당사가 1월 31일에 수취한 귀사의 주문을 전부 발송할 수 없었다는 것을 귀사에 알리게 되어 매우 유감입니다.)

② We regret having to draw your attention to the repeated delays in the execution of our order. (당사의 주문 이행에 반복되는 지연에 따라 귀사의 주의를 환기하게 시켜야만 한다는 것이 유감입니다.)

③ We regret(are sorry) that we cannot accept your offer as the price is too high. (가격이 너무 높아 귀사의 청약을 당사가 승낙할 수 없다는 것이 유감스럽습니다.)

④ We regret that we are unable to accept your order. (당사가 귀사의 주문을 승낙할 수 없다는 것이 유감이다.)

⑤ We are sorry we are not in a position to execute your order. (당사가 귀사의 주문을 이행할 수 없다는 것이 유감입니다.)

⑥ To our regret, we are unable to of service to you in this matter. (당사가 유감스럽게도 당사는 이러한 문제에서 귀사에 도움이 될 수 없습니다.)

⑦ We regret to inform you that it is beyond our power to co-operate with you in this matter. (이러한 문제에서 귀사와 협조하는 것이 당사의 권한 밖에 있다는 것을 통지하게 되어 유감입니다.)

시황 표현 형용사

• active(활발한)	• irregular(불안정한)	• sensitive(민감한)	• animated(활기 있는)
• long(강세의)	• booming(폭등하는)	• lull(소강의)	• brisk(활발한)
• firm(견고한)	• steady(착실한)	• strong(강세의)	• health(건전한)
• stationary (변동 없는. 안정된)	• erratic(변동이 심한/불안정한)	• reluctant(거래가 부진한)	• excited(흥분한) (feverish)
• advancing (상승하는, rising)	• stiffening(강세의, hardening)	• improving(호전되고 있는)	• bullish(강세의)
• unchanged(불변의)	• narrow(한산한)	• lifeless(활기 없는)	• limited(제한된)
• bearish(약세의)	• short(약세의)	• softy(내림세의)	• depressed(부진한)
• easy(수요가 적은, 약세의)	• declining(하락하는, falling)	• dull(활발하지 않은, slack)	• sinking(하락하는, falling)
• uneven(고르지 못한)	• spotty(고르지 못한)	• stagnant(부진한, flat)	• weak(약세인, 저조한)
• inactive(활기가 없는)	• quiet(한산한, 활발하지 않은)		

Model letter 8 난방설비 구매권유

CHOSUN EXPORTERS, LIMITED

446-29 Hoo-um-dong, Yong-san-ku,

Seoul, Korea

2nd February, 20--

US Trading Corporation

46 Broad Street

New York, N.Y. 10036

U.S.A.

Gentlemen :

What would you say to a gift that gave you a warmer and more comfortable home, free from draughts and a saving of over 20% in fuel costs?

You can enjoy these advantages not just this year but ever year, simply by installing our "Silver" panel system of double-glazing. Can you think of a better gift for your entire family?

The enclosed folder will give you some of the reasons why "Silver" is the most completely satisfactory double glazing system on the market, thanks to a number of features not provided in any other system.

Remember that the panels are precision made by experienced craftsmen who do nothing else, to fit your particular windows.

Remember too, that you will be dealing with an old established company that owes its success to the satisfaction given to scores of thousands of its customs.

There is no need for you to make up your mind now. First let us give you a free demonstration in your own home without any obligation of any kind, but if you are looking for an investment with an annual average return of over 20%, here is your opportunity.

If you post the enclosed card to reach us by the end of this month, we can complete the installation for you in good time before winter sets in.

Very truly yours,

CHOSUN EXPORTERS, LIMITED
Dae-shik Lee
Marketing Manager

DI : gk
Enc. 1 booklet

Notes

- free from draught(draft) 외풍이 없는
- install 설치하다 cf. installment 할부금
- panel system of double-glazing 이중 유리로 된 창틀 설비
- folder 접은 책자
- precision made 정밀하게 제조된
- owe to ~덕분에(owe a to B A가 B 덕분에)
- there is no deed for you to make up your mind 결심하다

= You need not make up your mind(make up one's mind 결심하다(resolve, decide, determine)
- without any obligation of nay kind **하등의 부담 없이**
- an investment with an annual average return of over 20% **연평균 20% 이상의 수익** (= 수익(earnings, gains, proceeds))
- in goods time **좋은 때에, 곧**

3 권유장 관련 통신문

Model letter 1 간행물에 자사의 소개 게재 요청

Dear Sirs,

We take the liberty of introducing ourselves to you as the most reputable stationary exporters in Korea, who have been engaged in this line of business since 1960.

We have been enjoying a good sale of Electronic goods., and are now desirous of expanding our market to your area,

We shall, therefore, appropriate it very much if you will kindly introduce us to the relative importers by announcing our requirements in your publications as follows :

"A Korean export firm of Stationery Goods is now making a business proposal for Electronic goods, which are said to have built up a high reputation at home and abroad. Contract them by addressing your letter to The Hana Trading Co., C.P.O Box 333, Seoul, Korea.

We solicit your close attention to this matter.

Faithfully yours,

Notes

- take the liberty of ~을 스스럼없이 하다. 실례를 무릅쓰고(외람되이) ~을 하다
- be engaged in ~에 종사하다(= engaged oneself in)
- introduce oneself to ~에게 자기를 소개하다
- have been enjoying a good sale ~이 잘 판매되어 재미를 보다

단어 및 어휘연구 ··· **다음과 같이**

- Our terms are as follows:
- Our terms are as below;
- Our terms are as underlie.

Model letter 2 동업자의 변경

Dear Sirs,

I inform you that, in consequence of the lamented death of my late respected partner. Mr. Omally a change has become necessary to take place in our firm, and that, in order to continue this business I formed a partnership with Smith who was in our firm as a Manager for over fifteen years, and we will devote ourselves as heretofore to the trade of woollens.

Kindly note that the name of our firm shall be continued as "Smith Trading Co."

We request a continuance of your confidence and support, and refer you to the signature of the new partner at foot.

Faithfully yours,

Notes

- in consequence of ~의 결과로(= as a result of)
- lamented death 애석한 죽음 cf. the late lamented = 고인
- take place 발생하다.
- devote oneself to ~에 전념하다.
- refer one to ~을 참조하다.
- at foot 서신 끝에 기재한

Model letter 3 회사의 합병

Gentlemen,

We have much pleasure in informing you that the two firms hitherto carrying on business under the names of Korea Trading Co., Ltd.. and Park's Mulsan Co., Ltd. will amalgamate on and after the 27th of April, 2009 under the firm name of

KOREA & PARK'S Co., Ltd.

The combined firm will trade in the sane manner as heretofore at the above address, to which all communications be sent in the future.

Taking advantage of this opportunity, we thank you sincerely for all the confidence and favors you have bestowed upon our two firms individually and solicit a continuance of the same under the new arrangement, No. effort shall be lacing on our part to merit your patronage.

Very Faithfully yours,

Notes

- hereto **지금까지**(= up to this time, so far)
- carry on **경영하다**(= run, manage)
- amalgamate **합병하다**.(= fuse)
  - 흡수합병은 'merger', 신설합병은 'consolidation'을 사용
- on and after **~로부터**
- in the same manner as heretofore **종전과 같은 방법으로**
- bestow **부여하다. 쏟다.**
- solicit **간청하다.**
- under the new arrangement **새로운 배치하에서, 합병된 새 회사에도**
- merit **-을 받을만하다.**(= deserve)
- patronage **애호**

단어 및 어휘연구 … **최선을 다하다.**

- do our best	- do the utmost
- make(exert) every effort	- make all possible efforts
- make every endeavor	- do all in our power
- do everything we possibly can	- do as far as we can

* We will do our best to ship the goods within stipulated date.

Model letter 4 여행용 가방 거래제의

Gentelmen :

Your name and address

Yours faithfully,

D.B. Park
Sales manager

Model letter 5 회신

Gentlemen,

I want to thank you for allowing me to come by and talk more about our products and services we offer to the hotel industry.

I know that price is a big factor for your Hotel Group as well as service after the sale. There is no other company in the industry that provides the product and the service on the same level as we do.

If you can give us some idea of the number of air conditioners, TVs, electronic doorlocks, ice machines, room safes and video surveillance equipment that you anticipate to install during the coming 12 months, we would be able to determine the competitive pricing and services for you.

We look forward to serving your Hotel Group and I welcome your call at any time

Sincerely,

Notes

- as well as ~뿐만 아니라
- safe 금고
- come by = drop by = drop in 우연히 들르다
- give one an idea of ~에게 ~을 알게 하다
- video surveillance equipment 비디오 감시 장비
- anticipate 예상하다
- install 설치하다

Useful Expressions

1. We have heard from the Chamber of Commerce in our city that you are in the market for Electric Appliances.
   귀사가 전기 기구를 구매하고 싶다는 것을 당시 상공회의소로부터 알았습니다.

2. We are specialists in silk goods.
   폐사는 견직물 전문업체입니다.

3. We specialize in this line.
   폐사는 이 품목을 전문으로 취급합니다.

4. We would like to enter into business relations with ABC Co. Ltd.
   ABC회사와 거래관계를 맺고 싶습니다.

5. It is our wish to enter into business relations with the above named company.
   상기 지명한 회사와 거래관계를 맺고 싶습니다.

6. We are writing you with a keen desire to enter into business connections with you.
   귀사와 밀접한 거래관계를 맺고자 하는 열망으로 서한을 보냅니다.

7. As to our terms and conditions of business, we would welcome your suggestions.
   폐사의 거래조건에 대해서는 귀사의 제안을 환영합니다.

8. No other firms can compete with us in either quick delivery or high quality.
   어떤 다른 회사도 신속한 인도나 고품질에 있어서 폐사와 경쟁이 될 수 없습니다.

9. Please quote us the best prices on the basis of F. O. B.Yokohama.
   FOB 요코하마 조건으로 최상의 가격을 제시하여 주십시오.

10. We have enclosed our samples and price list.
견본과 가격표를 동봉했습니다.

11. We look forward (are looking forward) to your early reply.
당신의 조속한 회답을 고대합니다.

12. We have been informed of your standing and reputation from the said bank.
상기 은행으로부터 귀사의 재정 상태와 평판을 통지받았습니다.

13. We are pleased to inform you that our business will be turned into an limited company on the 1st May.
5월 1일부로 폐사는 주식회사로 개편하게 되었으므로 통지하여 드립니다.

14. Notice is hereby given that the partnership will be discontinued, owing to the retirement of Mr. A. S. Kim.
김 안수 씨의 퇴사로 인하여 단독 경영체가 되었기 알려드립니다.

15. Replying to your inquiry of the 10th inst., we are unable to offer you plates of the size you specify.
귀사의 이달 10일 자 문의 서신에 대한 회신입니다. 귀사가 요구하신 크기의 접시는 당사로서는 오퍼할 수 없습니다.

16. We received on the 1st May your valued favour dated 30th April.
귀사의 4월 30일 자 서신을 5월 1일 접수하였습니다.

17. Kindly give us an order sheet in confirmation of the message by telephone of this morning.
오늘 아침 전화로 통지하신 주문을 확인하기 위하여 주문서를 송부해 주시길 바랍니다.

18. I have much pleasure in confirming my verbal order of this morning.
오늘 아침 구두주문을 확인합니다.

필수암기 UCP 주요 조문 (1/4)

Article 1 Application of UCP

The Uniform Customs and Practice for Documentary Credits, 2007 Revision, ICC Publication no. 600 ("UCP") are rules that apply to any documentary credit ("credit")(including, to the extent to which they may be applicable, any standby letter of credit) when the text of the credit expressly indicates that it is subject to these rules. They are binding on all parties thereto unless expressly modified or excluded by the credit.

Article 2 Definitions

Complying presentation means a presentation that is in accordance with the terms and conditions of the credit, the applicable provisions of these rules and international standard banking practice.

Confirming bank means the bank that adds its confirmation to a credit upon the issuing bank's authorization or request.

Honour means:

a. to pay at sight if the credit is available by sight payment.
b. to incur a deferred payment undertaking and pay at maturity if the credit is available by deferred payment.
c. to accept a bill of exchange ("draft") drawn by the beneficiary and pay at maturity if the credit is available by acceptance.

Negotiation means the purchase by the nominated bank of drafts (drawn on a bank other than the nominated bank) and/or documents under a complying presentation, by advancing or agreeing to advance funds to the beneficiary on or before the banking day on which reimbursement is due to the nominated bank.

- to be continued p.122 -

제3장

조 회

I 신용조회 및 회신

1 신용조회의 의의

신용조회란 새로운 거래를 시작하기 전에 상대방의 신용도와 신용거래능력 등에 대한 판단을 위하여 필요로 하는 신용정보를 조사, 분석하는 것을 말한다. 국제무역은 지리적인 격리성과 경제·사회·문화적, 법·제도상의 차이가 큰 환경에서 수행되기 때문에 거래 당사자들은 국내 거래에 비해 상대적으로 큰 무역위험에 노출된다. 심지어 부도덕한 거래당사자가 고의적으로 Market claim을 제기하거나, 의무이행에 불성실한 태도를 보임으로써 어려움에 처하는 사례도 빈번하게 발생하고 있다. 따라서 거래를 시작하기 전에 상대방에 대한 재정상태(Capital), 거래 및 경영능력(Capacity), 상도덕성(Character), 경영환경 및 경기(Conditions)와 담보력(Collateral) 등의 신용정보를 수집·분석하여 거래관계를 개설할 것인지 아닌지 또는 어느 정도의 범위 내에서 거래할 것인지 등에 대해 검토할 필요가 있다.

신용조회처(Reference)로는 상대방의 거래은행이 자주 이용되며, 동종업자가 이용되기도 하는데, 이를 각각 은행조회(Bank Reference), 동업자조회(Trade Reference)라 한다. 그밖에도 해당업종의 조합, 상업흥신소나 상업회의소, 국내외의 공관이 신용조회처로 이용되기도 한다.

신용조회서의 내용은 ① 상대방을 알게 된 경위 ② 신용조회의 대상이 되는 회사와 그 소재지, ③ 신용조사 의뢰를 하는 이유, ④ 조사를 의뢰하고자 하는 내용, ⑤ 조사내용에 대한 비밀유지와 조사비용부담의 약속 등으로 구성된다.

2 신용조회 관련 통신문

Model letter 1 신용조회

April 15, 20--

Dear Sirs,

We learned your esteemed name as a reference from the below firm in Seoul who would like to enter into business relations with us.

Kotex Co., Ltd., 532-5, Sinsa-dong Gangnam-gu, Seoul, CPO Box 333

We are interested in knowing their main items, your candid opinion on their financial responsibility, business mode, and general reputation in your country. We shall, therefore, be much obliged if you could give us enough information on them.

We assure you that all information will be kept strictly confidential and will be used for our files only.

We look forward to hearing from you soon.

Yours very truly,

Notes

- financial responsibility **재정능력, 지불능력**
  = financial ability, financial standing(status, position)
- strictly confidential **극비로** (= in strict confidence)
- for our files only **당사의 서류용으로만(즉, 비밀로)**

단어 및 어휘연구 … ~ **거래하다**

- commence(open, set up, start, begin, take up) business, 영업을 개시하다.
- open(enter into, start, establish) business (relations, connections) with, ~와 거래를 개시하다, open account with
- We with to do business with you,

- We are desire of doing business with you
- We wish to have(establish, enter into) business relations(connections) with you.
- We would like to open an account with you.
- We are in business with them. We have trade relations with them
- We are engaged in trade business with them.

Model letter 2 회신

April 29, 200-

Dear Sirs,

In response to your request of April 15, we are happy to inform you that Kotex Co, Ltd., has set up business in Seoul since 20-- as General Importers & Exporters, and has enough capital volume for their requirements.

For more than twenty-two years, they have kept a current account with us, and always given enough satisfaction to us and their customers. And their latest financial status show us a healthy conditions.

We trust that the above information, which is given for your confidential use and without responsibility on our part, will prove helpful to you. But we shall be pleased to be of any further services to you if you require more details.

The enclosed note show the charges which we have paid on your behalf, for which we ask you to settle soon

Yours very truly,

Notes

- General importers & exporters **종합수출입상**
  cf. 종합무역상사, General Trading Company
- current account **당좌계정**

단어 및 어휘연구

동봉하다

- We enclose(are enclosing) herewith our catalog.
- Enclosed (herewith) is our catalog
- Please find our catalog in the attached sheet.

~에 대한 응답으로

10월 25일자의 서한에 대한 응답으로
In response(reply, answer) to(= Replying to, Answering) your letter of October 25.

① In reply to your inquiry of November 15, we are glad to inform you that Kims & Co, are doing business on a sound basis and we have every confidence in them. (11월 15일자의 귀사의 조회에 대한 응답으로 김씨 상사는 건전한 기반 하에 사업을 영위하고 있고 당사가 동사를 전폭적으로 신뢰하고 있다는 것을 알리게 되어 기쁩니다.)

② Replying to your letter of July 15, we are please to quote you as follow. (7월 15일자의 귀사의 서한에 대한 응답으로 당사는 다음과 같이 귀사에게 견적을 하게 되어 기쁩니다.)

Model letter 3 신용조회

Dear Sirs,

Messrs. Watson & Jones of New York wish to open an account with us and have given us your name as a reference.

We should be grateful if you would supply us with what information you can about the firm's general standing and say whether in your opinion, they are likely to be reliable for credit up to £500, and whether, they settle their accounts promptly.

We enclose a stamped, addressed envelop and shall be only too glad to render you a similar service should the need arise.

It is hardly necessary to add that any information you supply will be treated in strict confidence.

Yours very truly,

Notes

- reference 조회, 문의
- as a reference 신용조회처로서 조회처를 의미할 때는 a reference 또는 references와 같이 사용
- a stamped, addressed envelope 주소가 기재되고 우표를 붙인 봉투
- confidence 비밀, 신용

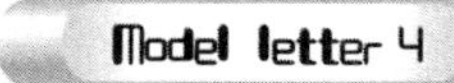

Model letter 4 회신

Dear Sirs,

We are pleased to state that the firm referred to in your letter of April 20 are a small but well-known and highly respectable firm, who have been established in this town for more than twenty-two years.

We ourselves have now been doing business with them for over five years on quarterly-account terms and although they have not as a rule taken advantage of our cash discounts, they have always paid their accounts promptly on the net dates.

The credit we have allowed the firm has at times been well above the £500 you mention.

We hope this information will be helpful and understand that you will treat it as confidential.

Yours faithfully,

Notes

- respectable 존경할 만한, 훌륭한 a small but well-known and highly respectable firm (소규모이나 유명하고 매우 존경할만한 회사)
- cash advantage 현금할인, 대금결제방식을 open account나 D/A 방식에서 송금방식이나 D/P 또는 L/ 방식으로 전환함에 따른 할인
- take advantage of ~을 이용하다 although they have not as a rule taken advantage of our cash discount(비록 동사가 당사의 현금할인과 같은 것을 이용한 예는 없지마는), Our terms of payment are 5% off the invoice amount at 60 days after sight. (당사의 결제조건은 일람후 60일 지급으로 송품장 금액의 5% 할인입니다만, 귀사에 10%의 특별현금할인을 해 드릴 수 있습니다.)
- net 순, 정미의, 에누리없는,
- They have always paid their accounts promptly on the net dates. (동사는 언제나 꼭 제날짜에 신속히 결제해 주었습니다.)
- net price 정미가격, 할인이나 에누리 및 commission이 포함되지 않는 가격
- at time 이따금, 때때로(= occasionally, now and then) cf. on time(정각에, 꼭 맞게, 제때에), in time(시간에 맞게, 시간 안에, 늦지 않게)

Model letter 5 동업자를 통한 신용조회

Dear Sirs,

We have just received information to the effect that you have a business relationship with The Hong Kong Importing Co., Inc. It is our wish to enter into business connections with the aforementioned company.

We therefore request that you give us any accurate information you have about that company in regard to productivity, efficiency, credibility and so on.

We would greatly appreciate any assistance you may be able to provide. We undertake to keep all information strictly confidential.

We are looking forward to receiving your favorable reply.

Yours faithfully,

Notes

- business relationship 거래관계
- accurate 정확한
- efficiency 능률
- assistance 지원, 도움
- aforementioned 전술한
- in regard to - 에 관하여
- credibility 진실성

단어 및 어휘연구

~와 관련하여

1월 15일 자의 귀사의 서한과 관련하여

- with(in) regard(respect, reference) to (=regarding to, respecting to, concerning to, referring to, relating to, in connection with, as regards) your letter of July 15.
- In reference to your order the 2nd of this month, we have to tell you that we find it impossible to, obtain the cloths at (for) the moment. (이번 달 2일 자의 귀사의 주문과 관련하여 당사는 지금은(당분간) 옷감을 입수하는 것이 불가능하다는 것을 알게 되었다는 귀사에 알려드립니다.)

~에 거래처를 가지고 있다.

connections 거래처 = customer, client, buyer, patron

- have connection in (~에 거래처를 가지고 있다.)
- have connection with (~와 거래관계가 있다.)
- in your market(district, area, region, zone, block) (귀 시장(지역)에)
- They have connection in ~ (동 상사는 ~에 거래처를 가지고 있다.)
- We have connection in your country. (당사는 귀국에 거래처를 가지고 있습니다.)
- They have no connections with traders in your market. (동 상사는 귀 시장에 있는 무역업자와 거래관계가 없습니다.)
- Do you have any connections in our city? (귀사는 당 도시에 거래처를 갖고 있습니까?)

Model letter 6 회신

Dear Sirs,

Your letter of Sept. 10 was received yesterday and the contents were well understood.

We therefore wish to inform you that The Hong Kong Importing Co., Inc. is a company of high standing.

They have business connections not only with us but also with X. Y. Z., U. A. C. and Johnson Co., Ltd. The success of their products and branches throughout the world speaks for itself.

While we can not be held responsible for any problems, we are happy to offer our services to you anytime.

Faithfully yours,

Notes

- contents **내용**
- therefore **그러므로**
- success **성공**
- product **제품**
- branch **지점**
- throughout the world = all over the world **전 세계적으로**
- make ourselves responsible for ~**에 대해 책임을 지다.** (take responsibility for, be accountable for ~, take charge of, be in charge of, answer for)

Ⅱ 무역조회 및 회신

1 무역조회의 의의

무역조회(inquiry)는 상거래관계 개시 전의 예비단계로 상품매매에 필요한 정보, catalog, 가격표(price-list), 견적가격(quotation)을 요청하거나 수량, 선적조건, 보험, 결재조건 등을 문의하는 것을 말한다. Inquiry는 우편 또는 전신으로 하며 이를 작성할 때는 ① 관심품목의 명시와 가격 ② 수요규모 및 구매상품의 명세 ③ 주문내용의 구체적인 설명 ④ 수요량에 따르는 선적시기 ⑤ 기타 요구 사항 등으로 기재한다.

답신은 신속 정확해야 하고 정중하고 짜임새 있는 것이 되도록 다음과 같은 요령으로 작성하여야 한다. ① Inquiry에 대한 감사의 뜻, ② 조회에 대한 답변(지나치게 과장하거나 복잡하게 하지 말 것), ③ 동봉한 Catalog나 Price List에 대해 필요할 때

보충설명, ④ 조속한 주문이 유리한 시황이라면 그 이유와 함께 조속히 주문해줄 것을 권고하는 말. ⑤ 맺음말

2 무역조회 관련 통신문

Model letter 1 전기제품에 대한 Catalog 요청

Gentlemen :

Thank you very much for your letter of June 10, proposing to do business with us in Electronic Machinery.

From your letter we are glad to learn that you are specially interested in shipping Electronic Machinery, and in these lines we may say that we are specialists.

We are prepared to accept your proposal so long as your goods prove suitable for our market in price and quality. Will you be good enough to send us a copy of your latest catalog and a price-list?

As to settlement of account, we are agreeable to your terms.

We thank you for your courtesy in marking the proposal and hope we may soon be able to work with you to our mutual advantage.

Very truly yours,

Notes

- specialists 전문가
- be prepared to ~할 준비가 되어 있다.
- suitable for our market 당 시장에 적합한
- the latest catalogue 가장 최신의 카탈로그(= the most up-to-date catalogue)
- settlement of account 지급(= payment)
- be agreeable to your terms 귀사의 조건에 동의하다
- to our mutual advantage 상호의 이익을 위해(= to our mutual benefit)

Model letter 2 회신

Gentlemen:

We acknowledge with thanks your letter of July, in which you expressed your willingness to open an account with us.

As requested, we have sent you separately one set of our complete catalog and enclose herewith our price list giving our lowest possible prices.

Before starting actual business, however, we should like to know if you would fall in with our general terms and conditions which we are enclosing.

If you have no objection to any of the clauses, you are requested to sign it and return the duplicate to us, keeping the original with you.

We congratulate ourselves upon having opened relations with you and look forward to doing business for a long time.

Your Very truly,

Notes

- acknowledge **수령하다**(= receive)
- willingness **바램, 소망**
- went you separately **별봉으로**(= under separate cover)
- fall in with **찬성하다**(= agree, accept)
- duplicate **부본**, to make out in duplicate(정부 2통을 작성하다),
  cf. original(원본), duplicate(2통), triplicate(3통), quadruplicate(4통), quintuplicate(5통), sextuplicate(6통), septuplicate(7통), octuplicate(8통), 9 copies(9통), 10 copies(10통)

단어 및 어휘연구 ~한 바와 같이

- as requested	- as advised	- as instructed	- as specified
- as pointed out	- as suggested	- as recommended	- as proposal

Model letter 3 면제품에 대한 상품조회

August 5, 200-

Gentlemen:

Having heard from The New York Chamber of Commerce that company is a leading firm specializing in Cotton Goods, we wish to make a purchase of Men's Cotton Shirts from you. We would appreciate receiving your best CIF New York with earliest delivery schedule.

We would also like to have two samples with Color Swatches by air mail.

If your goods are satisfactory in quality and delivery, we will place an order of 500 dozen on a trial basis and can make repeat orders with you in the near future.

We look forward to your early reply.

Cordially yours,

Notes

- having heard from 소식을 듣고(= hearing from, receive a letter from)
- best(lowest, minimum, rock-bottom) price 최저가
  (cf. retail(wholesale) price 소매(도매)가격, contract price(계약가격), fixed price(정찰가), invoice price(송장가격), quoted price(견적가격))
- color swatches 색상 견본 조각
- specializing in ~을 전문으로 하다.
- CIF New York 뉴욕항 도착 운임·보험료 포함 가격조건
- on a trial basis 시험으로(cf. initial(trial) order, 시험주문)

Model letter 4 회신

Gentlemen:

Thank you very much for your letter of August 5, 200- along with your excellent purchasing proposal.

As requested, we have already dispatched Silk Samples and Silk Swatches by Fed Express Speed Post.

From the enclosed price list you will notice that our prices are exceptionally low and this sacrifice is entirely due to our recognition of the necessity of price cutting in order to develop our sales in your market.

Since the market is now slow and prices are generally low, this is a good opportunity for you to buy. European buyers, however, seem to be picking up in activity.

Therefore, we advise you to buy the goods before the recovery reaches a peak.

Consequently, we can not keep the price effective more than two weeks from the date of this letter and we wish to receive your order by return mail.

We hope that this will meet with your immediate approval.

Very truly yours,

Notes

- your excellent purchasing proposal 귀사의 훌륭한 구매제안
- as requested 귀사의 요구에 따라서(= ccording to your request)
- be entirely due to 전적으로 기인하다.
- price cutting 가격 인하(가격할인)
- recognition of the necessity of pricing cutting 가격 인하의 필요성
- market is slow 시황이 부진하다. 침체되다
- picking up in activity 활동력이 회복되고 있다.

단어 및 어휘연구 ··· **meet**

- We will meet your requirements.(= satisfy, 충족시키다), meet the requirement, meet your request, meet the demand
- I can not meet your price.(=cover)
- This will meet with a ready sale(=face, 대응하다)
- We will meet the claims with counter-claim.(맞서다)
- We will meet all our debts(=pays, 지불하다, 갚다)
- We will meet the promissory notes.
- We will meet the premium for the insurance.

Model letter 5 견본 무료제공 요청

Dear Sirs,

We are pleased to inform you that we have received your letter of July 3 and sample No. PJG-0015, PJS-0215, ARS-3100, ARS-3200 and ARS-3300.

The samples you sent are passed over to our customs for their perusal and they informed us that they are satisfied with your quality and prices.

Also they want to ship the goods before the end of september by direct vessel from Korea to Las Palmas.

Beside of this, we sincerely request you to treat this samples in gratis for sample charges for this case only.

We have announced to our client that all sample are free of charge due to our misunderstanding of your price list which indicated all samples are free of charge except sample No. PJG-0015 and PJS-0215.

As your know it is common practice to supply samples free of charge in International transactions.

Looking forward to hearing good news from you soon, we remain.

Yours faithfully,

Notes

- for their perusal **그들이 숙독하도록, 그들이 상세히 검토하도록**
- by direct vessel **직항선에**(환적 없이 목적항까지 운송)
- beside of this **이에 더하여**
- in gratis **무료로, 대금을 바지 아니하고**
- client **고객** cf. 잠재고객(potential/prospective) client
- common practice **일반적이다, 보통이다.**

Model letter 6 견본대금 청구

Dear Sirs,

Thank you very much for your letter of July 3 showing your interest in our an paper samples. We are proud of our high quality paper refined through several decades to the point of perfection,

We have not received, however, the charges for two samples, namely PJG-0015, PJS-0215. All other samples are free of charge, but PJG-0015 and PJS-0215 are, as clearly stated in the price list, not free.

It is because these two are the most expensive products of our producer, who cannot furnish us with them free of charge.

If we cannot receive your payment, we must pay out of our account. As this is the first time for us to consider exporting direct to your country, we billed you with a 45% special discount.

Therefore, would you make the payment for PJG-0015 and PJS-0215 by the end of August? If you have further questions on this point, please fax us.

We are looking forward to your payment as well as your order for our high quality paper.

With best reqards.

Yours faithfully,

Notes

- art paper 아트지
- several decades 수 십 년간, 대체로 4~50년간
- point of perfection 완벽이라는 점에서, 완벽을 기한다는 관점에서
- pay out of our account 우리의 계정에서 지급되다. 우리가 지급하다. 귀사가 견본대금을 지급하지 않으면 우리가 대신 지급하여야 한다.
- furnish(provide/supply) A with B A에게 B를 공급하다
- looking forward to ~을 기대하다. to 다음에는 동사가 와서는 안 되며, 동명사나 명사가 와야 함

단어 및 어휘연구 … **A에게 B를 제공하다**

- furnish(supply, favor, provide) A with B
- Would you please furnish us with information for their business company? (동 상사의 거래 능력에 대한 정보를 제공해 주시겠습니까?)
- Please favor us with information on their financial standing. (동 상사의 금융 상태에 대한 정보를 알려 주시기 바랍니다.)

Model letter 7 견본대금 지급거절에 대한 회신

Dear Sirs,

Your facsimile memo of July 3, 20— on the payment for the 2 samples. We have studies your memo of July 3 carefully. Your stated, in the memo, that you refuse to pay for the two samples we have sent because you accepted them free of charge.

We have checked the copy of our letter and the price list we sent you on June 3 together with the samples. The letter and price list show that, in addition to the footnote on the price list, we stated as follow :

"We are sending you this letter with three sample sheets of art paper for free and two other at 45% reduced price."

This is because those two items have highly intricate transparent patterns and dusted with gold and silver. and are so expensive that our producer cannot supply them free of charge. We have decided to wait for your payment until April 31. You can mail us your check or remit the amount to our bank account shown in the price list.

Since established in 1926, we have had direct contact with the first class pater producers here. We shall be happy to send you any other samples (free or billed) you are interest in. Please let us know any time.

Yours very truly,

Notes

- free of charge 무료 • price list 가격표 • show 보여주다, ~로 확인되다.
- as follows 다음과 같이, follows는 비인칭 동사로서 항상 복수로 사용되어야 함
- intricate transparent patterns 복잡한 투명도안
- dusted with gold and silver 금가루와 은가루가 뿌려진
- free or billed 무료이거나 또는 대금을 받는

Useful Expressions

1. Thank you for your inquiry of May 1.
   5월 1일 자 귀 조회에 대하여 감사합니다.

2. Please tell us all you know about the Hong Kong Co., Inc
   홍콩회사에 관하여 알고 계신 모든 것을 말씀해 주십시오.

3. We would also like to know the financial status of the said company.
   또한, 상기 회사의 재정 상태를 알고 싶습니다.

4. Please inform us in confidence of your opinion about their financial standing.
   죄송하오나 극비로 그 상사의 재정 상태에 관한 귀사의 의견을 통지해 주십시오.

5. How long have you been in business relations with them?
   귀사는 얼마나 오랫동안 그들과 거래를 하여 왔습니까?

6. What are the terms of payment?
   결재 조건은 무엇입니까?

7. Please send us your sample with your best terms.
   최선의 거래조건과 함께 귀사의 견본을 보내 주십시오.

8. We should be obliged if you would let us know your lowest prices for the following goods
   다음 상품의 최저 가격을 알려 주시면 감사하겠습니다.

9. Please send us your best blue cotton shirting at prices ranging from 5d. to 7d. per yard.
   야드당 5펜스에서 7펜스로 변동한 가격으로 최고급의 청색 면 셔츠 감을 보내 주십시오.

10. We are enclosing our requirements. Please quote C.I.F. Hong Kong on the best refined sugar.
당사의 요구조건을 동봉합니다. 최고급 정제 설탕의 홍콩 도착 운임 보험료 포함 가격을 제시하십시오.

11. Please let us know what discount you can grant if we give you a large order.
대량 주문을 하면 어느 정도의 할인을 해 주는지를 알려 주십시오.

12. Any information you may give us about their credit standing will be treated strictly confidential.
귀사가 그들의 신용 상태에 관하여 당사에 제공하는 어떠한 정보도 극비로 처리될 것입니다.

13. Any expenses to be incurred in connection with this inquiry please charge to our account.
이 조사에 관련되어 발생된 비용은 당사 계정에 기장하십시오.

14. The firm enjoys an excellent reputation among the business circle here.
그 상사는 이 곳 실업계에서 평판이 뛰어납니다.

15. The firm has become insolvent.
그 상사는 지급불능이 되었습니다.

16. Messrs. Smith & Co,, of your city, desire to open an account with us, and have given us your name as a reference.
귀사 스미스상사는 폐사와 거래관계를 희망하고 있으며, 신용조회처로 귀하를 통지하여 주었습니다.

17. We thank you in advance for whatever information you will tive us, strictly in confidence.
극비로 어떠한 통지를 받든 대단히 감사히 여길 것이오며, 미리 사의를 표합니다.

청약과 승낙

I 청약의 기초개념

1 오퍼의 의의

오퍼(청약)란 청약자(offeror)가 피청약자(offeree)에게 일정한 상품을 일정한 조건으로 매매하고자 하는 의사표시이다. 청약은 다음의 요건을 갖추어야 한다.

첫째, 1인 또는 그 이상의 특정인에 대한 의사표시이어야 한다. 불특정인에 대한 의사표시는 단순한 청약의 유인(invitation to make offers)으로 간주된다.

둘째, 내용이 충분히 확정적이어야 한다. 제안(proposal)이 물품을 표시하고, 수량이나 대금을 지정하거나 그 결정을 위한 조항을 두고 있는 경우에 그 제안은 충분히 확정적인 것으로 간주된다.[3)]

셋째, 승낙이 있으면 그에 구속된다는 의사가 있어야 한다. 즉, 피청약자의 승낙으로 계약이 성립되면 청약자는 그 계약의 내용을 이행하여야 한다.

구속의 의사는 첫째, 청약에 승낙기간을 지정하거나 "irrevocable" 또는 "firm" 등과 같은 표시를 함으로써 청약이 철회될 수 없음을 명시하거나, 둘째로 청약이 철회할 수 없는 것이라고 상대방이 신뢰하는 것이 합리적이며 또는 그 청약을 신뢰하여 실제로 행동을 취한 경우, 예컨대 피청약자가 생산설비를 갖춘다든지 원료를 구매한

---

3) 다만 가격을 정하지 않고도 계약을 성립시키고자 하는 당사자들의 의사표시가 있다면, 가격이 확정적이 아니더라도 계약을 성립시킬 수 있다. 이때의 가격은 계약체결시 당해 거래와 유사한 상황에서 매도되는 물품에 대하여 일반적으로 청구되는 가액으로 정해진다. 즉 계약체결시 객관적으로 통용되는 가격이 계약대금이 된다.(CISG 제55조)

다든지, 사람을 고용하는 경우가 이에 해당한다. (CISG 第16조 제2항)

따라서 단순한 가격표나 카탈로그 또는 광고물을 보내는 것은 청약이 아니라 청약의 유인이며, 의향서(letter of intent)도 계약의 내용은 확정되어 있지만, 법적 구속의사가 없으므로 청약이 될 수 없다.

청약은 상대방에게 도달한 때에 효력이 발생한다. 청약의 방법은 반드시 서면(writing)으로 행할 필요는 없으므로 구두로 행하는 것도 가능하나 실무에서는 보통 전보, 팩시밀리 또는 일정한 서식을 갖춘 청약서(offer sheet)를 사용한다.

2 오퍼의 종류

오퍼에는 매도인의 매도의사표시인 Selling offer와 매수인의 매수의사표시인 Buying offer로 구분할 수 있으나, 실무에서는 주로 Selling offer가 많이 이용된다. 오퍼는 그 내용에 따라 다음과 같이 구분된다.

selling offer → [① firm offer / ② free offer / ③ conditional offer / ④ counter offer] ← buying offer

(1) **확정오퍼(Firm Offer)**

확정오퍼란 청약자가 승낙기간을 지정하고 있거나 승낙기간을 정하지 아니하였더라도 그 오퍼가 확정적(firm), 취소불능(irrevocable)이라는 것을 표시하고 있는 오퍼를 말하며, 취소불능청약(irrevocable offer)이라고도 한다. 확정오퍼는 승낙기간 또는 합리적 기간 내에 상대방이 승낙의 의사표시를 하면 오퍼의 내용대로 계약이 성립된다.

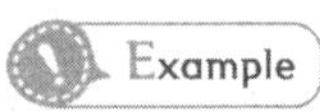

"We offer you firm subject to your acceptance reaching us by June 20 as follows."

 단어 및 어휘연구 ··· **subject to**

규정하고 있는 사항이 법률이나 다른 조항에서 규정하고 있는 내용 등을 조건으로 하는 경우에 그러한 것들이 당해 규정에 우선한다는 것을 표시하는 문언이다.

① 당해 규정의 성립이나 효력발성의 조건이 되거나 성립이나 해석의 근거가 되는 경우(governed by 또는 in accordance with로 대체가능)

"Subject to the availability of funds from the Export-Import Bank of Korea, the Seller hereby agrees to sell the Machinery on a deferred payment basis as hereinafter more specifically set out."

"Each individual contract to be made hereunder be always subject to the terms and conditions of this Basic Sales Agreement."

② 단서나 예외가 되는 경우

"Subject to the provisions concerning force majeure in Article 16, the Contractor execute the Works in strict accordance with the Construction Schedule attached hereto."

(2) 자유오퍼(Free Offer)

승낙기간이 지정되어 있지 않거나 확정적임을 표시하지 아니한 오퍼를 말하며 불확정오퍼라고도 한다. 불확정오퍼는 상대방이 승낙의 의사표시를 하기 전까지는 청약자가 일방적으로 청약의 내용을 철회 또는 변경할 수 있다.

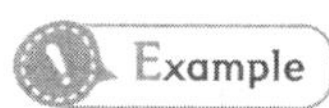

"We offer you the following merchandise on the terms and conditions mentioned hereunder."

(3) 조건부오퍼(Conditional Offer)

청약자의 청약내용에 조건이 붙어 있는 청약을 말하며, 피청약자의 승낙만으로는 계약이 성립되지 않고 다시 원청약자의 최종확인(confirmation)이 있어야만 계약이 성립되는 청약이다.

① 선착순매도조건오퍼(Offer subject to Prior Sale)

매수인이 승낙의 의사표시를 하는 시점에 물품의 재고가 있어야만 계약이 성립된다는 것을 조건으로 하는 오퍼로 "offer subject to being unsold(잔매조건부)"라고도 한다. 이 오퍼는 재고를 처분하고자 여러 곳에 동시에 오퍼 할 때 이용된다. 먼저 승낙의 의사표시를 한 자에게 매도할 것을 조건으로 하고 있으므로 결국 상품의 매진과 동시에 그 효력이 소멸한다.

② 승인오퍼(Offer on Approval)

오퍼와 함께 현품을 보내서 상대방이 실험 또는 사용해 보아 만족할 것을 조건으로 하는 오퍼로서, 상대방이 만족하지 아니하면 일정 기간 내에 반품할 수 있다. 이와 비슷한 것으로서 그 현품을 일정 기간 팔다가 남으면 반품할 것을 조건으로 하는 "Offer on Sale or Return"도 있다.

③ 확인조건부 오퍼(Offer subject to Confirmation)

"Subject to our final confirmation"이라는 단서가 붙은 오퍼를 말한다. 이밖에 "Offer without engagement", "Offer subject to change without notice" 또는 "Offer subject to market fluctuation" 등과 함께 상대방의 승낙만으로는 계약이 성립되지 아니하며, 이에 대하여 다시 원청약자의 최종확인이 있어야만 계약이 성립된다. 시장 상황, 환율변동이나 비용증가의 가능성이 있는 경우에 이용된다.

④ 반대오퍼(Counter Offer)

매도인의 청약에 대하여 매수인이 가격, 수량, 선적조건 등에 관하여 청약내용의 일부 변경 또는 추가 등 새로운 조건을 제의를 해오는 오퍼를 말한다. 반대오퍼는 원청약에 대한 거절인 동시에 새로운 청약을 제의하는 상대방의 의사표시이므로 반대청약이 있으면 원청약의 효력은 상실된다.

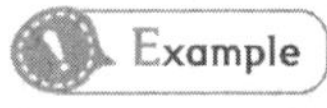

"Your offer dated May 7 is too high. We can accept the offer at USD 15 per piece CIF New York."

3 오퍼의 승낙(Acceptance)

원칙적으로 청약(offer)은 승낙(acceptance)이 있음으로써 계약의 성립된다.[4] 승낙이란 피청약자(offeree)가 청약자에 대하여 그 청약에 응하여 계약을 성립시킬 목적으로 행하는 의사표시를 말한다.

승낙이 법적으로 유효하게 되어 계약을 성립시키기 위한 요건은 다음과 같다. ① 유효기간 이내의 승낙일 것, ② 오퍼의 모든 조건에 대한 완전하고도 무조건적(unqualified)인 승낙일 것, ③ 오퍼에 대한 승낙 방법을 청약서에 지정한 경우 그 방법에 의한 승낙일 것 등이다.

이러한 요건을 갖추지 못하게 되면, 예를 들어 유효기간이 경과하여 승낙이 이루어진 경우나 승낙을 의도하고 있으나 원 청약 내용의 변경을 포함하는 응답은 원 청약에 대한 거절이면서 동시에 새로운 청약(counter offer)이 된다.

승낙의 의사표시는 진술뿐만 아니라 기타의 행위에 의해서도 가능하다. 예컨대 물품의 발송, 대금지급, 물품의 수령, 신용장의 개설 등에 의해서도 승낙이 가능하다. 그러나 청약에 대한 침묵이나 부작위는 그 자체만으로는 승낙이 되지 못한다(CISG 제18조). 다만 당사자간의 합의나 관행 또는 관례에 의해 침묵이 승낙이 될 수도 있다.[5]

---

4) 예외적으로 승낙이 없어도 계약이 성립된 것으로 간주되는 경우는 다음과 같다. ① 피청약자가 청약의 내용을 실행한 경우(대금결제 등), ② 교차청약의 경우, ③ 청약에 의하여 또는 당사자가간에 확립된 관례나 관행에 따라 상대방이 청약에 대한 승낙통지 없이, 물품의 발송이나 대금의 지급과 같은 행위를 함으로써 승낙의 의사표시를 할 수 있는 경우에는 그 행위가 이루어진 시점에 승낙의 효력이 발생한다.

5) 승낙 없이 계약을 성립하기로 당사자간에 합의한 경우 또는 관행적으로 그렇게 계약을 체결해 온 경우, 그리고 승낙을 의도하고 있고, 청약의 조건을 실질적으로 변경하지 아니한 부가적 조건 또는 상이한 조건을 포함하는 청약에 대항 응답 등이다. 이때 청약자가 그 상위에 이의를 제기하지 않을 경우에는 조건변경된 승낙의 내용대로 계약이 체결된다. 실질적 변경이란 대금, 대금지급, 물품의 품질과 수량, 인도의 장소와 시기, 당사자 일반의 상대방에 대한 책임 범위 또는 분쟁 해결에 관한 조건의 변경을 의미한다(CISG 제19조).

Ⅱ 청약 관련 통신문

Model letter I 칼라 텔레비전에 대한 확정 오퍼

October 7, 20--

Gentlemen :

We have received with thanks your inquiry of 5th October, requesting us to quote the prices for Color Television Sets.

Concerning the above, we offer you firm subject to your reply being received here by Monday, 21st October, as specified below:

500 Color Tv Sets each, Model SSE 2000 @£500 stg. and Model SSE 3000 @ £800 stg. per set CIF London, shipment to be effected within 6 weeks after receipt of your offer.

We are sure that you will find our prices attractive. The market here is enjoying an upward trend, and we have no further stock available to off at the same price.

We advise you not to overlook this opportunity and hope to receive your prompt order by facsimile.

Yours very truly,
Seoul Trading Co., Ltd.
Min-ho Kang
General Manager

Notes

- enjoying an upward 시장 상황이 상승하는 추세, 시장이 활황인
- do not overlook this opportunity 이번 기회를 간과하지 않다. 놓치지 않다.(= do not miss this opportunity, do not let this opportunity go)

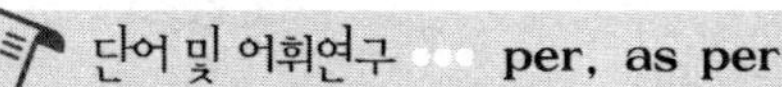

① your shipment per(= by) s/s Arirang(아리랑호 편으로)
the order per(= by) your letter of April 5.
per(= by) check : 수표로
② as per price list attached(= as indicated in)
as per enclosed copy of our cable(=as shown in)
as per sample, as per 다음에는 관사를 사용하지 않음

Model letter 2 반대청약

october 9, 200-
Seoul Trading Co., Ltd.
C.P.O. Box 777
Seoul, Korea

Gentlemen :

Thank you for your firm offer of 7th October.

Your goods meet our requirement in quality. But after careful examination of your quotation, we had an impression that your prices are rather stiff.

As your are aware, competition on this line is very keen, while the market becomes dull. Moreover when we compared the prices of your makes with those of other suppliers, we found that your prices are higher by over 5% than others.

In due consideration of market conditions, we ask you to reduce your prices to @ £470 stg. for Model SSE 2000 and @ £750 stg. for Model SSE 3000. Your kind allowances will be of help to an increase in your market share.

Unless you can book at these figures, we are afraid that this business will fall through.

Yours very truly,
America International Co., Inc.
Richard C. Anderson

Notes

- we had an impression that ~라는 생각이 들다, be under an impression that(~하다고 생각하고 있다.), make an impression on(~에게 인상을 주다, ~를 감동시키다.)
- your prices are rather stiff 귀사의 가격이 꽤 높은 편이다.
- competition on this line is very keen 이 계통 제품의 경쟁이 치열하다.
- the market becomes dull 시장 상황이 침체되다. 불황이 되다.
- in due consideration of ~을 고려하여, ~의 사례로서
- market share 시장점유율, Your kind allowances will be of help to an increase in your market share.(귀사께서 할인을 해 주신다면 귀사의 시장점유율이 증가하는 데 도움이 될 것이다.)
- book 기입하다, 표를 발행하다, 예약하다, (화물을) 탁송하다.
- figure 총액(amount)의 의미로 사용, They sell at high figures.(비싸게 팔고 있다.). He is good at figure.(그는 계산에 밝다.)
- Unless you can book at these figures 귀사께서 이 금액(가격)에 송부해 주실 수 없다면
- we are afraid 유감이지만 ~라고 생각하다.
- fall through 실패하다, 그르치다, 실현되지 않다.

Model letter 3 반대청약에 대한 대안의 청약

We have received your counter offer of 9th October requesting more reduction of prices.

As we have already allowed you a special discount of 3 percent our normal discount to the trade of 5 percent, your counter offer hardly covers the production cost. We, therefore, decided to consider your suggestion in two ways.

First, we can accept your counter offer providing you raise your order over 200 sets each.

Second, we offer you at prices of £ 480 stg. for Model SJC 1526 and @£770 stg. for Model SJC 1530.

This is our best offer for this initial order and we will be unable to offer at the same price in the future.

As we are anxious to materialize business in this opportunity, we hope you will accept one of our alternative without delay.

Yours faithfully,

Notes

- discount to the trade 동업자 할인, 5%의 정상 동업자 할인에 추가하여 3%의 특별할인을 하였기 때문에
- your offer hardly covers the production cost 귀사의 청약은 거의 생산비에도 미치지 못 한다.
- providing ~을 조건으로, 만약 ~이라면(= if)
- materialization business 사업을 실현하다. 거래관계를 맺다.

단어 및 어휘연구 ··· **cover**

- Supplies of the tin easily cover the present demand(= meet)
- Insurance covers the loss.(= provides for)
- The letter covers the matter(= deal with)
- The regulation covers the matters you have raised(= apply to)

Model letter 4 면셔츠에 대한 확정오파

October 10, 200-

Dear Sirs,

We have the pleasure of acknowledge your letter of August 30. requesting us to quote the most favorable price on cotton shirts and we make the following offer subject your acceptance received here by October 25 as follows :

Article : Cotton Shirts.
Quality : Subject to our catalog item Style No. 20.
Quantity : 1,000 dozen.

Price : @US$15.20 per dozen CIF New York.
Shipment : During November.
Payment : Under Irrevocable L/C at sight to be opened in our favor.
Inspection: Seller's inspection to be final.

We regret that our prices were not low enough to meet your requirements, we are sure that these goods are much better in quality than any other brand we have ever on sale and yet their price is quite reasonable.

The demand for these goods is very strong both at home and abroad. A rush of orders is now coming every day and we are afraid we will run out of stock one of these days.

Therefore, the above revised is the best price we can make at present since the high quality of our goods can't be maintained at lower prices.

In fact, our revised price is closely calculated and we shall not be able to make any further price reduction in spite of our eagerness to start business.

We trust you will accept it without delay.

Yours faithfully,

Notes

- on sale 판매중인 cf. for sale 팔려고 내놓은
- rush of orders 주문쇄도, 주문 폭주
- run out of stock 품절되다
- one of these days 근일 중에

Model letter 5 선착순 매도조건부 오퍼(Offer Subject to Being Unsold)

Gentlemen :

We have the pleasure of presenting the following goods as below:

22,000 "Dried Anchovy" Art. No. 1 @U.S.$ 1.10 per lb
22,000 "Dried Anchovy" Art. No. 2 @U.S.$ 1.20 per lb.
The prices are based on C.I.F. Hongkong.
Prompt shipment.
Terms as usual.

Owing to the brisk demand of fresh anchovy in the market during the fall and winter, it will be absolutely impossible for us to stock abundant processed products at such low prices, and we trust you are in a position to avail yourselves of this opportunity without delay.

Yours truly,

Notes

- Offer Subject to Being Unsold 선착순 매도조건부 오퍼
- Dried Anchovy 마른 멸치
- Art. No. = Article Number 품목번호
- fresh anchovy 싱싱한 멸치
- processed products 가공품
- be in a position to = be able to
- avail oneself of ~을 이용하다
- without delay 지체 없이, 속히

Model letter 6 Offer Sheet 양식

OFFER SHEET

Dear Sirs,

We take pleasure in offering you the following goods on the terms and conditions set forth below.

Description	Quantity	Unit Price	Amount
KOREAN AGAR-AGAR STRIP, 200-crop 2nd Grade, inspected and passed by our government	3,500lbs	CFR New York @US$ 2.10 per lb. FOB Busan, Korea @US$ 2.00 per lb.	US$ 7,350.00 US$ 7,000.00

1. Payment : By irrevocable and confirmed L/C in our favour.
2. Shipment : By the first available steamer for your port after receipt of L/C.
3. Packing : Export standard gunny bales in pressed condition (each bale measuring about 3.3 cft.).
4. Quality : As sample.
5. Origin : The Republic of Korea.
6. Validity : This offer is valid until September 21, 20--.
7. Remarks : The prices quoted above are net prices.
   We are hoping to be favoured with your order.

Yours very truly,

KOREAN AGAR-AGAR PRODUCTS CO., LTD.

Notes

- by irrevocable and confirmed L/C 취소불능확인신용장에 의해
- set forth = appeared
- in our favour 폐사를 수익자로 하여
- favor - with ~에게 ~을 주다

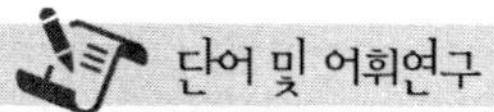

단어 및 어휘연구

~에 규정된

- set forth - mentioned - specified - provide for

유효하다

- The offer is valid until June 10(effective, open, good, in effect, in force)
- The validity of the offer is June 10.
- The expiry date of the letter of credit is June 10.
- The letter of credit expires of June 1.
- We off you firm subject to your acceptance(being) received here by noon June 10.

Model letter 7 주문거절

Gentlemen :

Thank for your order No. 3 received today.

Unfortunately we do not feel that the trade discounts which you have requested, viz. 30 percent, can be met since we only allow a 25% trade discount to all of our customers.

As you may agree, our prices are extremely competitive and it would not be worthwhile supplying on the allowance you have asked for. Therefore, in this case, we regret that we have to turn down your order.

Yours very truly,

Notes

- trade discount 동업자 할인(도매할인)
- viz. 즉, 라틴어 videlicet의 약자, namely로 읽음
- turn over 거절, decline이나 reject 보다 완곡한 표현

Model letter 8 가격인하 거절 및 대체품 제시

Dear Sirs,

"JAGUAR" SNEAKERs

ORDER NO. WK-508

We thank you for your order of June 10 for these shoes, which is receiving our immediate attention.

As for your request for a reduction in price, we regret that this is not just possible. We would very much like to accommodate you in this matter, but we have already cut our prices down to the absolute minimum.

You will perhaps agree that other shoes offered at better prices are of considerably different quality.

We would recommend VARE/FOOT/WEAR range on pp.12-14 of the catalogue enclosed as an excellent substitute. These are reliable shoes and will enjoy a guaranteed life of six months.

They sell at prices slightly higher than "JAGUR" Sneakers. To help you introduce them into your market, we are prepared to offer on them a special discount of 5%.

This offer is valid until July r, and we would like to know if you care to avail yourselves of this.

Yours faithfully,

Notes

- reduction in price 가격할인(= price reduction)
- We would like to accommodate you 귀사의 편의에 도모하고 싶다. (we would like to help you)
- cut our prices down to the absolute minimum 가격을 최저로 인하하다
- You will perhaps ~ 아마도 귀사께서는 ~하리라고 생각됩니다.
- at better prices = at low prices
- of considerably different quality = much lower in quality
- slightly 다소, 약간(= somewhat, more or less, rather)
- offer a special discount 특별할인을 해주다(= offer a introduction discount)
- This offer is valid 이 오퍼는 ~까지 유효합니다.(= effeictive, good) until ~, This offer effects in force until ~, This offer expires(is expire, shall expire)
- avail yourselves of this 본 오퍼를 수락하다.
  cf. avail oneself of ~을 이용하다(= make use of)

Model letter 9 가격할인을 요청하는 반대오퍼

October 15, 20--

Dear Sirs,

We are in receipt of your firm offer dated October 10 for 1,000 dozen of Cotton Shirts, Style No. 20 at US$15.20 per dozen CIF New York for November shipment, for which we have just cabled you a counter offer as below contents.

In view of the current price in this market your price is rather high.

You must remember that the competition in this line is very strong and that your competitors are offering lower prices than yours.

We would like to transact most of our business with you and we have cabled you a counter offer, asking for further discount. How about reducing your price somewhat, to US$14.20 per dozen?

If you can come down to this level, we prepared to give you a substantial order but so unless you can accept this price the business will fail through.

Hoping you to accept our price soon to our mutual encouragement and benefit.

Yours faithfully,

Notes

- in view of -을 비추어 볼 때(고려하여)
- current price 현시가(= ruling price)
- rather high 다소 비싼(= rather stiff, somewhat strong, slightly high)
- How about reducing your price somewhat, to US$14.20?
  값을 조금만, 예를 들면 다스 당 14.20달러로 내리는 게 어떻습니까?
- come down to this level 이 가격수준까지 내리다.
- give you a substantial order 상당한 양의 주문을 하다
- fail through 실패하다, 그르치다(= come to nothing fail)
- to mutual encouragement and benefit 서로의 격려와 이익을 위하여

Model letter 10 회신(반대오파)의 수락

Dear Sirs,

We accept your counter offer of October 15 in order to execute the first transaction with you.

In the course of our negotiation by cable with you, we were reluctantly forced to cut our price to a point where no margin of profit is left to us.

Frankly speaking, we cannot think of any specific objection to your proposal, and would certainly consider it to our mutual benefit to come to a concrete arrangement.

Please note that your limit price barely covers the cost of production, and therefore

We shall be unable to maintain our quality without any increase in price for your future orders.

We will proceed with the execution of this order immediately upon receiving your advice of the establishment of a letter of credit. Awaiting your L/C No. and Purchase Note by return.

Yours faithfully,

Notes

- in the course of ~**하는 동안(과정)에**(= while(during) we are)
- be forced to ~**하지 않을 수 없다.**(= obliged, compelled, bound)
- no margin of profit **이익이 전혀 없는**
- specific objection **명확한 반대**
- concrete arrangement **구체적인 협정(체결)**
- limit price **지정가격, 제한가격, 할인가격**
- barely cover the cost of production **제조한 원가를 거의 커버하지 못하다.**

단어 및 어휘연구 **~하지 않을 수 없다.**

- be compelled(obliged, forced, bound) to+동사원형
- be obliged to
- have no choice but to+동사원형
- there is no other way than to+동사원형
- there is nothing to be done(for it) but to+동사원형

① owing to the breakdown of our manufacturing plant, we are obliged to ask you for two weeks' extension of delivery. (당사의 제조기계의 고장으로 인하여 당사는 귀사에게 인도의 2주 연장을 요청하지 않을 수 없습니다.)

② Through the recent advance in sugar, we have been compelled to rise the price of the sweets somewhat. (최근 설탕가격의 급등으로 당사는 어느 정도 사탕 가격을 올리지 않을 수 없었습니다.)

③ Unless the goods arrive here in a week, we shall have to cancel the order. (1주일 이내에 물품이 도착하지 않는 경우 당사는 주문을 취소할 수밖에 없습니다.)

Model letter 11 주문품에 대한 대체품 오퍼

Dear Sirs,

Thank you for your letter of the 12th May enclosing your order for 800 yards of 36 inches wide "Aqualine" watered silk.

We are sorry we can no longer supply this silk. Fashions are constantly changing and in recent years the demand for watered silks has fallen to such an extent that we have ceased to produce them. In their place we can offer you our new "Gossamer" brand of rayon. This is a finely woven, hardwaring, non-creasable material with a most attractive luster.

The large number of repeat orders we regularly receive from lending distributors and dress manufacturers is clear evidence of the widespread popularity of this brand. At the low price of only £0.85 a yard this rayon is much cheaper than silk and its appearance is just as attractive.

We are makers of other clothes in which you may be interested and are sending you a full range of pattern by parcel post. All these are selling well in many countries and we can safely recommend them. We can supply all of them from stock and if, as we hope, you decide to place an order, we could meet it within ten days.

Yours faithfully,

Notes

- watered silk 물결무늬가 있는 견직
- in their place 그들 대신에
- non-creasable 구겨지지 않는
- with a most attractive luster 매우 호감 있게 광채 나는 색상으로
- safely recommend 안심하고 권하다
- meet 충당하다, 충족하다
- We are enclosing ~, We have enclosed ~, enclosed you will find~, enclosed please find~, please find enclosed~, enclosed is ~ 동봉하여 보내다

Useful Expressions

1. In response to your inquiry of July 20, we offer you our Lion Blanket No.123 as follows:
   7월 20일 자 귀 조회에 대한 회답으로 라이온 표 모포 No.123을 오퍼 합니다.

2. We are in a position to offer cotton goods at these lowest prices because we can purchase them from a large manufacturer.
   대규모 제조업자로부터 매입할 수 있기 때문에 싼 가격으로 면직물을 오퍼할 수 있습니다.

3. (a) This offer is open until May 7.
   (b) This offer is available until May 7.
   (c) This offer is effective until May 7.
   (d) This offer is good until May 7.
   (e)This offer is in force until May 7.
   이 오퍼는 5월 7일까지 유효합니다.

4. (a) This offer is subject to your reply received by July 2.
   (b) This offer is subject to (receiving) your reply by July 2.
   (c) This offer is subject to your reply reaching us by July 2.
   이 오퍼는 7월 2일까지 귀사 회답을 받을 것을 조건으로 한다.

5. This offer expires on May 12.
   이 오퍼의 유효기간은 5월 12일로 끝납니다.

6. We regret to inform you that we cannot accept your offer. Your prices are too high.
   유감스러우나 귀사의 오퍼를 수락할 수 없습니다. 귀사의 가격은 너무 비쌉니다.

7. The prices you quoted are much higher than those of other manufacturers.
   귀사가 메긴 가격은 다른 제조업자의 가격보다 훨씬 비쌉니다.

8. Our prices are always competitive.
폐사의 가격은 언제나 저렴합니다.

9. We will make you a rebate of 2%.
폐사는 2%의 환불을 해 드리겠습니다.

10. Will you please send us sample of the best note-papers you can offer of the following kinds :
아래의 종류 가운데서 오퍼할 수 있는 최고급 서한 용지의 견본이 있으면 보내주십시오.

11. We have an inquiry today from a client who desires to import some Chinese sheep wool, and shall be glad to receive samples and quotations FOB Hong Kong.
중국산 양모의 수입을 희망하는 고객으로부터 오늘 문의가 있었으니 견본 및 FOB 홍콩가격을 보내주십시오.

12. We are enclosing a copy of our recent catalogue with a few sample which may possibly interest you, and shall be glad to hear from you at any time.
최신판 카탈고그 1부에 견본 몇 개를 첨부하여 송부합니다. 이에 대해 마음에 드실 것으로 사료되오며, 언제든지 연락해 주시기를 부탁드립니다.

13. In the unlikely event of none of these sample suiting you, we can submit others.
만약 이 견본 가운데 마음에 드시는 것이 없으시면 다른 것을 제공하겠습니다.

14. Receiving your samples, we have shown them to their buyers.
귀하의 견본을 받고 그것을 구매자들에게 공람(供覽)시켰습니다.

15. In accordance with your wish, we are sending you enclosed our latest price list.
귀하의 희망에 따라 최신 정가표를 동봉하여 송부해드립니다.

제5장 주문과 수락

I 주문의 의의

일반적으로 매매계약은 수출업자의 청약(offer)에 대해 수입업자가 승낙(accept)하거나, 수입업자의 주문(order)을 수출업자가 수락(acknowledge)함으로써 성립된다. 주문이란 매수인이 매도인에게 구매하고자 하는 물품의 명세와 거래조건 및 구매의사에 관한 명시적 의사표시를 말하며, Buying Offer와 동일한 성격을 가진다. 주문서는 매도인으로부터 받은 Offer, 견본, 상품목록 및 가격표 등을 참조하여 매수인이 주문을 보낼 때 사용된다.

주문서에는 다음과 같은 내용이 포함된다. ① 관련서한 등 참조표시, ② 주문상품의 상품명, 품종, 번호, 품질, 수량, 가격, 카탈로그 번호 등, ③ 선적조건, ④ 가격조건, ⑤ 포장방법 및 하인

실무에서는 수출업자가 Firm Offer를 하고 수입업자가 지정기간 내에 Accept를 한 후에 賣約書(Sales Note)와 買約書(Purchase Note)를 교환하는 것이 보통이다. 그러나 실제에 있어서는 주문서(Order Sheet) 대신에 Purchase Note 그리고 주문승낙서(Acknowledge of Order) 대신에 Sales Note로 대용하는 경우가 많다.

매도인은 매수인의 주문을 수락하는 의사표시로서 매약서(sales note)를 발송하는데, 이를 주문수락서(acknowledge of order)라고 한다. 주문수락서 작성시 고려할 사항은 다음과 같다. ① 주문을 수락한다는 의사표시 및 감사의 뜻, ② 주문에 대한 상대방의 참조번호 및 주문내용 재확인, ③ 선적시기, 선박명 등의 지시사항 재확인 및 결제방법의 제시, ④ 주문품을 만족스럽게 조달할 것임에 대한 약속, 지속적 거래

를 희망한다는 의사표시 등이다.

Ⅱ 주문 관련 통신문

Model letter 1 시험주문

Dear Sirs,

Further to our letter of 14th instant, we have been successful in obtaining a small trial order for Lighters you sent us some time back, as per particulars given in the order sheet attached hereto, and shall be obliged if you will kindly let us have your Sales Note in duplicate mentioning the prices we have stated in the Indent, and as soon as we receive this we shall include this too in the letter of credit we will be opening in respect of the other orders we have already place with you.

The difference in price should be placed to the credit of our account, and please follow the instructions we have given in respect of our last order, and the documents should be in the same manner as the ones you have already sent us,

In this case too, we have undertaken to import the goods under our own name, and therefore the Sales Note should be under our own name and licence.

There is every possibility of obtaining some good orders for Gents and Ladies Fountain Pens of good quality, and if you can supply these, we shall be obliged if you will let us have immediately on receipt of this letter various samples, together with your CIF prices.

Please give the matter your early attention.

Yours faithfully,

Notes

- further ~외에도, 그 밖에, ~에다가 또(= in addition, besides)
- of 14th instant 이달 14일 자의
- small trial order 소액의 시험주문
- some time back 얼마 전에
- particulars 상세한 내용, 명세(= details)
- Sales note 매약서
- mentioning 기재한
- indent 위탁구매, 상품 구매를 직접 하지 않고 대행기관에 위탁하는 것
  cf. 위탁판매, consignment
- as soon as we receive this we shall include this too in the letter of credit we will be opening in respect of the other orders we have aleady place with you. (이것을 접수하는 즉시 이전에 귀사에 드린 다른 주문에 대해 개설할 예정인 신용장에 이것 또한 포함시키겠습니다.)
- difference in price 가격차이
- to place to the credit of our account 당사계정의 대변에 기입하다.
- please follow the instructions we have given in respect of our last order. (지난번 주문에 관해 말씀드린 당사의 지시에 따라주시기 바랍니다.)
- In this case too, we have undertaken to import the goods under our own name, and therefore the Sales Note should be under our own name and licence. (이번 건도 당사 명의로 수입을 수행하는 것이므로 매약서는 당사 명의와 수입면허로 하여야 합니다.)
- gent 남자, 신사(= gentleman)
- There is every possibility of obtaining some good orders for Gents and Ladies Fountain Pens of good quality. (품질 좋은 신사용 및 숙녀용 만년필에 대한 상당한 주문을 받을 가능성이 많다.)

Model letter 2 첫 주문

Gentlemen :

We have duly received with many tanks your full catalog and price list together with each one sample of your color television.

We have pleasure in enclosing our Order Sheet No. 9001. If you accept our order, please send us by return Fax the duplicate thereof, with your signatures, as an order acknowledgement.

Upon receipt of it, we'll request our bankers to open letter of credit for the amount of this order and you'll be duly advised of it through their correspondent bank in Seoul.

The goods we ordered are urgently wanted by our customs here, so, we ask you to ship them by a first available vessel.

In order to make the delivery efficient, please ship our order through our affiliated company, Evergreen Shipping (Korea) Co., Ltd.(Tel : 02-8808230)

This is a trial order. If your goods prove satisfactory upon arrival, we are sure to give you our main order in a large quantity within the near future.

Yours very truly,

KOREA EXPORTING CO., LTD.

Notes

- by return Fax 회신 팩스 편으로
- an order acknowledge 주문 확인
- be duly advised of it 정히 그에 대한 통지를 접수하다.
- correspondent bank 환거래은행
- a first available vessel 최초로 이용가능한 선박
- if your goods prove satisfactory upon arrival 만약 귀사의 물품이 도착한 즉시 만족스러운 것으로 입증된다면
- main order 본 주문

Model letter 3 주문에 대한 승낙

Dear Sirs,

We have duly received your Order Sheet No. 9001 of July 30, which we acknowledge with thanks. We have booked your for 1,500 units of color television Model No. 300.

As requested, we have enclosed the duplicate of your Order Sheet, duly signed by us, as an acknowledgement.

To confirm this business in detail, we will send you by Fax our Sales Note within a few days.

We trust that you will have a good turnover and this order will be the first step to a long and mutually profitable business relationship between you and us.

Yours faithfully,

Notes

- book an order 주문을 기장하다.
- as request 요청에 따라서(= in accordance with your request)
- in detail 상세히
- Sales Notes 매약서(매도계약서)
- in time for your next sales season 귀사의 다음번 판매시즌에 맞도록
- a good turnover 훌륭한 (많은) 판매고
- a long and mutually profitable business relationship 장기간의 그리고 상호 유익한 거래 관계

단어 및 어휘연구 … in accordance with, according to

① in conformity with의 의미
in accordance with your request(=in compliance with your request, as requested)
in accordance with the instructions given by you
in accordance with the regulations
in accordance with the specifications of our contract
② according to today's newspaper
according to today's CNN weather forecast
according to the statistics available from the Ministry of Trade and Industry.

Model letter 4 주문에 대한 거절

Dear Sirs,

Thanks for your valued order of June 30 for our new Model No. 300. We highly appreciate your interest in our goods. But it has been our business policy to accept only a order exceeding US$10,000.00, we are therefore unable to fill your order.

May we recommend you the following company, our selling agent in your country which, we believe, would accept an order of US$10,000.00 or less.

T. Kennedy & Co., Ltd,
3000 W. 30th Street,
Chicago, J11 60836.
U. S. A

If you contact them directly, they will, no doubt, pay their best attention to your order. We will be also writing to them about your order.

Thank you again for your interest in our goods and we look forward to an opportunity of serving you again in the near future.

Yours faithfully,

Notes

- your valued order 귀사의 소중한 주문
- fill your order 귀사의 주문을 이행하다(= fill, fulfill, carry out)
- no doubt 의심할 여지가 없이
- pay attention to ~에 주의하다.

Model letter 5 주문품에 대한 대체품의 추천

Dear Sirs,

Thank you for your order for 150 units of "Gold Moon" Brand Color Television.

Unfortunately, they were sold out 2 weeks ago on account of an unexpected rush of order from Japan and will not be available again before the end of this year.

As an excellent substitute, we recommend you "Silver Moon" Brand Color Television which is in our stock and slightly higher in price, but much better in quality and which, we believes, is more suitable for your market.

For your reference, we have already airmailed you a copy of the catalogue and price list, which will convince you that "Silver Moon" Brand is another profitable line of business.

Upon receipt your initial order accompanied by L/C at sight in our favour, we will ship the goods by a first available vessel.

We are looking forward to your early reply with a keen desire to start mutually profitable business with you.

Yours faithfully,

Notes

- unexpected rush of order 예상치 못한 주문의 쇄도
- available 이용할 수 있는, 인수 가능한, 이용 가능한(판매 가능한), 유효한
- an excellent substitute 훌륭한 대체품
- For your reference 귀사의 참고를 위해서(= for your information, for your guidance, for your reply)
- initial order (which is) accompanied by L/C 신용장이 수반되는 첫 주문
- with a keen desire to ~하고자 하는 강렬한 열망을 갖고

Model letter 6 주문확인

SUBJECT : Confirmation of your order No. WMC -ID-001

Dear Mr. Park,

We have just received your fax and purchase order No. WMC -ID-001, and are glad to confirm our acceptance of your order as it is.

Our Sales Note No. GSL-FED-1 in duplicate will follow this as an evidence of the conclusion of this contract. After your examination of it, would you kindly return to us the duplicate signed if there is nothing to amend in it?

We are waiting for your L/C to reach us within a week or so, by the end of this month at the latest, while you may rest assured that the shipment is done punctually as contracted.

We hope that this initial business will be the forerunner of future transactions mutually profitable to us.

Sincerely,

Notes

- as it is 그대로
- conclusion 체결
- in duplicate 두통으로
- rest assured 안심하다
- evidence 증거
- amend 수정하다
- at (the) latest 늦어도

단어 및 어휘연구 ··· 안심하다

- feel easy, feel at ease (rest), feel (be) relieved, be (rest) assured, be confident
- relax(vi) : 휴양하다 느긋하게 하다, 안심하다.

① We were greatly relieved at the news. (당사는 그 소식을 듣고 크게 안심하였습니다.)
② We confident of your success in new product. (당사는 신제품에서 귀사의 성공을 확신합니다.)
③ Be assured that you will find a ready sale for your goods in our market. (귀사는 당 시장에서 귀사 제품이 잘 팔릴 것에 안심해도 좋습니다.)
④ We assured you (Please be assured) that the matter will be attended to as instructed. (지시된 대로 그 건에 배려할 것을 귀사에 보증합니다.)(할 것이라는데 안심하십시오)
⑤ We assured you that the goods will sell well (meet with a ready sale) in our market. (물품이 당 시장에서 잘 팔릴 것이라고 귀사에 보증합니다.)

Model letter 7 위탁매입주문(Indent)

INDENT

No. 64

19-21 Victoria Street, New York
February 10, 20--

To : Messrs. Hopkins & Co.
Commission Agents and Shippers
41 King Street,
MANCHESTER, M60 2HB

Dear Sirs.

Please purchase and ship on our account, for delivery not later than March 31, the undermentioned goods, or as many of them as possible. Arrange insurance for amount of your invoice, plus 10% to cover estimate profit and your charges.

Yours faithfully,
for N. WHARFE & CO., LTD.
(signed)
Director

Marks etc.	Quality	Description of Goods	Remarks
N.W. 64 Nos. 1-12	48	H.M.V. Radiograms Model 1636 Walnut finish	Pack 4 per case
N.W. 64 Nos 13-37	25 bales	Grey Shirting Medium weight About 1,000 yards per bale	Pack in oil bags
N.W. 64] Nos. 38-39	4 gross	Assorted House Slippers Men's (1 1/2 gr.) Children's(1 gr.)	Pack in plain wooden case

Ship : By Manchester Lines Ltd.
Delivery : CIF New York
Payment : Draw at 60 d/s D/A, through Royal Bank of Canada, New York

Notes

- commission agent 중개상, buyer의 위탁에 따라 수수료를 받고 상품을 수입해주는 것을 업으로 하는 Broker를 말함
- commission agent and shipper 수입/수출업자의 위탁에 따라 수입/수출을 대신해주는 Broker
- on our account 당사의 계정으로, 당사의 계산으로(상품구매 비용을 부담한다는 의미임)
- arrange insurance for ~에 대한 보험을 체결하다
- estimated profit 희망이익, amount of your invoice, plus 10% to cover estimated profit and your charges(송장금액에 희망이익과 귀사 비용의 10%를 가산하여)
- Nos. 번호(= Number)
- radiogram 라디오 겸용 전축
- walnut finished 호두나무로 만든 것
- assorted house slippers 각종 가정용 슬리퍼
- liner 정기선

Model letter 8 주문서(Purchase Order)

PURCHASE ORDER

NO. WMC-ID-001

We purchase from you the following goods on the terms and conditions set forth below and on the reverse side hereof:

Description of Goods	Quantity	Unit Price	Amount
"Quick" Brand Golf Cart Model WMC-9 as per catalog and specifications	50 units	CPT Seoul @$11,300 per unit	US$565,000

Terms : An irrevocable L/C at sight
Shipment : By May 31, 200-, from New York
Insurance : To be covered by buyer
Packing : Ten (10) units to be stored in
a 40-foot container CRATE NO. C/T 1~50
Destination : Seoul, Korea MADE IN U.S.A.
Cables / Telexes / Faxes exchanged :
Yours of April 12 & 15, 20--
Ours of April 14 & 16, 20--
Remarks : GOLF SUPPLIES, LTD.

Shipping Marks

WMC

C/T No.
SEOUL VIA
PANAMA
MADE IN KOREA

- Signed -
Kim, Director
Import Department

Notes

- hereof 이 서면상의, 이 구매주문서의(= of this writing) cf. hereafter 이 ~의 이후에는 (= after this writing)
- hereby 이 ~에 의해(= by means of this writing)
- hereinafter 이 ~ 중의 이하에 있어서(= after in this writing, into this writing, hereunto)
- heretofore 이 ~ 이전에(= before this writing)
- thereof, therein, thereto here가 'this writing'인데 반하여 there는 'that writing'이며, 당해 계약서 이외의 문서를 가리킨다.
- the reverse side hereof 그 이면
- shipping marks 선적 화인(貨印)

Model letter 9 매약서 (Sales Note)

KOREA TRADING CO., LTD.

2-ka, Chongro, Chongro-ku, Seoul 100, Korea

Sales Note

March 15, 200-

No. ____________________

Messrs ____________________

____

We are pleased to confirm our sales to you as set forth below. If you find any discrepancy, please let us know immediately.

Please sign and return one copy.

1) Commodity :
2) Description :
3) Quantity :
4) Unit price :
5) Time of Shipment :
6) Payment :
7) Packing :
8) Insurance :
9) Inspection :
10) Shipping Sample :
11) Remarks :

Subject to the terms and conditions set forth on the reverse.

Accepted by: Seller:

Notes

- discrepancy 의견불일치
- reverse 배면

Model letter 10 가격인하 거절시 거래처 변경

Gentlemen :

Thank you for your letter of April 21 giving us your latest quotations for your textile goods.

We are, frankly, quite disappointed that you can offer a reduction of only US$ 2.00 per yard as compared with the order we gave you last November. You probably know that other manufacturers in your district have adjusted their prices.

We have been giving your goods special preference till now, but we must buy at more competitive price to increase our sales. Unless you can reduce your quotation substantially, we shall have to place our order elsewhere.

As we have to decide quickly, we would like to receive your prompt reply.

Yours very truly,

Notes

- only 아주, 매우(= only too, solely, very)
- compare with -과 비교(대조)하다.

Model letter 11 재주문에 대한 감사

Dear,

Thank you for your first repeat order for Clear Color II. We were confident that you could move more than 50 units a week, but your repeat order of 150 to cover two weeks shipment was more than we anticipated.

Please rest assured that our production capacity will not inconvenience you and we will deliver 150 units in two weeks without delay.

Our distributors in other districts have commented that the new price really triggered the slow placements since early this year and that we have done the right thing at the right moment.

Thank you again for your business and keep up your aggressive spirit.

Cordially,

Notes

- move 처분하다, 판매하다
- rest assured 안심하다
- inconvenience ~에게 불편을 느끼게 하다, 폐를 끼치다
- without delay 지체없이
- trigger 일으키다, 개시하다
- placement 대치
- aggressive 적극적인, 공격적인

Model letter 12 가격 할인 불가능을 알림

Dear Sir,

We thank you for your order of June 10 for these shoes, which is receiving our immediate attention.

As for your request for a reduction in price, we regret that this is not just possible. We would very much like to accommodate you in this matter, but we have already cut our prices down to the absolute minimum.

You will perhaps agree that other shoes offered at better prices are of considerably different quality.

We would recommend BARE/FOOT/WEAR range on pp.12-14 of the catalogue enclosed as an excellent substitute. These are reliable shoes and will enjoy a guaranteed life of six months.

They sell at prices sightly higher than "Jaguar" Sneakers. To help you introduce them into your market, we are prepared to offer on them a special discount of 5%.

This offer is valid until July 4, and we would like to know if you care to avail yourselves of this.

Yours very truly,

Notes

- reduction in price 가격할인(= price reduction)
- we would like to accommodate you 귀사에 편의를 도모하고 싶다(= we would like to help you)
- cut our prices down to the absolute minimum 가격을 최저로 인하하다.
- at better prices : at lower prices
- of considerably different quality = much lower in quality
- slightly 다소, 약간(= somewhat, more or less, rather)
- offer a special discount 특별할인을 해주다(= offer a introduction discount)
- this offer is valid until ~ 이 오퍼는 ~까지 유효합니다. (this offer effects in force until ~)
- avail oneself of -을 이용하다

Model letter 13 생산중단으로 인한 수주거절

Dear Mr. :

Thank you for your order dated March 31. Much as we like to fill it, we are sorry to inform you that we discontinued production of these conventional types two months ago due to competition and slow sales.

We are scheduled, however, from July 1, to resume production of the new types which should be cost-competitive and superior in function to the competitions.

The brochure, specifications, and price schedule are Enclosed. Please let us know if you are ready to rewrite your order for August shipment, as July production is fully booked.

May we look forward to hearing from you soon.

Yours truly,

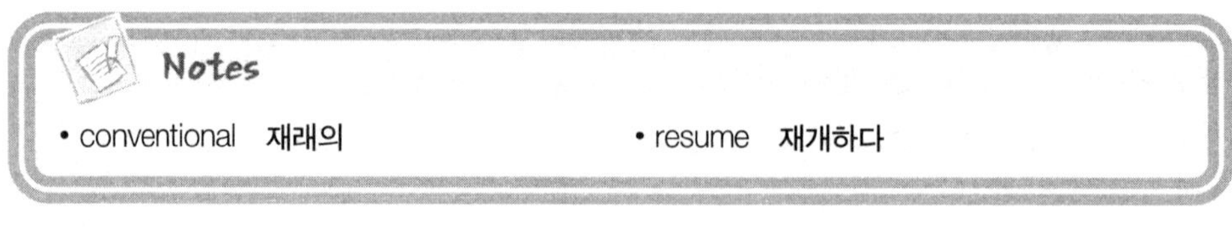

Notes

- conventional 재래의
- resume 재개하다

Model letter 14 계산서 작성오류에 대한 사과

Dear Mr. Arnaud:

As you informed us earlier today by phone, the invoiced order you sent is indeed incorrect. Your order should have been discounted 45% instead of 20%.

Perhaps we've done our promotional job on those brushes too well, our billing staff is now so used to allowing the 20% discount that in your case they forgot to add on the 25% trade discount.

We're in the process of recalculating your order with the correct 45% discount, and the new invoice should be processed on its way to you by the end of this week.

The new invoice replaces the original incorrect one in our files; simply disregard your copy of the original.

We do regret this slip and are happy to have the chance to set the matter straight. This month our store is featuring a promotion on a new line of high-quality acrylics; this will be offered to you at a 45% discount, which we will make sure you'll get it!

Sincerely,

Notes

- invoiced order 송장이 작성된 주문
- billing staff 계산서 작성직원
- process 복제하다
- replace 대치하다
- promotional 촉진의 ; 장려의
- trade discount 동업자할인
- on its way 도중에
- disregard 무시하다

단어 및 어휘연구

자신의 회사를 소개할 때

- We take this opportunity to introduce ourselves that ~
- We take the liberty in introducing ourselves as ~
- It is our great pleasure to introduce our company to you ~
- As for our company, we have two modern factories ~
- As you may know, we are one of the leading exporters of ~
- Taking this opportunity, we are pleased to introduce ourselves to you that ~
- We would like to introduce ourselves that we are dealing in the following items.
- We wish to introduce ourselves as one of the biggest ~

상대방에게 감사를 표할 때

- We wish to express our thanks to you whole-hearted which you paid to our president
- Tank you for your message of sympathy regarding ~
- This is to express our sincere thanks for your cooperation.
- We wish to thank you for your letter of October 1 espressing your congratulations on ~
- We deeply appreciate your courteous letter of 10th July `
- This is a note of our appreciation of your courtesy in sending us the ~
- please accept our thanks for the copies of your catalogue your sent us.

통신문에 동봉물이 포함되어 있을 때

- Enclosed you will fine here ~
- Enclosed please find ~
- We enclose herewith ~
- Enclosed is our price list and catalogue.

Useful Expressions

1. We are enclosing our order for 300 sets of Samsung Transistor Radio.
삼성 트랜지스터라디오 300대의 주문을 동봉합니다.

2. If you do not have them in stock, send us substitutes of the nearest quality.
만약에 재고품이 없는 경우 가장 가까운 품질의 대체품을 보내 주십시오.

3. Any items on this order which you cannot fill before June 25, should be cancelled.
이 주문에서 6월 25일 이전에 조달될 수 없는 물품은 취소해 주기 바랍니다.

4. Your most careful attention to this order will be highly appreciated.
이 주문에 대해서 세심한 배려를 해주신다면 감사하겠습니다.

5. Thank you for your order of February 3 for 3,000 dozen of silk handkerchiefs.
견 손수건 3,000 다스에 대한 2월 3일 자 귀사 주문에 대하여 감사의 뜻을 표합니다.

6. Your order will be shipped on the specified date.
귀사의 주문은 귀사가 지정한 날에 선적하겠습니다.

7. The first installment will be dispatched by the end of February.
분할 선적의 제 1회분은 2월 말까지 행하여질 것입니다.

8. We are sorry that we cannot accept the order at the price you specified.
유감스러우나 귀사가 지정한 가격으로는 귀사의 주문을 인수할 수 없습니다.

9. The goods are in bond.
물품은 보세창고에 들어 있습니다.

10. They do not sell goods on credit.
그들은 외상으로 물품을 팔지 않습니다.

11. We do not sell the goods by retail.
물품은 소매로 판매하지 않습니다.

12. We are in receipt of your favor of the 10th inst., with your order for five printing machines, which I herewith acknowledge with best thanks.
인쇄기 5대에 대한 주문서를 동봉한 금월 10일 자의 서신을 접수했습니다, 심심한 사의를 표합니다.

13. We have booked this order in accordance with your instructions, and shall forward the machines as soon as they will have been manufactured, which will be before the 16th inst.
귀하의 지시에 따라 이 주문을 기장(記帳)하였습니다. 기계는 제작되는 대로 발송하겠사오며, 금월 16일 이전에는 가능하리라고 봅니다.

14. We hope that this trial order will lead to an enduring connection with you.
이번의 시험주문으로 귀사와 영속적인 거래관계가 맺어지게 되기를 희망합니다.

15. We solicit a continuance of your order.
앞으로 계속하여 주문해 주시기를 간청합니다.

16. We have the honour to inform you that the Shirtings kindly ordered were duly shipped today, by s.s. "Arirang', sailing tomorrow, May 20th, from Seatle.
주문하신 셔츠지는 내일 즉 5 20일 시애틀시에서 출항하는 기선 아리랑호에 오늘 이상 없이 선적되었기에 이를 통지합니다.

17. We trust that the goods will reach you safely, and, as they have been carefully finished, we are confident you will be pleased with them,
그 화물은 무사히 귀하께 도착할 것으로 믿습니다. 아울러 이들은 신중하게 손질이 되어 있으므로, 만족하실 것으로 생각합니다.

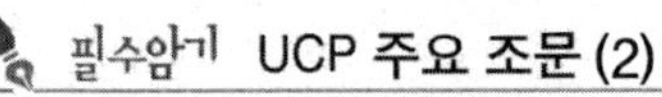

필수암기 UCP 주요 조문 (2)

Article 3 Interpretations

A document may be signed by handwriting, facsimile signature, perforated signature, stamp, symbol or any other mechanical or electronic method of authentication.

A requirement for a document to be legalized, visaed, certified or similar will be satisfied by any signature, mark, stamp or label on the document which appears to satisfy that requirement.

Branches of a bank in different countries are considered to be separate banks.

Terms such as "first class", "well known", "qualified", "independent", "official", competent or "local" used to describe the issuer of a document allow any issuer except the beneficiary to issue that document.

Unless required to be used in a document, words such as "prompt", "immediately" or "as soon as possible" will be disregarded.

The expression "on or about" or similar will be interpreted as a stipulation that an event is to occur during a period of five calendar days before until five calendar days after the specified date, both start and end dates included.

The words "to", "until", "till", "from" and "between" when used to determine a period of shipment include the date or dates mentioned, and the words "before" and "after" exclude the date mentioned.

The words "from" and "after" when used to determine a maturity date exclude the date mentioned.

The terms "first half" and "second half" of a month shall be construed respectively as the 1st to the 15th and the 16th to the last day of the month, all dates inclusive.

The terms "beginning", "middle" and "end" of a month shall be construed respectively as the 1st to the 10th, the 11th to the 20th and the 21st to the last day of the month, all dates inclusive.

- to be continued p.206 -

제6장 대리점

I 대리점의 의의

국내 또는 외국에 있는 타인의 위탁을 받아 상행위를 대리 또는 매개함으로써 그에 대한 보수로 일정한 수수료(commission)를 취득하는 것을 업으로 하는 자를 대리상(agent, commission agent, 또는 indent)이라고 한다.

대리상에는 판매를 대리하는 경우(selling agent)와 매입을 대리하는 경우(buying agent)의 두 가지가 있다. 판매 대리상은 대리권의 강도에 따라 독점 판매 대리상(exclusive or sole selling agent)과 그렇지 못한 이른바 한정판매 대리상(semi-exclusive selling agent)으로 구분된다.

독점판매 대리권이 대리상 협약(agent agreement)의 체결로 부여되면 그 상품과 지역에 관한 한 대리인의 인가나 동의 없이는 본사라 하더라도 상품판매를 직접 할 수 없게 된다. 따라서 해당 지역에 대한 모든 판매는 동 대리상을 통해서만 가능하고 만약 어떤 판매가 본사나 제3자에 의하여 이루어진 경우라 할지라도 그것이 마치 그 대리상을 통하여 이루어졌을 때와 다름없이 소정의 수수료 전액(full commission)이나 배당 구전(split commission)을 지급하는 것이 원칙이다.

이에 비하여 독점권을 부여하지 않는 대리상 계약의 경우에는 해당 지역 내에 복수의 대리상을 지정하거나 본점이나 제3자에 의한 계약 지역 내에서의 판매활동이 가능하고 판매에 대한 수수료의 지급도 판매자에게 귀속된다.

판매 대리점은 그런 의미에서 수입업자와 도매업자를 겸한 형태가 되어 외형상으로는 특약점(distributor, 일명 stockist)과 동일하게 보이지만 양자는 명확하게 구별

된다. 즉 Distributor는 본점과 어디까지나 대등한 관계에서 자기의 위험부담과 계산으로 거래하는 데 반하여 Agent는 본사에 종속된 지위를 유지하며 위험부담이나 계산의 책임이 본사에 있게 된다. 그뿐만 아니라 계약의 내용도 차이가 있어 Distributor는 Distributor Agreement와 Sales Contract가 체결되지만 대리점의 경우는 Agent Agreement로서 충분하다. 대리는 위탁판매(consignment)와 위탁구매(indent)로 구분이 된다. 판매의 경우 대리인은 매상계산서(account sales)와 대금(proceeds)을 보내고 수수료를 받는다. 매입은 상품매입을 해외에 대리시키고 수수료를 지급하는 것이므로 일종의 주문이라 할 수 있다.

대리점이 하는 기능과 유사한 기능을 갖는 것으로 Broker가 있는데, 이는 판매나 구매를 위해 제공된 서비스에 대해 그때그때 중개수수료를 받는 자를 말한다. 대리상을 위탁을 한 사람을 Principal이라고 한다. 대리상은 본사의 계산과 위험 아래 위탁받은 상행위만을 하는 것이므로 법률상 대금지급의 책임이 없으며, 특약이 있을 때만 대금지급에 대한 책임을 진다. 특약에 따라 지급책임을 지게 될 때, 그러한 지급보증에 대한 대가로서 지급되는 특별수수료를 Del Credere Commission(지급보증수수료)이라 하고, 이러한 특약에 관한 협약을 Del Credere Agreement(지급보증협약)라 하며, 그 협약에 의한 대리상을 Del Credere Agent(지급보증대리상)라 한다.

Ⅱ 대리점 관련 통신문

Model letter 1 대리점 소개의뢰

Dear Sirs,

We wish to sell our automatic copying machines in your country, and should like to be put in touch with a company or individual who would be willing to represent us.

The representative we are looking for should be experienced in this field, and should already be doing business with buyers of office equipment, having contacts with suitable outlets.

On our part we can offer up to British machines with an international reputation, which are already being sold in many countries in Europe.

We look forward to hearing from you.

Yours faithfully,

Notes

- in touch with ~과 접촉하여
- represent ~의 대리점을 맡기다(*We are represented in Tokyo. 폐사는 도쿄에 대리점이 있습니다.)
- reputation 평판

Model letter 2 대리점의 요청

Glough & Book Motorcycles Ltd.

Dear Sir,

We are large motorcycle retail chain, with outlets throughout the UK, and are interested in the heavy touring bikes displayed on your stand at the Milan Trade Fair recently.

As you are probably aware there is an increasing demand in this country for machines of this type due to increasing traffic congestion, environmental problems and the acceptance of the motorcycle as a common means of transport, rather than just a teenage phase.

And sales of larger machines have increased by more than 70 percent in the last two years.

We are looking for a supplier who will offer us a sole agency to retail heavy machines. At present we represent a number of manufacturers, but only sell machines up to the 600cc range, which would not compete with the 750cc, 1000cc, and 1200cc models you make.

We operate on a 10% commission basis on net list prices, with an additional 3% delcredere commission if required, and we think you could expect an annual turnover of more than £2,000,000. With an advertising allowance we would probably double this figure.

Our customers usually settle with us direct, and we pay our principals by bill of exchange on a quarterly basis.

You can be sure that our organization will offer you first class representation and excellent sales to guarantee the success of your products in this country.

We look forward to hearing that you are interested in our proposal

Yours faithfully,

Notes

- outlet 매출창구
- turnover 매상고
- advertising allowance 광고비

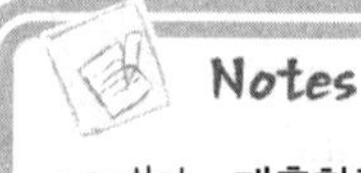

회신

Dear Mr. Glough :

We were pleased to receive your letter of March 1 and to see that you were interested in the machines we produce.

With regard to your offer, I should tell you straightway that we never use sole agencies anywhere in the world, but rely on merchants buying our products on their own account, then retailing them at market prices in their country.

We, of course, offer a 30% trade discount off net list prices and a further 5% quantity discount for sales above USD 100,000. We have found sole agencies tend to be rather restrictive both for ourselves and our customers.

As far as advertising is concerned, you will be pleased to hear that we have arranged for an extensive campaign which begins next month and features our heavy machines.

We are sending dealers throughout Europe brochures, leaflets, and posters to hand to their customers.

You may, on our account, arrange television advertising programs tailored to the special needs in your area. But you should consult with us in advance for expenses in excess of USD 2,000.

Our terms of payment are 60 d/s bills, documents against acceptance. Once again, thank you for writing to us, and please contact us if you have any more enquiries.

Yours truly,

Notes

- straight away 바로
- trade discount 동업자(도매) 할인
- feature 두드러지게 하다
- retail 소매하다(wholesale 도매하다)
- quantity discount 수량할인

Model letter 4 판매 대리점 희망

Dear Sirs,

We have learned from the Hong Kong Chamber of Commerce that you are one of the leading exporters of Korean products and are willing to establish a sole agency here with a view to opening up a new market for your products.

We are therefore writing you as we are very interested in entering into business relations with you.

For your information, we have been importing many kinds of Korean products since 1955. especially home appliances and general merchandise, and distributing them effectively.

We have close connections with many domestic wholesalers and retailers nationwide.

Our market research department reported that the market is expected to be very active and there will be a large demand for your goods.

So we are in a position to place a large order with you. If you are interested in doing business with us, please send us the terms and conditions of your Agency Agreement.

For any information concerning our standing and reputation, please refer to the Bank of Hong Kong, Hong Kong.

We look forward to your early and favorable reply. .

Yours very truly,

Notes

- the leading exporters 유수한 수출업체들
- a sole agency 독점대리점
- with a view to~ ~할 목적으로
- enter into business relations with~ = open an account with-
- for your information 참고로
- place an order with B B에게 -를 주문하다

Model letter 5 회신

Dear Sirs,

Thank you very much for your letter of August 22 expressing your eagerness to enter into business connections with us. We understood from your letter that you are interested in making an agency agreement with us.

As your market research shows, market conditions are increasingly active and there would be a great demand for our products.

As regards a sole agency agreement, we have no hesitation in appointing you our exclusive sales representative.

However, it is usual with us to enter into such a relationship only after examining the result of your sales efforts and the possibility of sales of our goods on a large scale in your market. And also we would like to contact the reference named.

Under such circumstances, we would like to propose doing business with you on a non-exclusive basis for a while.

If you would care to deal with us on such a basis, we will be pleased to give you further details of our business.

We hope we will be able to do business with you in the near future.

Very truly yours,

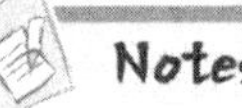

Notes

- as regards ~에 관하여
- market research 시장조사
- enter into ~를 개시하다
- on a large scale 대규모로

Model letter 6 대리점 제의거절

Dear Sirs,

We have the pleasure of acknowledging your letter of June 10th in which you proposed to do business as our sole agent in your city.

From your last letter, we learned that your mode of doing business and your distribution network would be very effective in allowing us to expand the market for our goods.

However, we regret to have to inform you that we have just found a business partner who wishes to offer us their services as our sole agent in your market.

However, we shall keep your name on our files, and we will write to you when a new business opportunity arises in your country.

We thank you very much for your kind proposal and hope we will be able to do business together in the near future.

Yours very truly,

Notes

- acknowledge 받다, 받았음을 확인하다
- distribution network 판매망
- mode of doing business 거래방식
- regret 유감이다

Model letter 7 판매 대리점 협정 [in letter style]

Dear Mr. :

This will confirm our agreement with you on your sales representation on a non-exclusive basis in the State of California, pertaining to our products.

You will pursue such leads as you may obtain or as we may supply to you. All sales will be made at such prices as mutually agreed.

You will use your best efforts to promote sales and obtain orders for us and at all times maintain goodwill between customers and the Company.

Our payment of commission to you will be made according to the schedule attached hereto, upon delivery of products sold.

It is understood that you are not our employee but an independent contractor and, as such, responsible for payment of all taxes due and payable by you.

This agreement will remain in effect until terminated by either of us. If the foregoing contains the basic terms and conditions of our agreement, please return the copy of this letter with your signature where indicated.

Very truly yours,

Notes

- pertaining to ~에 관계하는
- attach 첨부하다
- remain in effect 유효하다
- lead 선두
- employee 종업원

Model letter 8 판매 대리점 협정 [in letter style]

Dear Mr. :

We are pleased to appoint you as our exclusive sales representative to sell our products as listed separately on Schedule A.

1. Our prices may change from time to time.
2. Your territory where you can sell our products shall be in the States of Arizona, California, Colorado, Idaho, Montana, New Mexico, Nevada, Oregon, Utah, Washington, and Wyoming.
3. We will furnish you with all sales materials for the products and will keep them updated.
4. You shall use your best efforts to promote, market, and sell our products within the Territory and abide by our policies.
5. The period of your representation shall be for two years.
6. Your commission as set forth on Schedule B shall be paid on the 25th of the month for all shipments made during the preceding month.
7. You are an independent contractor and shall not be considered our partner or employee.
8. This agreement supersedes all prior agreements and shall be construed according to the laws of the State of California.

Please sign and return the copy to us. This formal agreement will be worked out by our attorney for legal execution soon. Meanwhile, you are authorized to start your sales representing us as stipulated above.

Very truly yours,

Useful Expressions

1. We wish to handle as an agent for the goods you are exporting now because we are commanding an extensive domestic market in this line.
당사는 이 품목에서 광범위한 국내 시장을 지배하고 있으므로 귀사 수출품에 대한 대리점을 맡고 싶습니다.

2. We have much confidence that we can play an important parts as a buying agent in your overseas trade.
당사가 귀사의 매입대리점으로서 중요한 역할을 할 수 있다고 확신합니다.

3. We understand paragraphs 2 and 3, but for the rest we can hardly agree.
제2장에 대해서는 동의하지만, 나머지에 대해서는 동의하기가 어렵습니다.

4. We wish to leave the question of your commission for future discussion.
귀사의 수수료에 대한 문제는 다음으로 미루고 싶습니다.

5. We note from the Trade News that our goods have bright prospects in your market.
무역소식지로부터 폐사의 물품이 귀 시장에서 전망이 밝다는 것에 주목합니다.

6. We are prepared to appoint you our selling agent for these products.
귀사를 이 제품의 판매 대리점으로 임명할 각오입니다.

7. We have been established here as the sole agent for Japanese cotton goods for twenty years.
폐사는 여기에서 일본 면제품 독점대리점으로 설립 된 지 20년이 됩니다.

8. We regret to say that we already represented in your market.
유감스럽지만 귀 시장에 이미 폐사의 대리점이 있다는 말씀을 드리게 됩니다.

9. We have received with thanks your letter of July 12th offering us your services as an agent for our canned goods.
폐사의 통조림제품의 대리점으로 봉사하겠다는 7월 12일 자 귀 서한을 감사하게 받았습니다.

10. We await your early and favorable reply.
조속하고 호의적인 회신을 기다립니다.

11. We are fully confident of meeting your requirements if you will entrust us with your agency for Korea.
만약에 귀사가 대 한국 대리권을 우리에게 맡겨주면 귀사의 요구를 충족시켜 줄 자신을 가지고 있습니다.

12. We have spent many years in the trade and have gained an intimate knowledge of the market for the type of merchandise you manufacture.
그 계통 무역에 다년간 종사하여 왔으며 귀사가 제조하는 종류의 상품에 대한 시장 사정에 우리는 매우 밝습니다.

13. Regarding the terms of agency, we make the following proposals, which we hope will be agreeable to you.
대리점 조건에 대하여 우리는 다음과 같은 제의를 하는 바 그것에 대하여 귀하도 동의할 수 있기를 바랍니다.

14. We would do our utmost to push the sale on your if you are disposed to entertain our commission rate.
당사의 수수료율을 수락하실 의향이라면 귀사를 위해 판매촉진에 최선을 다 하겠습니다.

제7장

무역계약의 체결

I 무역계약의 기초

1 계약서의 의의

무역계약은 통일된 서식, 방법 및 절차는 없다. 따라서 반드시 문서로 작성할 필요는 없지만, 후일의 분쟁에 대비하기 위해서 계약이 성립되면 양 당사자가 계약조항을 확인하고 서명한 계약서(written contract)를 작성해 두기도 한다. 계약을 문서화하는 방법으로는 다음과 같은 것이 있다.

① 성립된 계약의 내용을 일방의 당사자가 정리하여 기재한 계약서(contract sheet)를 정·부(original and duplicate) 2통으로 작성하여 서명한 후 상대방에게 송부하고, 상대방은 이를 검토한 후 1통에 서명하여 반송함으로써 각기 1통씩 보관하는 방법이다.

이러한 계약서를 매도인이 작성할 때에는 흔히 매도계약서(sales contract), 매약서(sales note) 또는 주문확약서(confirmation of order)가 사용되고, 매수인이 작성할 때에는 구매계약서(purchase contract), 매약서(purchase note), 또는 주문서(order sheet)가 사용된다.

② 매도인이 발행한 Offer sheet 자체에 매수인이 Acceptance의 서명을 하거나, 매수인이 발행한 Order sheet에 매도인이 Acknowledgement의 서명을 하는 방법이다. 이 때에도 서류를 정·부 2통으로 작성하여 각기 1통씩 보관한다.

③ 매도인이 확정오퍼의 전신이나 서신을 상대방에게 보내고, 상대방은 수락의 전신이나 서신을 보냄으로써 법률상의 서면계약서(written contract)의 효력을 갖

도록 하는 방법이다.

④ 계약규모가 거액이고 계약 내용이 복잡할 때, Sale note나 Purchase note로는 복잡한 거래조건을 충분히 포괄할 수 없으므로 일반적인 계약서(sales contract, contract sheet)를 작성하는 방법이다.

⑤ 동일 거래처와 반복거래가 지속될 것으로 예상되는 때에는 사전에 당사자 간의 합의에 따라 일반적(공통적)이고 기본적인 거래조건을 문서화하여 서명한 일반거래조건협정서(Agreement on General Terms and Conditions of Business)을 작성해두고, 개별거래 시에는 그때마다 필요한 내용(품명, 수량, 금액, 선적기간 등)만을 청약과 승낙만으로 합의하여 거래하는 방법이다.

2 계약서의 주요내용

무역계약의 내용은 매매당사자의 합의에 따라 결정되는 것이지만 대체로 다음과 같은 조항들이 포함될 수 있다.

---

(1) 표　　제(title of contract) 계약서의 제목
(2) 두　　서(headings)
　계약 일자(date of contract)
　계약 당사자(parties)
　계약 체결지(place of contract)
(3) 전　　문(premises) 계약체결 경위의 설명, 약인문구
　설명 문구(recitals, whereas clause, backgrounds clause)
　약인 문구(consideration wording)
(4) 본　　문(Operative Part)
　정의 조항(definition)
　주된 계약 내용에 관한 조항
　기타 계약상 일반조항
　계약 기간(period of agreement, duration, term)
　계약의 종료(termination)
　불가항력(force majeure)
　중　　재(arbitration)
　준 거 법(applicable law, governing law)
　재판관할(jurisdiction)
　통　　지(notice)
　다른 계약과의 관계(integration) 즉 완전조항(entire agreement)
　조문 표제(headings)

기타 조항
(4) 최 종 부
말미 문언(testimonium clauses)
서　　명(signature)
날　　인(seal)

첨부 문서(annex, appendix, attachment, addendum, exhibit)

---

(1) 표제(title of contract)

특별한 법적 효과가 있는 것은 아니므로 표시의 여하에 따라 계약 내용이 영향을 받는 것은 아니다. 다만 계약 내용을 한눈에 알아보기 쉽도록 하기 위한 것일 뿐이므로 생략되기도 한다.

(2) 두서(headings)

계약체결 일자 및 장소, 계약 당사자의 표시 및 설명 조항이 포함된다. 계약 당사자가 개인의 경우에는 주소와 Full name을 기재해야 하며, 법인의 경우에는 주 사무소의 소재지, 정확한 법인명 및 설립 준거법을 포함하여 기재한다.

(3) 전문(premises)

전문은 설명 조항과 약인 조항으로 구성된다. 설명 조항(recitals, whereas clause)이란 계약 체결에 이른 경위나 기초사실 등을 간단명료하게 표시하며, 보통 현재의 시제로 표현한다. 설명조항은 특별한 법적 효력을 갖지 아니하므로 계약 내용에 영향을 미치지 않지만, 본문 계약 조항만으로는 불명확한 때에 계약 당사자의 진의를 파악하는 기준이 될 수도 있다.

약인조항(Consideration clause)이란 "WHEREAS"라는 문구 다음에 관행적으로 대가의 존재를 확인하기 위해 기재되는 내용을 말한다. 영미법에서는 원칙적으로 요식계약(Formal Contract) 이외의 계약(Simple Contract)에서는 약인이 존재하지 않으면 계약이 성립하지 아니한다. 그러나 계약서 본문에는 어떠한 형태로든 당사자 사이에 존재하는 약인이 기재되는 것이므로 현대에 있어서는 별도로 약인문언을 기재하지 않는 때가 많다.

(4) 정의조항(definition)

계약서에서 여러 번 반복 사용되는 긴 문언이나 용어에 대한 의미를 미리 정의해둠으로써 번잡함을 회피하고 읽기 쉬운 계약서를 만들기 위해 두는 조항이다.

(5) 계약의 주된 내용에 관한 조항

계약체결의 목적이나 당사자 사이의 권리와 의무 관계를 명시하는 계약의 중심 부분이다.

(6) 계약기간

계약의 효력발생시기, 소멸시기, 연장 등에 관한 절차를 기재한다. 계약의 효력발생시기를 특별히 표시하지 않은 때에는 계약서를 작성하여 양 당사자의 서명이 이루어진 날, 그 날이 명확하지 않으면 전문 안에 기재되어 있는 계약서 작성일이 그 시기로 간주되는 것이 보통이다. 기간의 만료로 계약은 소멸하지만, 계약을 갱신할 것을 약정하려면 그 절차와 이에 따른 연장기간을 미리 정해 둘 필요가 있다.

(7) 계약의 종료

계약의 종료사유를 기재한다. 계약은 통상 계약의 이행, 계약의 기간만료, 해제조건의 성취, 약정 해제권의 행사 또는 법정 해제권의 행사로 종료·소멸한다.

계약의 기간만료 및 법정 해제권의 행사에 의한 계약의 종료는 당연한 것이므로 특별히 기재할 필요가 없으나, 해제조건과 약정 해제권의 발생 원인에 대하여는 장래에 발생 가능성이 있는 사태를 신중하게 고려하여 그 내용을 빠짐없이 명시해 두어야 한다.

(8) 불가항력조항(Force majeure clause)

매매당사자의 귀책사유가 아닌 불가항력으로 인하여 약정된 선적기일 내지 인도기일 이내에 선적 또는 인도를 하지 못한 경우 등과 같이 계약 의무를 이행하지 못한 때는 그 당사자는 면책된다는 것과 불가항력의 정의 또는 예시 및 면책받기 위하여 그 당사자가 해야 하는 조치 등을 그 내용으로 한다.

(9) 지연이행조항(delayed performance clause)

불가항력 때문에 계약이행을 하지 못한 때에는 그 이행기를 며칠간 연장한다는 것과 그렇게 연장된 기간 내의 계약 이행 및 연장된 기간 후의 계약 이행을 수용할 것인가의 여부, 연장 기간 후에도 여전히 불가항력의 지속이나 그 후속 사태의 여파로 계약이행이 불가능한 때의 처리문제 등에 관한 사항을 약정하는 조항이다.

(10) 계약의 양도(assignment clause)

제3자에 대한 계약의 양도제한에 관한 규정을 설정하는 조항이다. 영미계약법에서는 계약상의 권리 또는 의무는 당사자의 의사 또는 법률의 규정에 따라 일정한 조건으로 제3자에게 양도할 수 있다. 따라서 계약양도에 대해 별다른 규정을 하지 않은 때에는 계약양도가 가능하게 되므로 계약의 양도를 금지하려면 그 취지를 계약서에 명기해 두어야 한다. 계약양도에 대하여 조건을 붙이거나 일정한 절차를 요구하고자 할 때에는 그 조건이나 구체적 절차에 대하여 계약서에 명확히 규정하여 둘 필요가 있다.

(11) 중재조항(arbitration clause)

중재조항에는 중재에 회부될 사항, 중재의 장소, 중재기관, 중재절차 등을 기재한다.

(12) 재판관할 조항(jurisdiction clause)

소송시 어느 법원에서 소송을 진행할 것인지에 관해 기재하는 조항이다. 중재조항이 존재하더라도 중재에 붙일 범위 외의 사항에 대하여는 재판에 의하게 된다. 그 경우에 소송을 제기할 재판소를 당사자 간에 미리 약정하여 놓는 것이 재판관할이다. 이때 재판소의 지정을 막연히 한국재판소 또는 미국재판소라고 규정하기보다는 서울, 런던, 뉴욕 등 특정지의 재판소를 구체적으로 지정하여야 한다.

(13) 준거법 조항(governing law clause, proper law)

당해 무역(국제매매)계약에 관한 계약의 성립, 이행, 해석에 적용할 준거법을 정하는 조항이다.

(14) 완전합의조항(entire agreement clause)

계약체결의 이전 단계에서 그 계약과 관련되어 이루어졌던 의견교환이나 합의 또는 약속 등은 정식으로 체결된 계약의 내용에 완전히 흡수 통합되어 소멸되는 것이므로 그것들이 계약내용이 상치되더라도 과거의 것을 주장할 수 없고 오직 정식으로 체결된 계약내용만이 유효하다는 것을 명시하는 조항을 말한다.

(15) **권리불포기조항**(non-waiver clause)

일시적으로 계약상의 어떤 권리를 행사하지 않았다고 하여 이것을 그 후의 동 조항이나 조건의 이행 청구권을 포기한 것으로 간주하지 않는다는 조항이다. 따라서 어느 일방이 상대방의 계약조건 위반에 대해 이의를 제기하지 않았다는 것이 곧 이의제기를 포기하는 것 등으로 해석되어 그 위반과 관련되어 갖게 되는 권리가 박탈되지 않는다.

(16) **분리가능조항**(severability clause)

계약 내용의 일부가 어떠한 사유로 실효 또는 무효화 하더라도 그 계약 전체가 실효 또는 무효로 되는 것은 아니라는 조항을 말한다. 이러한 조항은 법원의 판결이나 법규의 강행규정에 의하여 계약 내용의 일부가 실효 또는 무효로 되는 경우에 계약 전체가 실효 또는 무효화 하는 것을 방지하기 위하여 설정되고 있다. 다만 계약조항의 중요한 부분이 실효되는 때에는 계약 전부가 실효되는 수도 있다.

(17) indemnificationn clause(**사후손실 보상조항**)

어느 일방의 계약불이행이나 제3자에 대한 의무 불이행으로 인한 손해에 대하여 배상할 것을 규정하는 조항이다. 경우에 따라서는 계약불이행에 따른 직접적인 피해뿐만 아니라 그 불이행에 따른 기대이익의 상실 등 간접피해까지 배상하도록 규정하기도 한다.

(18) Waiver of Sovereign Immunity(**주권면제특권 포기조항**)

무역계약의 당사자가 국가인 경우 이를 피고로 하여 소송을 제기한다 해도 상대방 국가는 주권국가라는 것을 이유로 하여 자국 이외의 어떠한 타국의 재판에도 응소하지 않을 수 있다. 이 원칙을 국가의 재판(관할)권 면제 또는 주권면제특권이라고 한다.

주권면제 포기조항(waiver of sovereign immunity clause)이란 국가 또는 정부기관과 무역계약을 체결하는 때에 일방 당사자인 국가가 이러한 주권면제특권을 포기하고 사인(私人)과 완전히 동일한 지위에서 채무 및 책임을 부담하고 소송 당사자가 되겠다는 것을 약정하는 조항을 말한다.

(19) **사정변경조항**(hardship clause)

계약체결 당시에는 전혀 예기하지 못했던 경제적 또는 정치적 사태가 계약체결 후에 발생함으로써 당초의 계약대로의 이행이 불가능해지거나 심히 곤란해져 계약의 본질적 변경이 불가피해진 때에 계약 내용의 변경을 요구할 수 있으며, 그때에는 상대방은 반드시 이에 응해야 한다는 조항으로 이행가혹조항이라고도 한다.

(20) **비밀유지조항**(secrecy clause)

무역거래나 기술도입(제휴)의 과정에서 알게 된 비밀정보를 보호하기 위해서 상대방의 비밀정보를 누설하거나 도용해서는 안 된다고 규정하는 조항을 말한다.

(21) **권리침해조항**(infringement clause)

매수인이 제공한 규격이나 사양에 따라 매도인이 물품을 생산하여 매수인에게 인도하였으나 그것이 제3자의 권리(특허권 등)를 침해하는 결과가 되었다면 모든 책임은 매수인이 부담하며 매도인에게는 아무런 피해를 주어서는 안 된다는 조항을 말한다. 반대로 매도인이 인도한 물품이 상표도용과 같은 지적소유권의 침해가 발생되거나 모조품으로 판명된다면 매도인이 그 책임을 지도록 약정해 두는 때도 있다.

(22) **제조물 배상책임**(product liability clause)

제조되고 판매된 물품이 소비자나 기타의 제3자의 신체 또는 재산에 손상 또는 손해를 발생시킨 때, 매도인과 매수인 가운데 책임을 부담할 것인가를 약정하는 조항을 말한다.

(23) **손해배상액예정조항**(liquidated damages clause, penalty clause)

계약당사자의 어느 일방이 계약을 위반할 때 청구할 수 있는 손해배상액을 미리 설정해 두는 조항이다. 상대방의 계약위반 사실을 입증하거나 손해액을 산정하는 것은 그리 쉬운 일이 아니므로 이와 관련된 조항을 미리 약정해 두는 것이 바람직하다.

(24) **면책승인조항(Releases clause)**

계약이 만료되면, 이후에는 어떤 법적 소송도 제기하지 않겠다는 약속으로 서구기업 사이에 일반화되어 있는 조항으로서 계약서와는 별도로 면책승인서를 받아 두기도 한다.

(25) **보증조항(warranty clause)**

계약과 일치하는 물품의 인도의무와 하자 있는 물품을 인도하였을 때의 조치에 대한 내용을 규정하는 조항이다.

(26) **claim clause**

클레임의 제기절차와 방법 등을 정하는 조항이다.

(27) **escalation clause(신축조항)**

Plant(산업설비)나 선박, 대형 기계류처럼 제조공정에 장기간이 소요되는 물품의 경우에 각종 원부자재의 가격상승에 대응하여 가격 변경(조정)을 할 수 있도록 하기 위한 조항이다.

(28) **계약의 수정, 변경**

계약서의 수정, 변경은 구두 또는 서면에 의한 합의로써 할 수 있다. 그러나 당사자 사이의 권리와 의무와 관련된 중요한 계약 내용의 일부 수정변경에 관하여는 그 방법과 절차를 미리 약정하여 둠으로써 장래의 불필요한 분쟁을 피하도록 하여야 한다.

Ⅱ 무역계약서의 실례

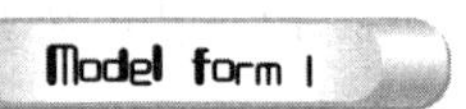

Agrement on General Terms and Conditions of Business

It is hereby agreed between the Seller, Kangnam Trading Co., Ltd., Seoul,

Krorea and the Buyer, Hanover Trust Co., Inc., New York, U. S. A. that all business shall be conducted on the following terms and conditions :

(1) Business : Business is to be transacted between Sellers and Buyers as Principals to Principals, on their own account and responsibility for the sale of the Seller's Sporting Goods in New York.
(2) Quality : The Sellers are to supply the Buyers with samples free of charge and the quality of the goods to be shipped should be fully equal to that of the sample on which an order is given.
(3) Quantity : The minimum quantity for an order is to be the standard contents of one package. Assortment of various articles is to be accepted so long as the total amount exceeds USD20,000.
(4) Price : Prices are to be quoted in U.S. Dollars on the basis CIF New York unless otherwise specified.
(5) Firm offer : Firm offers are to remain effective for forty-eight hours after the time of dispatch, excluding Sundays and National Holidays.
(6) Orders : Except in cases where firm offers are accepted all orders are to be subject to the Seller's final confirmation.
(7) Discount : The special discount of 3 percent from the contract price is to be accepted on an order exceeding 5,000 pairs in quantity.
(8) Packing : Proper export wooden case packing is to be carried out, each case bearing the mark 〈W.S.〉 with port mark, running case numbers and the county of origin.
(9) Shipment : Shipment is to be made within the time stipulated in each contract, except in circumstance beyond the Seller's control. The date of bill of lading shall be taken as conclusive proof of the date of shipment. Unless expressly agreed upon, the port of shipment shall be at the Seller's option.
(10) Force Majeure : The Sellers shall not be responsible for the delay in shipment due directly or indirectly to force majeure including mobilization, war, riots, civil commotion, hostilities, blockades, requisition of vessels, prohibition of export, fires, floods, earthquakes, tempests, shakes, strikes, lockouts and any other contingencies, which prevent shipment within the

period stipulated. In the event of any of the aforesaid causes arising, documents proving its occurrence or existence shall be submitted by the Sellers to the Buyers without delay and furnish a certificate substantiated by the Korea Chamber of Commerce and Industry.

(11) Insurance : All shipments are to be covered on ICC(B) including War Risks for the invoice amount plus ten percent, and the insurance policy is to be made out in U.S. Dollars and claims payable at New York.

(12) Payment : Draft is to be drawn at 60 d/s under irrevocable Letter of Credit which should be opened in favor of the Sellers immediately upon contract, with full set of transport documents, viz. Bill of Lading, Insurance Policy, Commercial invoice and other documents which contract required.

(13) Claim : Buyer's claims, if any, shall be made by cable within 10 days from the date of final discharge of goods at destination and certificates by recognized surveyors shall be sent by mail without delay.

This Agreements shall be valid on and after May 25, 20--.

HANOVER TRUST CO., INC.	KANGNAM TRADING CO., LTD.
(signed)	(signed)
P. Samuelson	J. J. Jung
Vice President	Director, Trading Department

Notes

- as principal to principal **당사자 대 당사자**
- one's own account **(각자) 자신의 계산으로**
- supply A with B **A에게 B를 공급하다.**
- free of charge **무료로**(= gratis, for nothing, without payment) cf. commercial value (유상으로)
- unless otherwise specified **별도로 명시하지 않는 한** cf. unless expressly agreed upon(명시적으로 합의하지 않는 한), unless by mutual consent(상호 동의 없이는)
- remain effective **유효하다**(be valid, be good, be open)
- exclude **제외하다**

- except in cases where ~한 경우를 제외하고는
- subject to ~을 조건으로 하여(= conditional on, conditionally on)
- discount 가격할인(= allowance, concession, deduction, reduction)
- carry out 실행하다(= execute, fulfill, complete, accomplish, perform)
- running (case) Number 일련번호(= serial number, consecutive No)
- shipment is to be made (by seller) 선적을 이행되어야 한다.
- make shipment 선적을 이행하다(= effect shipment, ship)
- except in circumstances 사정이 있는 경우를 제외하고는
- be at one's option ~가 선택하다.
- taken as conclusive proof 결정적인 증거로 간주되다.
- beyond the seller's control 매도인으로서는 불가항력적인
- in the event of 만일 ~의 경우에는(= in case of)
- in be responsible for ~에 대해 책임을 지다(= answer for)
- mobilization 동원
- riot 폭동, 소동
- civil commotion 내란
- hostilities 적대행위, 교전
- blockades 봉쇄
- requisition 징발
- prohibition 금지
- tempest 대폭풍우
- lockout 직장폐쇄
- contingencies 우발적 사고
- in aforesaid 앞서 언급한
- occurrence 발생, 사건, 사고
- existence 존재
- cover (on) 보험에 들다
- payable 지급해야 하는(= must be paid)
- claim payable at New York 손해배상 청구액의 지급지는 뉴욕으로 한다.
- SRCC 동맹파업, 폭동, 시민소요(strike, riots and civil commotions)
- for account of ~의 비용부담으로, ~의 계정으로(at the account of ~)
- under ~에 의거하여, ~과 일치하도록(= based on, in compliance with)
- open (신용장을) 개설하다(= establish, arrange, issue, furnish)
- viz 즉, 말하자면(videlicet, namely, that is to say)
- in triangle 삼각형 안에
- claim 보험금
- TPND 도난, 발하, 불착위험 담보(= theft, pilferage, non-delivery)
- be valid 유효하다(= be effective, be open, be good)
- can not be amicable settled 자치적(우호적)으로 해결될 수 없다면
- whose award 중재인(arbitrator)의 판정
- viz. namely로 읽음 ~과 교환으로, 맞바꾸어(against)

bear

- The buyer should bear the cost of commission(= pay, 부담하다)
- You should bear the transport charges.
- We will bear the entire(ultimate) responsibility for the damage(= assume, 책임지다)
- The firm should bear the liability form the payment)
- The product bears our mark(= carry)
- The cheque bore the drawer's signature.

중단된 거래를 재차 시도하는 경우

- Please refer to our last letter of ~
- Through we have not continued our business relation since ~
- Six months have passed since you placed order with us ~
- During the last season, we have no communication with ~
- With reference to our circular letter dated May 26, in which ~
- We refer to the meeting with our director in the Mandarlin Hotel in your end.
- Further to our previous communication, we would lime to provide you for ~

Model form 2 판매특약점계약서

DISTRIBUTORSHIP AGREEMENT

This Agreement, made and entered into on this first day of Jan, 20— by and between KOREA Trading Co., Ltd. a corporation duly organized and existing under the laws of the KOREA and having its principal office at ---------- (hereinafter referred to as "Manufacturer") and America Trading Co., Inc. a corporation duly organized and existing under the laws of the state of New York, U.S.A. having its principal office a --------- (hereinafter referred to as "Distributor").

WITNESSETH

WHEREAS, Manufacturer wishes to appoint Distributor the exclusive distributor for the products (as hereinafter defined) in the territory of the United States of America.

WHEREAS, Distributor wished to accept such appointment as an exclusive distributor.

IN CONSIDERATION OF the mutual convenance contained herein, the parties herto agree as follows :

Article 1. Definitions

In this Agreement except where the context otherwise requires, the following terms and expressions shall have the meanings respectively defined as follows ;

a. "Products" means those products which are mentioned in the attached Annex.

b. "Territory" means the United States of America.

Article 2 Appointment and Acceptance

a. During the term and subject to the conditions hereinafter set forth, Manufacturer hereby appoints Distributor as an exclusive distributor for the products in the Territory, and Distributor accepts such appointment. During the term of this Agreement, Manufacturer shall not, either directly or indirectly, sell the products in the Territory without the prior consent of distributor.

b. Distributor shall not purchase, import, sell, distribute, advertise or otherwise deal in products competitive with or similar to the products in the Territory.

Article 3 Orders and Shipment

a. In placing orders with Manufacturer, Distributor shall clearly describe the products and quantity required, and shall include precise instructions for packaging, invocing and shipping.

The orders shall not be binding unless and until they are accepted by Manufacturer in its discretion. Manufacturer agrees to supply Distributor with products to enable fulfillment of the minimum purchase as set forth in Article t hereof. Manufacturer agrees to extend its best efforts to accept all orders as submitted by Distributor in excess of said minimum purchase.

b. Manufacturer shall be responsible for packaging the products in such manner to ensure except for perils of the sea sage and undamaged delivery.

Article 4 Price and Payment

a. The prices of the products shall be determined in accordance with the price lists attached hereto and made a part hereof, which price list may be changed from time to time by the Manufacturer with 30 days prior notice.

b. Within 30 days after receipt of Manufacturer's confirmation of order, Distributor shall open an irrevocable Letter of Credit in favor of Manufacturer, issued by a first class, international bank, satisfactory to Manufacture.
c. Currency of Payment shall be in United States Dollars.

Article 5 Minimum Purchase

a. Distributor guarantees minimum purchase of the products from Manufacturer in the following amount, on a CIF BUSAN basis :
   (1) First year U$100,000
   (2) Second year U$250,000
   (3) Third year U$450,000
   For the purpose of this Article, the products shall be considered purchased when shipped by manufacturer.
b. When Distributor has fulfilled the minimum purchase guarantee as stipulated in Article 5 a, this Agreement shall automatically be renewed for a period of three years. The minimum purchase amount for any three year period shall not be less than U$1,500,000 and not less than U$350,000 for each year of said period, and said purchase volume shall be subject to the same conditions as aforesaid. As long as this volume is reached, the Agreement shall be automatically be extended by successive three years period subject to Article 13, provided, however, that each successive period shall require a 10% increase of the minimum purchase volume.
c. If Distributor fails to purchase the minimum amount as stipulated in Article 5 a and 5 b, Manufacturer may terminate this Agreement by a written notice as hereinafter provided for in Article 14 a(b) within one month after the expiration of the three years period of this Agreement, but Distributor shall have no other liability in connection therewith.

Article 6 Technical Assistance

a. Manufacturer engages thenselves to supply Distributor with necessary Technical Assistance by means of informative and illustrated materials and to sen all advertising materials suitable for promotion and advertising of the products.
b. Manufacturer shall train a reasonable number of technical personable either in Korea or on site in the Territory by consent of both sides if it becomes

necessary dut to introduction of any new Products or generally in order to achieve better installation and maintenance standards. Costs for round trips, meals, lodging, and other expenses of the dispatched personal of Distributor or Manufacturer for training shall be borne by Distributor.

c. The above Technical Assistance shall be implemented in English language.

Article 7 Spare Parts

a. Distributor shall keep a sufficient level of spare parts in order to privide an efficient After Sales Services. Manufacturer shall also advise Distributor of the required spare parts and any stocking will be discussed and mutually agreed before orders are placed.

b. Manufacturer shall supply to distributor spare parts for the products so long as Distributor continues to purchase the products pursuant to the terms and conditions of this Agreement and for two years after the last shipment of the products to Distributor. The price of the Spare Parts shall be consented by both parties. And at Manufacturer's suppliers directly for two years after the last shipment.

Article 8 Inspection and Warranty

a. Promptly after the receipt of the products, Distributor shall inspect or shall cause its qualified agent to insure that the quality standards, as agreed to by the parties in writing, have been met. If any of the products or any part of a products is found not to be in compliance with the quality standards. Manufacturer shall supply Distributor free of charge replacement for the products or the part of a product not meeting the quality standards, and/or shall indemnify the Distributor against any loss and damage suffered by the Distributor.

b. Manufacturer warrants the products at the time of shipment shall be free from defects in material and workmanship. This warranty does not extend to any of the said products which have been : (1) subject to misuse, neglect, accident or abuse, (2) improperly repaired, or altered or modified in any way, and (3) used in violation of instructions furnished by Manufacturer.

c. Claims by Distributor in regard to any defect in the products must be in writing and be dispatched by Distributor with full particulars within one(1) year after receipt of the products.

Article 9 Distributor's Responsibility

a. Distributor shall maintain adequate stocks of the products throughout the Territory to meet its customer's demand in time. Distributor shall maintain adequate stocks of replacement parts, facilities and qualified mechanics throughout the Territory and shall provide reasonable after sale-services to its customers.

b. Distibutor shall undertake for its own account, advertisement, and sales promotions of the products and devote its best efforts toward obtaining the largest sales volume of the products in the Territory.

c. Whenever Manufacturer shall render to Distributor any complaint as to products from any dealer or customer in the Territory. Distributor shall immediately make investigation and take a proper action.

Article 10 Report

Distributor shall make quarterly repots to Manufacturer on the sales of the products, the inventory of the products and parts therof, general market conditions and others as Manufacturer requires.

Article 11 Trademark

a. Distributor recognized that any of trademarks, designs, copyrights and other proprietary right, used on or embodies in the products("Proprietary Rights") shall remain the exclusive property of Manufacturer. Distributor shall not have or acquire any right, title or interest in proprietary rights : provided, however, that Distributor may with the consent of Manufactorer indicate that it is an authorized distributor of the products. Upon termination of this Agreement for any cause. Distributor shall cease holding itself out as a distributor of the products and cease using in any way Manufacturer's name or its proprietary rights or nay material similar thereto.

b. Distributor shall not alter, deface, remove, cover or mutilate in any manner the trademark, serial or model numbers, brand or a Manufacturer's name attached or affixed to any of the products, without the consent of Manufacturee.

Article 12 Status of Distributor

a. This Agreement does not in any way create the relationship of principal and agent between Manufacturer and Distributor : and under no circumstances shall Distributor be considered to be the agent of Manufacturer. Distributor shall not act or attempt to act, or in any manner assume or create, or attempt to assume or create, any obligation, liability, representation, warranty or guarantee on behalf of, or in the name of Manufacturer.

b. Distributor shall at all times comply with all applicable laws, regulations, and orders of any government of the Territory or political subdivisions thereof relating to or in any way affecting this Agreement and Distributor's performance hereunder, including the obtaining of any required licenses, permits or approvals.

c. Distributor shall not disclose to any third party, without the prior written consent of Manufacturer, or use for any purpose other than the performance of its obligations under this Agreement, any confidential information concerning the products or business affairs of Manufacturer (including, but not limited to, prices, discounts or product specifications) which it receives directly or indirectly from Manufacturer, or which it requires or develops in the course of its transactions withj Manufacturer.

Article 13 Term

a. This Agreement shall become effective upon signing and shall continue in full force and effect for a period of three years from the date hereof, unless earlier terminated pursuant to Article 14, and shall thereafter be automatically extended for successive three year periods of time unless, three months prior to the expiration of the term or any extension therof, an notice of intention to finally terminate is given in writing by one party to the other.

b. Upon the extension of this Agreement in accordance with Article 12 a, the minimum purchase amount for each period shall be renewed and a new minimum purchase amount shall be mutually agreed upon in writing by the parties within two(2) months after commencement of each new period.

Article 14 Termination

a. This Agreement may be terminated at the option of Manufacturer, effective upon thirty(e0) days prior written notice of termination given to Distributor, in the event of the happening of the following events :

(1) Should Distributor becomes bankrupt or insolvent, or have its business placed in the hands of a receiver, assignee or trustee, whether by voluntary act or otherwise : or

(2) Should Distributor fail to meet the minimum annual purchase requirements or otherwise fail to meet promptly any of its obligations pursuant to this Agreement : or

(3) Should Distributor be acquired by, or should itself acquire, in whole or in part a manufacturer of the products which in the reasonable judgement of Manufacturer completes to material extent withj the products ; or

(4) Should Distributor attempts to assign this Agreement or any rights hereunder without Manufacturer's prior written consent ; or

(5) If Distributor ceases to function as a going concern or to conduct its operations in the normal course of business.

b. All monies owed to Manufacturer upon termination shall become immediately due and payable and no cancellation or termination of this Agreement shall serve to release Distributor or its successors or assigns from any obligations under this Agreement.

Article 15 Force Majeur

Neither party shall be liable to the other partly foir nonperformance or delay in performance of any of its obligations under the Agreement due to war, revolution, riot, strike or other labor dispute, fire, flood, acts of government or any other causes reasonably beyond its control. Upon the occurrence of such a force majeur condition, the affected party shall immediately notify the other party of any further developments with evidence proving its occurrence. Immediately after such condition is removed, the affected party shall perform such obligation with all due speed.

Article 16 Governing Law

This Agreement shall be interpreted and governed by the laws of the Republic of Korea.

Article 17 Arbitration Law

All disputes, controversies or differences which may arise between the parties out of or in relation to or in connection with this Agreement or for the breach thereof shall be finally settled by arbitration in Seoul, Korea in accordance with the Commercial Arbitration Rules of the Korean Commercial Arbitration Board and under the law of Korea. The award rendered by the arbitrator(s) shall be final and binding upon both parties concerned.

Article 18 Miscellaneous Provisions

a. Notices : Any notice required or permitted to be given hereunder shall be in writing, and may be given by personal service, registered airmail, or by cable, facsimile or telex if confirmed on the same day in writing by registered airmail.

b. Entire Agreement-Amendments : This Agreement constitutes the entire understanding of Manufacturer and Distributor with respect to the subject matter hereof. No amendment, modification or alteration of any term of this Agreement shall be binding on either party unless the same shall be made in writing and executed by or on behalf of the parties hereto.

c. Assignment and Succession : This Agreement shall inure to the benefit of and be binding upon the parties heto and their respective successors. No assignment of this Agreement shall be valid without the prior written consent of the other party hereto.

d. Waiver : Any waiver hereunder must be in writing, and the failure of any party at any time to require the other party's performance of any obligations under this Agreement shall not affect the right subsequently to require performance of the obligation.

   Any waive of any breach of any provision of this Agreement shall not be construed as a waiver of any continuing or succeeding breach of such provision or a waiver or modification of the provision.

e. Serverability : If any one or more of the provisions contained in this Agreement shall be declared invalid, illegal or unenforceable in any respect under any applicable law, the validity, invalid, illegal or enforceability of the remaining provisions contained herein shall not in any way be affected and in such case the parties hereto oblige themselves to reach the intended purpose of the invalid provision by a new, valid and legal stipulation.

f. Headings : The section headings herein are included for purpose of convenience only any shall not affect the construction or interpretation of any of the provision of this Agreement.

IN WITNESS WHEREOF, the parties hereto have caused this Agreement to be executed by their respective duly authorized officers.

MANUFACTURER,	DISTRIBUTOR,
Korea Trading Co., Ltd.	America Trading Co., Ltd.
(signed)	(signed)
Vice President	President

Model form 3 Bonded Processing Trade Contract

THIS CONTRACT IS MADE AND AGREED on this Seventeenth day of July, Two Thousand by and between the following parties concerned :

Cohan Bros., Inc. hereinafter referred to as party A,
having their head office at 25
Pedder St., Hong Kong, and

Koryo Mulsan Co., Ltd. hereinafter referred to as Party B,
having their head office at Room 205,
Bando Bldg., Seoul, Korea.

1. Party A exports to Party B Rayon Yards as specified in the attached sheet, and Party B exports to Party A Rayon Fabrics after bonded processing as specified in the attached sheet.
2. Party B guarantees the quality of the Rayon Fabrics to be shipped will

conform to the samples already confirmed by Party A.

3. Party A establishes the 1st Credit in the amount of US$ 50,000.-- approx. in favor of Party B, and then Party B opens Credit in favor of Party A in the amount which is to be proper for processing the ordered quantity.
4. Shipments are to be carried out partially as agreed upon by parties A and B, and establishments of Credits after the 1st Credit are to be made partially as agreed upon in consideration of execution of the 1st Credit.
5. The term of this contract is one year, and further extension and/ or renewal may be possible after consultation by Parties A and B.
6. In performance of this contract, both Party A and Party B are always to cooperate to their best sincerity and care. In case any loss may be incurred by breach of this contract by either party, the party breaking this contract is to compensate the other party for the loss.
7. Unilateral cancellation of this contract is prohibited unless Parties A and B agree upon beforehand.
8. This contract shall be put into effect promptly after signed by both parties concerned hereto.

In witness whereof the parties concerned have hereunto set our hands and seals in duplicate in the presence of the undersigned witnesses in Hong Kong on the day and year afore-mentioned.

(Party A)	COHAN BROS., INC.
	George M. Cohan
	President
(Party B)	KORYO MULSAN CO., LTD.
	Chang Do Harn
	President

Made and subscribed by the above named parties in the presence of

W.R. Hoskins

Soodong Chung

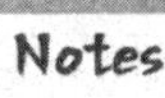

Notes

- bonded processing 보세가공
- breach 위반, 불이행
- unilateral 일방적인
- carry out 실행하다
- compensate 보상하다
- bilateral 쌍방의

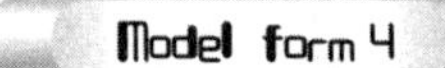

Sole Agency Agreement

This Agreement entered into between Seoul Trading Co., Ltd., (hereinafter called Principal) and J. Smith & Co., Inc.

1. Appointment : Principal appoints Agent as his sole agent to solicit orders for the merchandise stipulates in Article 3 from customers in the territory stipulated in Article 2, and Agent accepts such appointment.
2. Territory : The territory covered under this Agreement is confirmed to the United States of America (hereinafter called Territory).
3. Merchandise : The merchandise covered under this Agreement is confined to staples, tops, yarns and fabrics of Korean origin (hereinafter called Merchandise).
4. Exclusiveness : Principal may not, directly or indirectly, sell Merchandise for Territory through any channel other than Agent, and Agent may not sell, distribute or promote the sale of any other line similar to Merchandise produced or manufactured in Korea. Further, Agent may not solicit or accept orders for the purpose of selling or delivering Merchandise outside Territory. Principal shall refer to Agent any inquiry or order for Merchandise which Principal may receive from others within Territory.
5. End-User and End-Use : Agent shall inform Principal of the End user's name and his End-Use in each case of transaction before Agent sells Merchandise in Territory.
6. Expenses : Agent shall bear all the expenses incurred in connection with the sale of Merchandise including traveling, cable, telex, postal and other incidental expenses. Principal shall, likewise, bear his own traveling, cable, telex and postal expenses.
7. Commission : Principal shall pay to Agent commission in U.S. currency at

the rate of 3% of the net invoice price of Merchandise on all orders obtained by Agent and received and accepted by Principal, provide, however, that no such commission shall be payable until Principal receives the full amount of payment due.

8. Offer : All cable and/ or telex offers will be considered "firm" subject to reply being received within three days from and including the day of despatch, unless otherwise stated. Sundays and National Holidays at both ends are excepted.
9. Trade Terms : The trade terms used between Principal and Agent shall be governed and interpreted by the provisions of the latest Incoterms.
10. Information and Report : Both Principal and Agent shall periodically and/ or at the request of either party furnish information and market reports to promote the sale of Merchandise as much as possible.
11. Trade Marks, etc. : Agent may not use, directly or indirectly, in part or in whole, Principal's signature or name or any other mark owned by Principal in any way in connection with Agent's business except in the manner and to the extent that Principal may specially and expressly consent in writing. Further nothing herein contained may be construed as transferring any patent, trade mark or design in Merchandise. In case any dispute or claim arises in connection with the above right or rights, Principal reserves every and all rights to cancel this Agreement at his discretion and hold himself free from any liability arising therefrom.
12. Duration : This Agreement shall be valid for a period of one year commencing from the 10th day of May, 200__ and shall be automatically renewed thereafter on a year to year basis unless either party gives the other party a three month's written notice to terminate this Agreement. No change, modification and amendment of this Agreement are binding upon Principal and Agent unless made in writing and signed by both parties.
13. Arbitration : All disputes, controversies, or differences which may arise between Principal and Agent, out of or in relation to or in connection with this Agreement, or for the breach thereof, shall be finally settled by arbitration in Seoul Korea in accordance with the Commercial Arbitration Rules of Korea Commercial Arbitration Board. The award rendered by the arbitrator(s) shall be final and binding upon both parties.

14. Governing Law : This Agreement shall be governed in all respects by Korean law.

Principal :
Seoul Trading Co., Ltd.
(signed)
President

Agent :
J. Smith & Co., Inc.
(signed)
President

Notes

- appointment 임명
- be confined to ~에 한정하다
- exclusiveness 배타성
- territory 지역
- Korean origin 한국원산

단어 및 어휘연구

회신이 지연된 경우

- We are very sorry for not having replied you more sonner.
- Please accept our apologies for the delay in replying.
- Due to our president's business trip schedule, we could not attend to your inquiry.
- Forgive us for our belated letter.

신용조회에 회신하는 경우

- Your bank has been referred by ~
- YOur name was given by ~ as their credit reference.
- ~ has advised us to get in touch with you concerning their standing.
- Your name is already familiar to us and please permit us to write to ask you about ~.

신용조회처에 회신하는 경우

- In reply to your credit inquiry of July 21, ~
- Replying your inquiry of ~, we are pleased to advise you ~.
- With reference to the above company , we have the pleasure in informing that ~
- In response to your inquiry of February 26, ~

신용조회처를 제시할 때

- We wish to refer you to ~'
- Regarding to our reference, please contact ~
- Our standing will be obtained from ~
- As for our credit standing, you may check with ~

Useful Expressions

1. We have acquired your name and address from the New York Chamber of Commerce.
   뉴욕 상업회의소로부터 귀사명과 주소를 알았습니다.

2. Considering the rapid expansion of your market, we are looking for some reliable firms who wish to open an account with us.
   귀 시장의 신속한 확대를 고려하여 폐사와 거래관계를 개시하고 싶은 믿을만한 상사를 찾고 있습니다.

3. Please inform us whether or not you are willing to establish business relations with us.
   폐사와 거래관계를 맺고 싶은지를 알려주십시오.

4. The market is very active due to the upward tendency of economic conditions.
   경제상황의 상승경향으로 시황은 매우 활황입니다.

5. We can refer you to the Bank of Tokyo, regarding our standing and reputation.
   폐사의 재정 상태와 평판에 관하여는 도쿄은행에 조회하십시오.

6. Please let us know your main lines and terms and conditions of business.
   귀사의 주 품목과 거래조건을 알려주십시오.

7. We are not in a position to accept your proposal due to an inactive market.
   활기 없는 시황으로 인하여 귀사의 제의를 수락할 수 없습니다.

8. We would not like to do business with you unless you can favor us with the best prices.
   귀사가 최저가격으로 하실 수 없다면 귀사와 거래하고 싶지 않습니다.

9. A fairly large demand is expected for these items because of the coming summer season.
다가온 여름철 때문에 이 품목에 대하여 꽤 많은 수요가 예상된다.

10. As to the terms of business, we make it our custom to trade on an Irrevocable Letter of Credit.
거래조건에 관하여는 취소불능신용장으로 거래하는 것을 관례로 하고 있습니다.

11. Our requirements are now fully covered for some time to come, and we therefore greatly regret that we have to cancel our order with you,
폐사는 금후 당분간 소요량이 충분히 확보되어 있기 때문에 유감스럽지만, 주문은 취소할 수밖에 없겠습니다.

12. Our client refuses to raise his limit of prices for the textiles ordered in ours of 5th inst., so uless you see your way to undertake it on his terms, please consider it as cancelled.
금월 5일 자 본인 서신에서 주문한 직물은 폐사의 거래처에서 지정가격 인상을 거절하고 있으므로, 그 조건수락이 어려우시면 이는 취소되는 것으로 알아주시기 바랍니다.

13. We have already written to you twice urging dispatch, and as you have failed to deliver these goods on the date named, we are obliged, very regretfully, to cancel this order.
서면으로 두 차례나 지급 발송을 독촉하였으나, 지정일에 그 물건을 인도해 주시지 않았기 때문에, 매우 유감이오나 이 주문은 취소할 수밖에 없습니다.

14. We have none of this particular make in stock at the moment, and, owing to the great pressure at the mills, we are afraid we cannot guarantee delivery within less than three months of receipt of orders,
현재 이 특제품의 재고는 품절되었습니다. 또한, 공장도 크게 붐비고 있기 때문에 주문접수 후 3개월 안에는 인도를 보증할 수가 없습니다.

제8장

대금결제와 신용장

I 신용장의 의의

1 신용장의 정의

신용장(Letter of Credit, L/C)이란 수입상(발행의뢰인)의 요청에 따라 수입상의 거래은행인 신용장 발행은행이 수익자(수출상)가 제시한 환어음과 서류가 신용장에서 요구하는 조건과 일치하면 틀림없이 그 환어음에 대한 지급(payment), 인수(acceptance), 연지급(deferred payment) 및 매입(negotiation)하겠다고 확약한 증서를 말한다.

신용장방식은 수출상이 선적을 하고도 대금회수가 불가능하게 되는 신용위험(credit risk)과 수입상이 대금을 지급하고도 상품입수가 불가능하게 되는 거래위험(mercantile risk)을 완화하여 원활한 무역거래가 이루어지도록 해준다.

2 신용장 거래의 당사자

(1) 발행의뢰인

매매계약에서 신용장 방식으로 거래하기로 약정한 경우 매수인(buyer)인 수입업자(importer)는 매매계약에서 규정한 조건에 따라 자기의 거래은행에 신용장 발행을 의뢰하는 발행의뢰인이 된다.

발행의뢰인은 은행으로부터 신용을 부여받는다는 점에서 Accredited buyer(수신매수인), 신용장발행의뢰인인 동시에 개설자라는 점에서 Opener(개설자), 또 화물의 수하인이라는 점에서 Consignee(수하인), 어음의 결제인이라는 점에서 Accountee (어음결제인) 등으로도 불린다.

(2) 발행은행

발행의뢰인과의 신용장발행계약(commercial letter of credit agreement)에 따라 신용장을 발행하는 은행을 개설은행(opening bank) 또는 발행은행(issuing bank)이라고 한다.

(3) 수익자

수익자(beneficiary)란 발행된 신용장으로부터 이익을 받는 수출업자(exporter)인 매도인(seller)을 말하며, 화물을 선적하는 선적인(shipper)이다. 또한 신용장의 사용자(user), 어음발행인(drawer), 신용수령인(accreditee) 또는 지명인(addressee)으로도 불린다. 그리고 양도가능신용장의 양도를 받은 양수인은 제2의 수익자(second beneficiary)라고 한다.

(4) 통지은행

신용장의 발행은행은 신용장의 발행사실과 그 내용을 수익자에게 직접 통지하거나 수익자의 소재지에 있는 발행은행의 본·지점 또는 환거래은행(correspondent bank)을 이용하여 통지한다. 신용장 발행 사실을 수익자에게 통지하는 은행을 통지은행(notifying bank, advising bank) 또는 전달은행(transmiting bank)이라 한다.

(5) 확인은행

신용장발행은행 이외의 제3의 은행이 그 신용장에 자신이 어음의 인수·지급을 할 것이라는 약속을 추가하는 행위를 신용장의 확인(confirm)이라고 하며, 확인을 하는 은행을 확인은행(confirming bank), 확인은행의 확인을 받은 신용장을 확인신용장(confirmed credit)이라 한다.

(6) 매입(할인)은행

매도인은 선적을 완료하면 신용장 조건에 따라 매수인 또는 발행은행 앞으로 환어음을 발행하고 여기에 신용장에서 요구하는 서류를 첨부하여 은행에 매입(할인)을 의뢰한다. 이 어음을 매입(negotiate)하는 은행을 매입은행 또는 할인은행(negotiating bank)이라 한다.

(7) 지급은행

신용장발행은행으로부터 당해 신용장의 수익자가 발행한 환어음을 지급하도록 지시를 받은 은행을 지급은행(paying bank)이라 한다.

(8) 인수은행

어음의 지급인은 기한부어음(time bill, usance bill)을 인수(acceptance)함으로써 어음소지인에 대한 주된 채무자로서 만기일에 지급할 의무를 진다. 그런데 신용장발행은행이 수익자가 발행한 환어음의 직접적인 인수인이 되지 않고, 런던이나 뉴욕 등에 있는 거래은행 또는 신용장의 통지은행 등이 어음의 인수인이 되도록 하는 때가 있다. 이와 같은 인수인을 인수은행(accepting bank)이라 한다.

(9) 결제은행

신용장의 결제통화가 수입국이나 수출국의 통화가 아닌 제 3 국의 통화일 때에는 발행은행의 거래은행이 발행은행의 지시에 따라 대금을 결제하는 경우가 있는데, 이 은행을 결제은행(settling bank)이라고 한다. 어음을 매입한 은행에 대금을 상환해 주는 은행이라고 해서 상환은행(reimbursing bank)이라고도 한다.

3 SWIFT 신용장

(1) SWIFT의 개념

SWIFT란 국제은행간금융데이터통신협회(Society for Worldwide interbank Financial Telecommunication)의 약자이다. SWIFT는 국제간의 대금결제 등을 위한 은행 간 데이터통신의 연결망(network)을 기획하고 운영하는 것을 목적으로 설립되었다. SWIFT는 신뢰성과 보안성이 높다. 따라서 SWIFT에 가맹한 은행들은 국제간의 지급, 각종 거래에 따른 확인 및 국제은행 업무에 관련된 통신을 SWIFT 통신망을 통해 EDI 방식으로 교신함으로써 보다 신속하고 정확하게 처리할 수 있다.

(2) SWIFT 신용장

SWIFT에 의한 신용장 발행은 신용장의 서식(format)이 Code화 되어 있고, 현재

KTNET에서 SWIFT에 의한 신용장 통지업무를 EDI 방식으로 서비스하고 있다. SWIFT 신용장의 표준형식은 Massage Type(MT)로 정형화되어 사용되고 있는데, 예컨대 신용장 발행은 MT700이 사용되며 신용장에 기재되는 내용이 많을 경우에는 MT701을 추가로 사용하게 된다. SWIFT 시스템에 의해 사용되고 있는 Massage Type는 〈표〉와 같다.

[표준통신문 형식]

메시지 포맷	서비스 내용
MT700	화환신용장의 발행, 발행된 신용장 조건들을 표시
MT701	화환신용장의 발행, MT700에 연속되는 신용장의 내용 2쪽
MT705	화환신용장의 사전통지문, 완전한 신용장을 보내기 이전에 사전 정보사항으로 보내는 신용장의 사전통지문
MT707	화환신용장의 조건변경 통지문, 조건변경사항을 통지
MT710/711	제3은행의 화환신용장 통지, 신용장을 다른 은행으로 통지
MT/720/721	화환신용장의 양도
MT730	화환신용장의 수신확인
MT732	하자 있는 서류를 접수한 은행의 하자인수 통지
MT734	하자 있는 서류를 접수한 은행의 인수거절 통지
MT740	발행은행이 상환은행으로 보내는 상환수권서의 발행
MT742	대금상환청구
MT747	상환수권서의 조건변경
MT750	하자통지
MT752	지급, 인수, 매입의 수권
MT754	지급, 인수 매입의 통지
MT756	대금상환 또는 지급의 통지

(3) SWIFT 신용장의 구성

SWIFT 전신문의 1면은 "Covering letter"로 화환신용장을 통지은행에 통지한다는 내용과 수익자로 하여금 신용장 조건을 확인하고 이상이 있으면 발행의뢰인에게 즉시 연락하라는 내용 등이 기재되어 있다.

제2면은 신용장 본문이다. 맨 위에 "AUTH. CORRECT WITH CURRENT KEY(현재의 키로 인증되고 정확하다)"는 문언이 삽입되어 있다. MT700 제2면에 기재되는 조항별 기재 내용은 다음과 같다.

[MT700에 의한 신용장의 CODE별 내용]

M(mandatory), O(option)

M/O	Tag	Field Name
M	20	Documentary Credit Number, 발행은행이 부여하는 신용장 번호를 표시
O	23	Reference to Pre-Advice, 사전통지를 보냈던 신용장의 경우 그와 관련된 참조사항을 표시. 예컨대 PREADV/141122 : 2014년 11월 12일 송부한 사전 통지문의 원본 신용장임을 의미
M	27	Sequence of Total, 전문의 총 쪽수에서 몇 번째 쪽인지를 표시
O	31C	Date of Issue, 발행은행이 발행 일자로 간주하는 일자를 표시, 아무런 표시가 없으면 이 전문이 발송된 일자를 발행 일자로 간주
M	31D	Date and Place of Expiry, 서류가 제시되어야 하는 마지막 일자와 장소를 표시, 신용장의 유효기일과 장소를 대부분 수출국을 기준으로 하지만, 수입국으로 하는 수도 있으므로 이 경우에는 수입국까지의 서류도착 기일 잘 참작하여 미리 매입을 의뢰해야 한다.
M	32B	Current Code, Amount, 신용장의 통화 및 금액을 표시
O	39A	Percentage Credit Amount Tolerance, 신용장 금액의 과부족 편차를 표시, 수량과 금액을 몇 % 범위에서 과부족이 허용되는지를 표시, 환어음 발행은 원칙적으로 신용장 금액을 초과할 수 없으나, special instructions의 내용에 따라 초과 발행할 수도 있다.
O	39B	Maximum Credit Amount, up to, maximum 또는 not exceeding과 같은 문언을 사용하여 신용장 금액을 표시
O	39C	Additional Amount Covered, 수익자가 사용할 수 있는 추가금액(운임, 보험료, 이자 등)
M	40A	Form of Documentary Credit, 신용장의 종류를 표시, 아무런 언급이 없으면 취소불능신용장으로 간주
M	40E	Applicable Rules 준거문언을 표시. "UCP LATEST VERSION" 최신버전 LCCP 적용
M	41D	Available with~, by name and address 'with' 다음에는 신용장을 사용할 수 있는 은행명을 그리고 'by' 뒤에는 신용장의 사용방법을 표시, 신용장의 사용방법에는 payment, acceptance, negotiation, deferred payment의 4가지가 있음
O	42A	Drawee 화환어음의 지급인을 표시, 화환어음의 지급인은 발행은행이 되며 발행은행이 수건을 준 다른 은행이 될 수도 있다. 다만 발행의뢰인은 drawee가 될 수 없다.

M/O	Tag	Field Name
O	42C	Draft at ... 환어음의 지급기일을 나타냄, 일람불 또는 기한부가 표시됨
	42D	Drawee name and address 화환어음의 지급인을 표시, 화환어음의 지급인은 발행은행이 되며, 발행은행이 수권을 준 다른 은행이 될 수도 있다. 다만 개설의뢰인은 Drawee가 될 수 없다.
O	42M	Mixed Payment Details 혼합지급으로 사용이 가능한 경우 그것들의 결정에 필요한 지급일자, 금액 그리고 방법을 표시
O	42P	Deferred Payment Details, 연지급으로 사용이 가능한 경우 그것의 결정에 필요한 지급일자, 금액 또는 결정방법을 표시
O	43P	Partial Shipment, 분할선적의 허용 여부를 표시, 아무런 표시가 없는 경우 분할선적이 허용되는 것으로 간주
O	43T	Transshipment 환적이 허용되는지를 표시, 아무런 표시가 없는 경우 환적이 금지되는 것으로 간주
O	44A	Loading on board/Dispatch/Taking in Charge at/from 선적항, 발송지 또는 수탁지를 표시(해상운송 시 on board, dispatch는 항공, 우편, 육상 운송 시, taking in charge는 복합운송시 사용)
O	44B	For Transportation to ... 최종 목적지를 표시
O	44C	Latest Date of Shipment, 최종 선적일자를 표시
O	44D	Shipment Period, 선적이 가능한 기간을 표시
O	45A	Description of Goods and/or Service, 상품이나 용역의 명세를 표시
O	46A	Document Required, 수출상이 제시해야 할 서류에 관한 사항
O	47A	Additional Conditions, 추가조건을 표시
O	48	Period for Presentation, 선적 후 서류가 지급, 인수 또는 매입을 위하여 제시되어야 하는 제한기간을 표시
M	49	Confirmation Instructions 수신은행 앞 확인에 대한 지시사항을 기재, 예컨대 CONFIRM(수신은행에 신용장 확인을 요청함), MAY ADD(수신은행에 신용장의 확인을 허용함), WITHOUT(수신은행에 신용장의 확인을 요청하지 않음)
M	50	Applicant, 발행의뢰인, 즉 수입상
O	51A	Applicant Bank 발행의뢰은행
M	52A	Issuing bank, 발행은행
O	53A	Reimbursement Bank 개설은행에 의하여 상환을 이행하도록 수권 받은 상환은행명을 표시함
O	57A	Advice Through Bank 수익자에 통지하기 위해 경유해야 하는 은행명이 표시됨
M	59	Beneficiary, 수익자, 즉 수출상

M/O	Tag	Field Name
O	71B	Charges, 비용부담자, 수수료가 수익자 측의 부담인 경우에 주로 표시
O	72	Sender to Receiver Information 필요한 경우 발신은행이 수신은행에 제공하는 정보사항을 기술함
O	78	Instructions to the Paying/Accepting/Negotiating Bank 지급은행, 인수은행 또는 매입은행을 위한 지시사항을 기술

4 신용장거래의 절차

(1) 신용장의 발행 및 통지

① 매매당사자가 신용장에 의한 결제방식으로 하는 매매계약을 체결한다.

② 수입상(발행의뢰인)은 자신의 거래은행에 신용장의 발행을 신청한다.

③ 신용장 발급을 요청을 받은 발행은행은 발행의뢰인의 신용도, 거래조건 및 담보능력 등을 검토하여 신용장을 발행하여 자신의 환거래은행에 신용장 발행 사실을 수익자에게 통지하도록 요청한다.

④ 통지은행은 신용장 발행 사실을 수익자에게 통지한다.

(2) 운송서류의 제시

⑤ 신용장을 접수한 수출상은 수출물품을 선적하고 보험서류와 운송서류를 획득한다.

⑥ 수출상은 환어음과 기타 신용장에서 요구하는 서류를 갖추고 여기에 보험서류와 운송서류를 첨부하여 매입은행에 매입을 의뢰한다.

⑦ 매입은행은 수출상이 "일치하는 제시(complying present)"를 하면, 그 서류를 매입하고 대금을 지급한다.

⑧ 매입은행은 매입한 서류를 상환은행(있는 경우), 확인은행(있는 경우) 또는 발행은행에 보내어 대금의 상환을 요청한다.

⑨ 만약에 매입은행이 상환은행에 서류를 제시하였다면 상환은행은 약정된 금액을 매입은행에 상환해주고 그 사실을 발행은행에 통지한다. 확인은행에 서류를 제시하였다면 확인은행은 지급이행 또는 매입한 후 서류를 발행은행으로 보낸다. 발행은행에 서류를 제시하였다면 발행은행은 매입은행에 대금을 상환

한다.

⑩ 발행은행은 상환은행이 매입은행에 대금을 상환하였을 때는 상환은행에 그리고 확인은행이 지급이행 또는 매입하였을 때에는 확인은행에 대금을 상환함으로써 모든 결제과정이 종료된다.

(3) 대금결제 및 서류인도

⑪ 서류를 접수한 발행은행은 서류가 도착하였음을 발행의뢰인에게 통지한다.

⑫ 발행은행은 수입상에게 상품대금을 받고 선적서류를 수입상에게 인도해준다.

⑬ 서류를 입수한 수입상은 B/L과의 상환으로 운송회사에 화물은 인수한다.

⑭ 보험사고가 발생한 때는 보험회사에 사고통지를 하고 보험금을 받는다.

■ 매입신용장 거래절차 ■

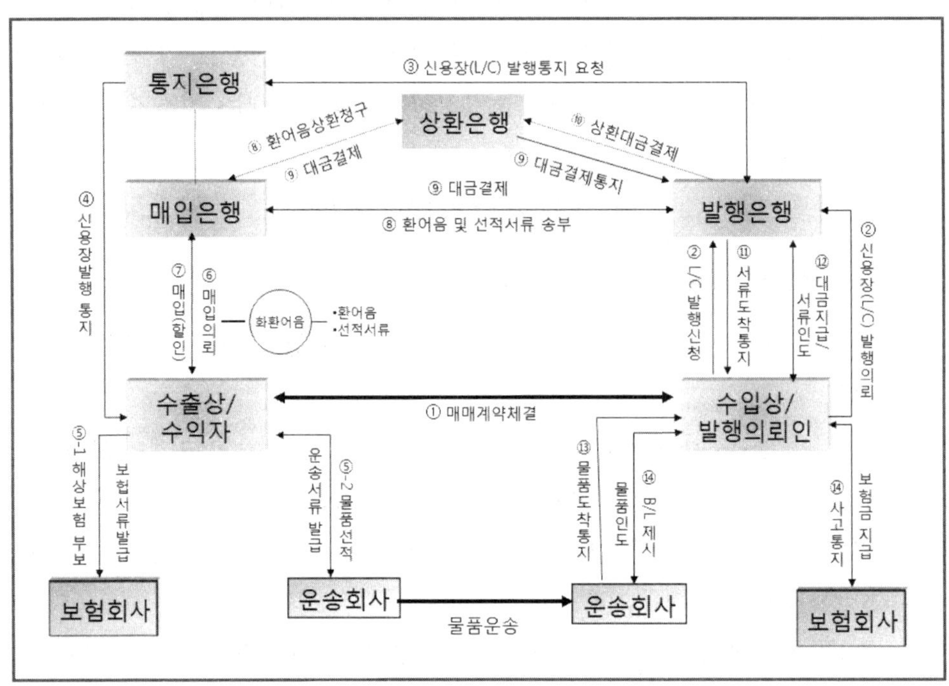

Ⅱ 신용장관련 통신문 및 L/C Model Form

1 신용장 관련 통신문

Model letter 1 L/C개설요청

Gentlemen :

Re : CONTRACT NO. 3939

We refer to our letter dated June 20, confirming acceptance of your order above.

We inquired you on July 7 by telex when you would issue a credit for this contract. Your reply read in part that they would attend to this in a week or so.

Our telex message is a week old, but apparently we have not received any further news on this matter.

Would you be good enough to look into the matter with good speed so that we may effect the contracted shipment without the slightest hitch.

Your prompt response would be highly appreciated, we wait for the early arrival of the Letter of Credit.

Your faithfully,

Notes

- a credit for this contract 본 계약의 결제를 위한 신용장
- attend to ~ 처리하다, 신중히 다루다(= give care and time to~)
- in a week or so 1주일 정도 걸리면
- is a week old 일주일 전에 발송되었다.(was dispatched a week ago)
- any further news on ~에 관한 어떤 소식도(any information on~)
- with good speed 즉시(immediately)
- without the slightest hitch 조금의 어려움 없이(= without difficulty, quite smoothly)

Model letter 2 L/C개설요청

Gentlemen :

Re : Your Order No. 1215

We regret very much to inform you that we have not yet received your credit opening advice, though your order has been confirmed on July 25, 200__.

We would very much appreciate it if you could expedite L/C opening by this week. Otherwise, due to price increase in raw material offer, we may be forced to add additional 5 percent to our previous offer.

On receipt of your L/C, we will pack and ship the goods at the first available opportunity and send you the shipping advice by fax.

Please understand our difficulties and open a credit soon.

Truly yours,

Notes

- regret to ~하게 되어 유감스럽게 생각하다.(be sorry to)
- We will appreciate it if you will ~해 주시면 감사하겠습니다.(= We will/or would appreciate ~ing)
- expedite 촉진시키다(hasten)

Model letter 3 L/C 개설독촉

Gentlemen:

Opening of the L/C for the order No.105

The letter of credit you promised to send us through Korea Exchange Bank, Busan has not reached us yet.

The time of shipment is fast approaching, and you will readily see how inconvenienced we are. Your order has already been with us and is ready to dispatch to Yokohama for scheduled loading on SS Puma.

In order to save time for mailing, please electronically send your L/C direct to our bankers as previously instructed.

Your speedy arrangements will be much appreciated.

Faithfully yours,

Notes

- inconvenienced 폐를 입은
- dispatch 발송하다
- electronically send 전송하다
- Your speedy arrangements will be much appreciated. (신속한 배려를 해주시면 매우 감사하겠습니다.)

Model letter 4 L/C 발행 통보

Gentlemen:

We are advised by the Bank of California of Los Angeles, that they have issues an irrevocable Documentary Letter of Credit No. HNB-1234 in your favor for USD10,000 available until September 20.

We are further informed that the copy of this credit was forwarded direct to you. Please chase and collect the Documentary Credit and confirm us by fax upon receipt of the Documentary Credit from advising bank.

We shall be glad to be of service to you in connection with negotiating your draft under this credit.

Faithfully yours,

Notes

- advise(inform, notify) ~ of(that S+V) ~에게 ~을 통지하다. 알려주다(= we are advised by A that ~)
- issue(= open, arrange, establish, furnish) an L/C in one's favor to cover A for B(금액) until ~ ~을 수익자로 하여 A에 대하여 B 금액으로(에 대해) ~까지 유효한 것으로 하여 신용장을 개설하다.
- be of service to ~ ~에게 도움이 되다
- negotiate a draft 어음을 팔다, 네고하다, 어음을 매입하다. (은행 입장에서) 어음을 결제하다.

Model letter 5 L/C 개설통지

SUBJECT : L/C No. BT-12345 for Sales Note No. GSL-FED-1

Dear Mr. Hill

Thank you very much for your confirmation of our order for 50 units "Quick" Brand Golf Cart Model WMC-9.

We are very happy to import it as an initial order, and are sure that it will prove to be comfortable and convenient for golf players in this country.

As contracted, we have just completed the procedures at our bank to open an irrevocable L/C in your favor.

As to the Sales Note, we have already returned to you the duplicate with our signature.

We look forward to your punctual shipment, and are also waiting for the safe arrival of the goods here.

Sincerely,

Notes

- prove to be comfortable and convenient **편안하고 편리한 것으로 입증되다**
- procedures **수속, 절차**
- punctual shipment **시간 엄수한 선적, 늦지 않은 선적**

Model letter 6 L/C 내도통지(통지은행이 수익자에게 보내는 서신)

Gentlemen :

R : L/C No. HNB-1234 for USD10,000

We please to advice you that we have received the L/C on 1st December, 20— by telex as a non-negotiable copy is enclosed herewith for your information only.

Our charges for advising the above item amount to Korean Won 30,000.

Please call on our counter, bringing with your signed letter of acknowledgement together with the appropriate payment, to collect this item as soon as possible.

Faithfully yours,

Notes

- collect **대금을 회수하다. 추심하다** (cf. freight collect 운임후불, 운임도착불, 운임미지급)

Model letter 7 L/C 조건변경 요청

Gentlemen :

Change of the opening bank of the L/C

We have received your letter of November 1, informing us of your prospective bank which would open the letter of credit.

Although we thank you for prompt attention to this matter, we have to say that the bank you mentioned in the letter is not acceptable.

When your representative came to Korea for negotiation, we were told that you would arrange an L/C through a mutually acceptable bank.

We understand that a mutually acceptable bank connotes a meaning that the opening bank should be appointed on our approval.

Under the circumstances, would you kindly ask one of the banks listed on the enclosed sheet of paper, cancelling the bank you mentioned?

Or we recommend you that the letter of credit to be opened by Second Rate Bank of Indonesia be confirmed at your cost by our bank.

We trust that you as a reputed house of international trading will surely accept this favor. We would appreciate your prompt attention.

Faithfully yours,

Notes

- prospective 유망한
- connote 암시하다, 내포하다
- favor 호의, 부탁
- mention 언급하다
- recommend 추천하다, 권하다

Model letter 8 L/C 연장신청

Gentlemen:

Extension of the L/C No. 12235

With respect to the subject letter of credit, we would like you to extend its validity from March 31 to April 30.

The manufacturers we assigned to process your order have reported to us with an apology that the order would take a couple of more weeks for an unexpected delay of schedule on the part of their subcontractors.

The subcontractors seem to have incurred an extraordinary delayed delivery of material to be applied as a vital ingredient to the product, and our expected shipment will be correspondingly delayed. We judge the cause somewhat beyond their control and permissible as well.

We would be much obliged if you would understand the situation we are put in and extend both the time of shipment and validity of the L/C accordingly. Interest cost and other charges incidental to the extension will be borne by us on receipt of your bill.

Your kind arrangement will be much appreciated.

Faithfully yours,

Notes

- extend 연장하다
- assign 임명하다
- subcontractor 하도급업자(하청업자)
- vital 매우 중요한
- as well 게다가, 그 위에
- validity 유효기간
- process 가공 처리하다
- incur 초래하다, 걸머지다
- ingredient 성분, 재료
- incidental 부수적인

Model letter 9 L/C의 접수

Dear Sirs,

We have received with thanks the letters of credit covering your orders Nos. 101.

Upon examination, however, we have found that the L/C No. 7340 for Order No. 101 to be shipped during this month, expires on 15th August. On the other hand, the only available vessel to your port during August is S/S "Yamato Maru" leaving Kobe on or around the 20th.

So we have cabled, as per copy enclosed, asking you to extend the validity and the shipment time of the L/C to the end of August and cable us to that effect by the 18th.

We trust that you will comply with our request, since the contract stipulates "during August" and the goods are ready for shipment.

Yours very truly,

Notes

- Upon examination 검토해 보니
- expire (기한이) 끝나다
- to that effect 그러한 취지로
- On the other hand 반면에
- S/S 증기선, 기선(Steam ship), 철선(Steel ship) cf. M/S(디젤선, Motor ship = M/V, Motor vessel)
- on or around = about, around ~일 경

Model letter 10 L/C의 취소

Dear Mr. Kim,

We thank you very much for your president's visiting our office and kindly accept our deepest apology for not having extended our warm reception to him because his schedule was very tight.

Today, our bank informed us the L/C No. 9RH2-02765/ 471-U442 is invalid and asked us to cancel it. We are so sorry for being unable to accept your shipment of hair dryer.

Indeed, this quality can not meet our requirements. Later, if you can produce this article with the better quality, please do not hesitate to tell us, we will not fail to place our order with you soon,

Thanking you, we remain,

Yours very truly,

Notes

- apology 사과
- not having extended our warm reception 우리의 따뜻한 환대를 주지 못했던 것
- invalid 무효의, 무효가 되는
- our requirements 폐사의 요구조건
- hesitate 주저하다
- fail to -을 못하다(cannot)
- not fail to 꼭 -하다 (이중부정)

Model letter 11 확인은행의 지정요구

Gentlemen:

Re: Confirmation of the L/C

We have received your recent letter informing us of an opening of a letter of credit. We were surprised at the same time that the L/C would be opened by a bank whose name is totally unknown to us.

It has been an agreement between you and us that the L/C would be opened by a mutually acceptable bank. It is regrettable that you did not comply with what has been agreed upon despite our repeated reminder.

We, therefore, ask you to let us appoint one of our bankers here to have them confirm the L/C in particular. This would be the most appropriate method thinkable under the circumstances where time is most important.

Since the opening of the credit was done without our consent and against the good faith, we would request that the confirmation fee be borne by you.

Please let us hear from you by the end of this week. If not, we will assume that request for confirmation was accepted. Thank you very much for your attention.

Faithfully yours,

Notes

- inform ~ of ~을 ~에게 알리다
- repeated reminder 반복된 독촉장
- appropriate method 적절한 방법
- comply with 동의하다
- consent 동의
- good faith 선의

Model letter 12 L/C 확인료의 분할 요청서

Gentlemen :

Re : Confirmation charges for the L/C

With respect to the confirmation of the L/C for our order, we would like you to understand that the bank we approached for the opening of the credit is the most locally accessible bank to us of all commercial banks in this country.

The other reasons why we used the Second Bank of People was that, firstly being our bankers they would take far lesser time until the credit is opened and secondly their credit is one of the best among banks of compatible credit standing.

We would admit, however, that the Second Bank of People may not fully satisfy such a rigid credit status of the internationally qualified banks as we initially agreed.

We will therefore accept your request as is proposed in your recent correspondence on condition that half of the confirmation fees that your bank will charge will be borne by you.

We hope that you would accept our counter-request appreciation extremely inconvenient locality we are located and good profit potentials that our business will bring.

Faithfully yours,

Notes

- confirmation 확인
- accessible 접근하기 쉬운; 얻기 쉬운
- satisfy such a rigid credit status 그러한 엄격한 신용상태를 충족시키다
- compatible credit standing 적합한 신용상태를 가진
- on condition that ~이라는 조건으로, 만일 ~라면(if)

2 L/C Model Form – 취소불능신용장

(1) LETTER OF CREDIT [UCP500에 의한 신용장]

<table>
<tr>
<td colspan="2">1) THE FIRST PACIFIC BANK OF CHICAGO
(Mid-Continental Plaza Wabash at Adams
Chicago, ILL., 60603
Cable address :
Telex No. : PO box :</td>
<td>3) <u>IRREVOCABLE</u>

<u>LETTER OF</u>

<u>CREDIT</u></td>
<td>4) <u>Credit No.</u>
(Issuing Bank's No.)

FPB96904892</td>
</tr>
<tr>
<td colspan="2"><u>2) Place and date of issue</u>
Chicago, USA 30 Aug 1998
□ Confirmation of our brief teletransmission of</td>
<td colspan="2"><u>5) Date and place of expiry</u>
10. SEP. 20--
at counter of Bank in Seoul</td>
</tr>
<tr>
<td colspan="2"><u>6) Applicant</u>
WAIKKI CO., LTD.
5002 North Clark Street Chicago, ILL., 60603, USA</td>
<td colspan="2"><u>7) Beneficiary</u>
KOREA TRADING CO., LTD.
Jungkok-dong Sungdong-ku, Seoul, KOREA</td>
</tr>
<tr>
<td colspan="2"><u>8) Advising Bank</u>
Korea Exchange Bank Seoul, Korea
Advising Bank's No.</td>
<td colspan="2"><u>9) Amount</u>
USD20,000.00(USDollars Twenty Thousand only)</td>
</tr>
<tr>
<td><u>12)</u>

<u>Partial Shipment</u>

□ allowed

□ not allowed</td>
<td><u>13)</u>

<u>Transshipment</u>

□ allowed

□ not allowed</td>
<td colspan="2" rowspan="2"><u>10) Credit available with</u>
THE FIRST PACIFIC BANK OF CHICAGO
(Mid-Continental Plaza Wabash at Adams
Chicago, ILL., 60603
by
11) □ sight payment/
□ deferred payment/
□ acceptance/
□ negotiation against the documents detailed herein.
□ and your drafts(□ at sight/ □ at days) drawn on us for full invoice value of goods.</td>
</tr>
<tr>
<td colspan="2"><u>14) Loading on board</u>
from Busan, Korea
<u>not later than</u> 10 SEP 20--
for transportation to Hong Kong</td>
</tr>
<tr>
<td colspan="4"><u>15) Documents required</u>
·Invoice(s) in quadruplicate
·□ Full set of original clean "On Board" bill of lading made out to the order of shipper endorsed in blank
□ Original airwaybill marked "for the consignor" signed by the carrier of his agent. marked "Freight □ Prepaid / □ Collect" and "Notify KOREA TRADING Co., Ltd, Seoul, Korea.
·□ Marine / □ Air <u>Insurance Policy or Certificate</u> for full CIF value plus 10% covering
□ Institute Cargo Clauses(A) / □ Institute Cargo Clauses(Air), □ Institute War Clauses(□ Cargo/ □ Air Cargo) and Institute Strikes Clauses(□ Cargo / □ Air Cargo).
·Packing List in quadruplicate
·□ Insurance covered by □ Applicant / □ ultimate buyer, 16) 1,000pcs LEATHER GARMENTS at USD20.00 per pc CIF
17) Each □ claim for payment/ □ draft accompanying documents must state: "Drawn under credit N0. FPB96904892 The First Pacific Bank Of Chicago, Chicago"</td>
</tr>
<tr>
<td colspan="4"><u>18) Documents to be presented for negotiation</u> within 10 days after the date of issuance of the transport document(s) but within the validity of the credit</td>
</tr>
<tr>
<td colspan="4"><u>19) Special conditions</u>(These shall prevail over all printed terms in case of any apparent conflict)
All banking charges outside U.S.A are for account of beneficiary
□ to be continued on next page</td>
</tr>
</table>

20) We hereby issue this irrevocable documentary credit in your favour which, except so far as otherwise expressly stated herein, is subject to "Uniform Customs and Practice for Documentary Credit (2007 Revision), International Chamber of Commerce Publication No. 600)" 21) □ We hereby engage that payment will be duly made against presentation of documents which conform with the terms of this credit. □ We hereby engage that drafts drawn in conformity with the terms of this credit will be duly accepted on presentation and duly honored at maturity. □ We hereby agree with the drawers, endorsers, and/or bona-fide holders that drafts drawn and negotiated in conformity with the terms of this credit will be duly honored on presentation so long as there has been strict compliance with the terms and conditions (including special conditions) of this credit save to the extent that the same have been amended in writing and signed on our behalf. Documentary evidence will be required of compliance with all conditions of this credit. This document consists of one signed pages. Your faithfully THE FIRST PACIFIC BANK OF CHICAGO	22) We cannot make any alterations to this credit without the opener's authority. Should any of its terms or conditions be unclear or unacceptable, the beneficiary of this credit must contact the opener directly. We shall insist on strict compliance with all the terms and conditions of this credit unless and until they have been formally amended in writing signed on our behalf or by tested telex or by such other method as shall have been agreed from time to time. The beneficiary of this credit is not entitled to rely on communications or discussions with us, the advising bank or the opener as in any way amending this credit. The attention of the beneficiary is also drawn to Articles 4 and 5 or UCP600. 23) Advising Bank's notification 24) Place, date, name and consignee of the Advising bank

Notes

① 신용장개설은행
② 개설일자 및 장소(place and date of issue)
③ 신용장의 종류
④ 신용장번호(credit number)
⑤ 유효기간 및 장소(date and place of expiry)
⑥ 개설의뢰인(applicant)
⑦ 수익자(beneficiary)
⑧ 통지은행(advising bank)
⑨ 신용장금액(amount)
⑩ 신용장의 사용방법(credit available with~)
⑪ 환어음에 관한 사항(by ~ 아래
⑫ 분할선적(partial shipment)
⑬ 환적(transsipment)
⑭ 선적항 등(loading on board/dispatch/taking in charge from/at)
⑮ 서류에 관한 사항(documents required)
⑯ 상품에 관한 사항
⑰ 환어음의 작성에 관한 사항
⑱ 서류제시기간(documents to be presented for negotiation)

⑲ 특수조건에 관한 사항(special conditions)
⑳ 신용장통일규칙 준거문언
㉑ 지급확약문언
㉒ 수익자가 주의해야 할 사항
㉓ 통지은행 확인란(advising bank's notification)
㉔ 매입은행에 대한 지시(place, date, name and consignee of the Advising bank)

(2) IRREVOCABLE CREDIT(BY CABLE)

THE NATIONAL BANK OF NEW YORK
120 Broad Street New York

IRREVOCABLE CREDIT No.1001

November 30, 20--

Haedong Trading Co., Ltd.

The credit airmailed through
The Kukmin Bank, Seoul Korea

Gentlemen :

We hereby authorize you to draw on The National Bank of New York, New York, for account of American Silk Store, Inc., New York up to the amount of Five Thousand Dollars($5,000) available by your drafts at sight for 100% invoice value of silk goods, CIF accompanied by :

Commercial Invoice in triplicate

Customs Invoice in duplicate

Marine Insurance Policy or Certificate in duplicate covered with the American Insurance Underwriters for 110% of invoice value including W.A. and War Clauses.

Packing List in triplicate

Full set of on board clean Bill of Lading drawn to the order of The National Bank of New York, New York, marked "Notify American Silk Store, Inc., New York", evidencing shipment from a Korean port to New York during the month of January 20--.

All drafts must be marked "Drawn under Credit of The National Bank of New York, No. 1001 dated November 30, 20--."

The amount of any draft drawn under this credit must be endorsed on the reverse hereof and the presentation of draft, if negotiated, shall be a warranty by the negotiating bank that such endorsement has been made. If the draft is not negotiated, this credit and all relative documents must accompany the draft.

We hereby agree with the drawers, endorsers and bona fide holders of drafts drawn under and in compliance with the terms of this credit, that such drafts will be honored on presentation to the drawees if negotiated or presented at this office on or before February 15, 20-- This credit is subject to the Uniform Customs and Practice for Documentary Credits(2007 revision, ICC Brochure No. 600).

Yours very truly,

Notes

- draw on (지급인) 앞으로 어음을 발행하다(value on)
- for account of (수입상) 수입상의 계정으로,
- up to the amount of ~의 한도까지(= for ~)
- available by your drafts 귀사의 어음에 의하여 이용 가능한, 그 이용은 귀사 어음발행으로 가능하다
- for 100% invoice value 송장금액 100%에 대한
- accompanied by ~이 첨부된
- in triplicate 3통
- in duplicate 2통
- covered with ~에 부보한
- War Clauses 전시약관
- Commercial Invoice 상업송장
- Customs Invoice 세관송장
- Marine Insurance Policy 해상보험증권
- W.A.= With Average 분손담보조건
- Full set 전 부수
- on board clean Bill of Lading 선적무고장 선화증권
- to the order of ~의 지시인에게
- marked "Notify American Silk Store, Inc". "American Silk Store, Inc.에 통지바람"으로 표시가 된
- evidencing shipment 선적사실을 증명하는
- endorse 이서를 하다
- negotiating bank 매입은행
- drawer 발행인
- bona fide holder 선의의 소지자
- reverse hereof 이 이면에
- all relative documents 모든 관계서류
- endorser 이서인
- drawee 지불인
- Uniform Customs and Practice for Documentary Credits(1995 revision) 화환신용장 통일규칙(1995년 개정)
- ICC 국제상업회의소(International Chamber of Commerce)

수입신용장(SWIFT MT 700)

ADVICE OF ORIGINAL LETTER OF CREDIT

L/C NO. : M1234 606NS00018 DATED 20○○, 6. 20

FOR : USDUSD 119,000.00

OUR REF. :

OPENEED BY : WOORI BANK, SEOUL DATED 20○○, 6. 24

DEAR SIRS,

WITHOUT ANY RESPONSIBILITY OR ENGAGEMENT ON OUR PART FOR POSSIBLE ERRORS, OMISSIONS, OR DELAYS IN THE TRANSMISSION THEREOF, WE ENCLOSE AN AUTHENTICATED MESSAGE ADVISING THE ISSUANCE OF THE CAPTIONED CREDIT.

YOU ARE REQUIRED TO EXAMINE THE CONTENTS OF THE CREDIT.

IF ANY OF THE TERMS/CONDITIONS DO NOT COMPLY WITH YOUR EXPECTATION, PLEASE CONTACT DIRECTLY WITH THE APPLICATION AS WE ARE BIT AUTHORISED TO VARY THE CREDIT WITHOUT INSTRUCTIONS FROM THE ISSUING BANK.

YOUR FAITHFULLY,

HANKOOK BANK

HONG KONG BRANCH

MANAGER

[FIRST COPY]

AUTH CORRECT WITH CURRENT KEY

FIN UAK	{ 1: F21NATAKRSEAXXX1203103247
{4: {117: date and time (YYMMDDHHMM)	: 971007 1421}
{451: acceptance/rejection :	0}}
{1: FIN MESSAGE/ session / OSN	F01 NATAKRSEAXXX 1203 103247}
{2: output Message Type	701 issue of a documentary credit

Input Time / MIR	1519 971007NATAAU33A04B0924666347
Priority / Delivery / Obsol.	Normal}

Text Block :

/27 : sequence of total	: 1/1
/40A : form of documentary credit	: IRREVOCABLE
/20 : documentary credit number	: M1234 606NS00018
/31C : date of issue	: ○○/06/24
/31D : date and place of expiry	: ○○/08/20 HONG KONG
/50 : applicant	: KOREA TOYS CO., LTD. 159-1SAMSUNGDONG KANGNAMGU, SEOUL, KOREA
/59 : beneficiary	: CHINA TOYS CO., LTD. RM 1000 CHAI WAN IND. CITY PHASE 1, 60 WING TAIRO, CHAIWAN H.K.
/32B : currency code amount	: USD 119,000.00
/39C : additional amount covered	: CFR PORT OF DISCHARGE
/39A : pct credit amount toterance	: 10/10
/41D : available with by name, address	: ANY BANK BY NEGOTIATION(or YOURSELVES BY NEGOTIATION)
/42C : drafts at	: AT SIGHT
/42A : drawee	: HONG KONG FIRST BANK LTD., HONG KONG (ADDR 2007, JARDINE HOUSE 1 CONNAUGHT PLACE, CENTRAL, HONG KONG)
/42M : Miixed payment details	: 50% 45 D/S FROM THE BL DATE 50% 420 D/S FROM THE BL DATE
/43P : partial shipment	: ALLOWED
/43T : transshipment	: NOT ALLOWED
/44A : on board/Disp/taking charge	: SHIDAO, CHINA(or ANY PORT IN 국명)
/44B : for transportation to	: BUSAN, KOREA
/44C : latest date of shipment	: ○○/08/10

/45A : descr goods and/or services

700PAIRS OF CHINESE GIANT BEAR TOY

SIZE : MIN 1.5 METERS AT USD170.00 CFR SHIDAO. CHINA

/46A : documents required

+SIGNED COMMERCIAL INVOICE IN QUINTUPLICATE

+PACKING LIST IN TRIPLICATE

+FULL SET OF CLEAN ON BOARD OCEAN BILL OF LANDING MADE OUT TO THE ORDER OF WOORI BANK MARKED FREIGHT COLLECT AND NOTIFY APPLICANT

+CERTIFICATE OF ORIGIN

/47A : additional conditions

+ ALL DOCUMENTS MUST BEAR OUR CREDIT NUMBER M1234 606NS00018

+ INSURANCE WILL BE COVERED BY BUYER IN HONG KONG

+ T/T REIMBURSEMENT NOT ALLOWED
+ OUANTITY 10PCT MORE OR LESS ALLOWED
+ THIRD PARTY DOCUMENTS ACCEPTABLE
+ SHIPMENT PRIOR THE DATE OF THIS CREDIT IS NOT ACCEPTABLE
+ PLEASE ACKNOWLEDGE RECEIPT OF THIS L/C MENTIONING : YOUR REFERENCE NUMBER AND THE EXACT DATE YOU ADVISE/CONFIRMED THIS L/C T ㅐ THE BENEFICIARY QUOTING
  OUR REFERENCE ILC000145246
+ MUST BE SHOW "FREIGHT PREPAID" AND THE FREIGHT AMOUNT IN FIGURES AND WORDS

/71B : charges	: ALL BANKING COMMISSIONS AND CHARGES INCLUDING REIMBURSEMENT CHARGES OUTSIDE KOREA ARE FOR ACCOUNT OF BENEFICIARY
/49 : confirmation instructions	: WITHOUT
/53A : reimbursement bank	: HONG KONG FIRST BANK LTD., HONG KONG(ADDR 2007, JARDINE HOUSE 1 CONNAUGHT PLACE, CENTRAL, HONG KONG)

/78 : instructions to the pay/acc/neg bk

DRAFTS MUST BE SENT TO DRAWEE BANK FOR YOUR REMBURSEMENT
AND ALL DOCUMENTS TO US BY COURIER SERVICE IN ONE LOT

/57A : advise thru bank - BIC	OKey BANK SEOUL
/40E : applicable rules	: THIS CREDIT IS SUBJECT TO U.C.P(2010 REVISION) I.C.C. PUBLICATION NO. 600)

Useful Expressions

1. We have opened an L/C for $13,500 in your favor
   귀사를 수익자로 하여 $13,500의 신용장을 개설하였습니다.

2. We will arrange an L/C with a bank listed in your letter. As soon as an opening bank has been decided, we will let you know accordingly.
   귀 서신에 있는 은행에서 신용장을 개설하겠습니다. 개설은행이 결정되자마자 그에 따라 알려 드리겠습니다.

3. What we asked you to do was to open an irrevocable letter of credit, not an revocable letter of credit. We ordinarily refer to an L/C as an irrevocable letter of credit.
   폐사가 해주시도록 요청했던 것은 취소가능신용장이 아니라 취소불능신용장이었습니다. 폐사는 통상 신용장을 취소불능신용장으로 지칭합니다.

4. Please amend (adjust) the L/C No. 1356 as follows;
   (1) Amount to US$1,500 (by US$100)
   (2) Validity to be extended till 30th April.
   (3) The words "equal" are to be deleted.(replaced by "about")
   신용장 제 1356호를 다음과 같이 변경해 주십시오.
   (1) 금액을 1,500美弗까지 증액할 것(100美弗 증액)
   (2) 기한을 4월 30일까지 연장할 것
   (3) 다음의 문언 "equal" 삭제 ("about"로 바꿀 것)

5. We would like to extend the time of shipment and the validity of the credit to March 10 and March 31 respectively.
   선적기간과 신용장의 유효기간을 3월 10일과 3월 31일까지 각각 연장하고 싶습니다.

6. Since we have extended the L/C No. 876 twice, we find it very difficult to do so this time.
폐사는 신용장 876호를 두 번 연장했기 때문에 이번에 연장한다는 것은 매우 어렵습니다.

7. We would like to point out that our bankers are so strict in extending credit and such amendment will be totally unacceptable.
폐사의 거래은행은 신용장 연장에 아주 엄격하므로 그러한 변경(연장)은 전혀 받아들여질 수 없으리라는 것을 지적하고 싶습니다.

8. We understand that the opening bank of L/C for this transaction was once approved by you and, therefore, we do not see why you reject it.
이 거래에 대한 신용장의 발행은행은 한때 귀사가 승인하였습니다. 그러므로 그것을 거절한 이유를 모르겠습니다.

9. We would like you to arrange for a letter of credit to be opened by the First Credit Bank of New York. Should you have any other bank in mind, please let us know accordingly.
뉴욕제일신용은행이 신용장을 개설하도록 배려하여 주셨으면 합니다. 어떤 다른 은행을 염두에 두고 계시다면 알려 주십시오.

10. In order to avoid unnecessary confirmation on the letter of credit we advise that the opening banks be agreed. We believe it will save us a lot of time and money.
신용장에 대한 불필요한 확인을 피하기 위하여 개설은행에 대하여 합의되었음을 통지해드립니다. 그럼으로써 시간과 금전을 절약할 것으로 믿습니다.

11. Our bankers are so strict that they will not overlook the slightest discrepancy between descriptions on the shipping documents and those on the L/C.
폐사의 거래은행은 아주 엄격하여 선적서류상의 명세와 신용장상의 명세간에 경미한 불일치라도 간과하지 않을 것입니다.

제9장

해상적하 보험

I 해상적하보험 계약과 부보

해상적하보험(Marine Cargo Insurance)이란 화물의 이동구간, 즉 운송구간에 있어서 해난(disaster at sea) 또는 항해에 관련된 우발적인 사고에 의해 발생하는 선박이나 적하에 대한 손해를 보험사고로 하여, 보험자가 그 손해를 보상할 것을 약속하고 피보험자가 그에 대한 대가로 보험료를 지급할 것을 약속하는 보험을 말한다.

해상보험계약은 해상에서의 손해에 추가하여 강이나 호수와 같은 내수(內水, inland waters) 또는 육상위험의 손해까지 확장하여 보상할 수 있으며, 건조(建造) 중의 선박, 선박의 진수 또는 해상사업과 관련 있는 유사한 사업의 손해까지도 해상보험증권에 의해 보상할 수 있다.(MIA 제2조)

1 해상적하보험 계약의 당사자

(1) 보험자

보험자(insurer)는 타인에게 손해를 보상할 것을 약속하는 당사자를 말하며, 언더라이터(underwriter)라고도 한다. 즉 보험자는 보험사업을 영위하는 자로서 피보험자로부터 보험료를 받고, 그 대가로 보험사고(해상위험)로 인한 손해보상을 약속한 자를 말한다.

(2) 피보험자

피보험자(insured, assured)란 피보험이익의 주체로서 보험사고가 발생할 경우 보험자로부터 손해보상을 받을 수 있는 자, 즉 보험계약으로부터 보호를 받는 자를 말한다.

(3) 보험계약자

보험계약자(insurance policy holder, party insuring)란 보험자와 보험계약을 체결하고 보험료를 지급하기로 약속한 자를 말한다. 보험계약자는 자신이 직접 보험계약을 체결할 수도 있으며, 자신의 대리인으로 하여금 보험계약을 체결하도록 할 수도 있다.

(4) 보험대리점

특정 보험자의 보험계약 체결 업무를 일정 기간동안 대리하거나 중재하는 것을 업으로 하는 자를 말하며, 이들은 특정 보험자로부터 업무를 위임받아 그를 위한 보조업무만을 수행한다.

(5) 보험중개인

불특정보험자를 위해 보험계약의 성립을 중재하는 것을 업으로 하는 자를 말한다. 보험대리인과는 달리 특정 보험자가 아닌 불특정 보험자나 피보험자로부터 업무를 위임받아 보험계약의 성립을 중재하는 업무를 한다.

2 해상적하보험 관련 용어

(1) 피보험이익

피보험이익(insurable interest)이란 보험의 목적의 멸실 또는 손상으로 경제적 피해를 당하게 되는 특정인(피보험자)과 보험의 목적 사이에 존재하는 적법한 경제적 관계를 말한다. 다시 말하자면 손해보험 계약에 있어 보험의 목적에 대해 보험사고가 발생하지 않음으로써 피보험자가 손해를 입지 않게 되는 이익이라 할 수 있다. 보험의 목적이란 보험사고 발생의 객체가 되는 대상을 말하며, 보험의 목적에 따라 선박보험, 적하보험 등으로 구분된다.

보험계약의 목적은 피보험이익이며 피보험이익의 대상인 재화 즉 보험의 목적 그 자체가 아니다.

(2) 보험가액

보험가액(insurable value)이란 보험사고 발생 시 피보험자가 당할 수 있는 손해의 최고상한액을 말하며, 이는 피보험이익을 경제적 가치로 평가한 금액이 된다. 피보험자 입장에서 보험가액은 보험에 가입할 수 있는 최고한도액이 된다. 적하보험에서의 보험가액은 통상 CIF 가격에 10%를 가산한 금액으로 하고 있다.

(3) 보험금액

보험금액(insured amount, sum insured)이란 피보험자가 실제로 보험에 가입한 금액으로 보험사고가 발생한 경우 보험자가 피보험자에게 지급하여야 할 금액의 최고한도가 된다. 보험금액과 보험가액이 동일한 경우를 전부보험(full insurance), 보험금액이 큰 경우를 초과보험(over insurance) 그리고 보험가액이 큰 경우를 일부보험(partial insurance, under insurance)이라고 한다.

(4) 보험료

보험료(premium)란 보험자의 손해보상에 대한 약속의 반대급부로 보험계약자가 지급하는 금전적 급부를 말한다. 통상 보험료율은 보험금액에 대한 일정률(%)로 표시되며, 보험료의 산출은 보험금액(CIF value × 110%)에 보험료율(premium rate)를 곱하여 산출한다.

(5) 보험금

보험금(amount)은 담보위험에 의해 손해가 발생한 경우 보험자가 피보험자에게 실제로 지급해야 하는 손해보상의 최고한도액을 말한다. 즉, 실제로 발생한 멸실·손실을 경제적 가치로 환산한 금액이다.

3 협회적하약관

(1) 구협회적하약관

가) 전손담보(Total Loss Only ; TLO)

전손담보조건이란 보험의 목적물이 전손되었을 때에만 손해를 보상하는 조건이며, 분손 즉 공동해손이나 단독해손은 보상하지 않는 조건으로 실제로는 그다지 이용되지 않고 있다.

나) 단독해손 부 담보(Free From Particular Average ; F.P.A.)

이 조건은 담보되는 위험에 의해 발생한 전손과 공동해손은 보상되지만, 단독해손인 분손은 원칙적으로 보상되지 않는 조건이다.

다) 분손 담보(With Average ; W.A.)

이것은 단독해손담보라고도 하며, 전손·공동해손은 물론 단독해손인 분손도 보험증권에 열거되어 담보하는 위험에 의한 손해인 한 모두 보상해 주는 조건이다.

라) 전 위험담보(All Risks ; A/R)

이 조건은 법률 또는 약관에 의해 면책되는 것 이외의 모든 멸실·손상을 보상해 주는 조건이다. 즉 All Risks 조건은 담보하는 위험 이외에 보험 증권에 열거되어 있지 않은 이른바 특약에 의해 담보하는 위험을 별도의 특약 없이도 담보한다.

(2) 신협회적하약관

가) Institute Cargo Clauses(A) ; 'A' 약관

I.C.C.(A)는 종래의 보험조건 중 전위험담보조건[I.C.C.(A/R)]과 유사한 조건으로서 종전의 All Risks 조건과 비교할 때 명칭만 변경되었을 뿐이고 실질적인 내용상의 차이점은 별로 없다. I.C.C.(A)에서 보험자는 열거된 면책위험을 제외하고는 모든 위험을 담보한다. 담보범위가 가장 큰 조건이다.

나) Institute Cargo Clause(B) ; 'B' 약관

I.C.C.(B)는 종래의 보험조건 중 분손 담보조건(I.C.C.[WA])의 담보위험이 명확하지 않았던 점을 보완하여 보험자가 보상하여야 할 담보위험을 구체적으로 열거함으로써 피보험자가 담보위험의 범위를 쉽게 이해할 수 있도록 한 것이다.

다) Institute Cargo Clause(C) ; 'C' 약관

I.C.C.(C)는 보상범위가 가장 제한된 보험조건으로서 종래의 보험조건 중 분손부담보조건(I.C.C.[FPA])과 담보위험이 유사하다.

■ 신협회적하약관[Institute Cargo clauses(A)(B)(C)] 대비표 ■

[담보위험]	A	B	C
◎ 위험약관(다음 손해를 담보함)			
① 화재 또는 폭발	○	○	○
② 본선 또는 부선의 좌초·교사·침목·전복	○	○	○
③ 육상운송용구의 전복·탈선	○	○	○
④ 본선·부선·운송용구의 타물과의 충돌·접촉	○	○	○
⑤ 피난항에서의 화물의 하역	○	○	○
⑥ 지진, 화산의 분화, 낙뢰	○	○	×
◎ 위험약관(다음 위험으로 생긴 보험목적의 멸실·손상			
① 공동해손희생손해	○	○	○
② 투하	○	○	○
- 파도에 의한 갑판상 유실	○	○	×
③ 본선·부선·선창·운송용구·컨테이너·리프트벤[6] 또는 보관장소에 해수·호수·하천수의 유입	○	○	×
① 본선·부선으로의 선적 또는 하역작업 중 바다에 빠지거나 추락한 포장당 전손	○	×	×
⑫ 공동해손약관(공동해손·구조료), 면책위험과 관련된 것은 제외됨	○	○	○
⑭ 쌍방과실충돌	○	○	○
[면책위험]	**A**	**B**	**C**
◎ 여하한 경우에도 다음의 손해는 담보하지 않음			
① 피보험자의 고의적 위법행위에 기인한 멸실, 손상 및 비용	×	×	×
② 통상의 누손, 통상의 중량, 용적상의 통상의 손실 및 통상의 자연손모	×	×	×
③ 포장 또는 준비의 불충분으로 인한 멸실, 손상 또는 비용	×	×	×
④ 피보험목적 고유의 하자 또는 성질로 인해 발생한 멸실, 손상, 비용	×	×	×
⑤ 지연이 담보위험에 의하여 생긴 경우라도 해당 지연을 근인으로 하여 생긴 멸실·손상 및 비용	×	×	×
⑥ 선주·관리자·용선자·운항자의 파산 또는 재정상의 채무 불이행으로부터 생긴 멸실, 손상 및 비용	×	×	×
⑦ 보험의 목적이나 그 일부에 대해 발행한 여하한 자의 불법행위에 의한 고의적인 손상이나 파괴	○	×	×
⑧ 원자력 또는 핵의 분열, 융합, 이와 유사한 반응 또는 방사능이나 방사성물질을 응용한 핵무기에 의한 멸실, 손상 또는 비용	×	×	×
◎ 불내항, 부적합면책약관			
① 피보험자 또는 그 사용인이 인지하지 못한 선박의 불내항성, 부적합으로부터 생긴 멸실, 손상 또는 비용은 담보하지 않음	×	×	×

6) Liftvan이란)컨테이너 이외의 유사한 용기를 말한다. 벤 또는 바스킷이라고도 한다.

◎ **전쟁위험약관**			
다음 사유로 인하여 발생한 멸실, 손상 또는 비용은 담보하지 않음			
① 전쟁, 내란, 혁명, 모반, 반란 또는 이로 인해 발생한 구내투쟁, 교전구에 의해 또는 교전구에 대해 행해진 적대행위	×	×	×
② 포획, 나포, 강류, 억지 또는 억류 및 그 행위의 결과 또는 행위의 기도	×	×	×
- 해적행위	○	×	×
③ 유기된 기뢰, 어뢰, 폭탄 또는 기타의 유기된 전쟁무기	×	×	×
◎ **동맹파업위험면책약관**			
다음의 멸실, 손상 또는 비용은 담보하지 않음			
① 동맹파업자, 직장폐쇄를 당한 노동자 또는 노동분쟁, 소요 또는 폭도에 가담한 자에 의하여 발생한 것	×	×	×
② 동맹파업, 직장폐쇄, 노동분쟁, 소요 또는 폭동의 결과로 생긴 것	×	×	×
③ 테러리스트 또는 정치적 동기로 행동하는 자에 의하여 발생한 것	×	×	×

Ⅱ 해상적하보험관계 통신문

Model letter 1 해상보험 문의

Dear Sirs,

We will be sending on behalf of our clients, Delta Computer Ltd., a consignment of 20 computers to N.Z. Business Machines Pty., Wellington, New Zealand. The consignment is to be loaded on to the SS Northern Sea which sails from Tilbury on May 23 and is due in Wellington on June 20.

Details with regard to packing and values are attached, and we would be grateful if you could quote a rate covering all risks from port to port.

As the matter is urgent, we would appreciate a prompt reply. Thank you.

Yours faithfully,

Notes

- on behalf of ~을 대신하여
- sails from Tilbury on May 23 and is due in Wellington on June 20 영국의 틸버리에 5월 23일 출항하여 6월 20일 뉴질랜드 월링턴 도착 예정인
- quote a rate covering all risks from port to port 항구로부터 항구까지 전 위험담보조건의 보험료를 견적하다
- As the matter is urgent 그 문제가 긴급하므로

Model letter 2 보험요율 문의

Dear Sirs,

Please quote us your lowest rate for marine insurance, ICC(C), including War Risk on a shipment of 10 cases of dyed cotton velveteen, valued at USD10,000 CIF Manila per m/v "White Bear" from Busan to Manila.

The ship will set sail from Busan on the 2nd of August and we hope to have your reply at your first convenience.

Yours faithfully,

Notes

- low rate 최저율
- marine insurance 해상보험
- War Risk 전쟁위험
- shipment 선적품
- dyed cotton velveteen 염색한 면 벨베트

Model letter 3 보험료율 안내

Dear Sirs,

In reply to your inquiry August 2, 20--, we quote you the rate of marine insurance at 30 cents per one hundred dollars ICC(A), including War Risk on the shipment referred to in your letter.

This is an exceptionally low rate, because many companies hesitate to take the risk at any premium whatever, due to the heavy average to which they are exposed in the China Sea owing to the present hostilities between Country A and Country B,

We look forward to doing business with you.

Yours very truly,

Notes

- 30 cents per one hundred dollars 100달러당 30센트. 0.3%
- referred to 언급한
- hesitate to take the risk 그 위험 부담을 주저하다.
- heavy average 극심한 훼손
- present hostilities 현재의 전쟁상태

Model letter 4 부보요청

Dear Sirs,

Please insure against all risks to the value of £1,500 on five cases of cotton piece goods, marked,

K.R.S	11/15

Singapore

and shipped for account of Kurt Richard & Sons, Singapore, on s.s. "Jehmoolpoh" sailing from Inchon on 17th November.

Be good enough to effect this at once, and let us have the policy together with a note of the charges.

Yours truly,

Notes

- cotton piece goods 면제품
- on board s.s. "Jehmoolpoh" 기선 "제물포"호에 적재하여
- sailing from ~에서 출항할
- effect 부보하다, 보험계약을 체결하다(= cover, open, provide)
  (cf. insure (금액) against(from) the risk(fire, all risk) on the cargo)
- effect this 부보하다(to effect insurance)
- policy 보험증권
- together with ~과 함께
- a note of the charge (소요) 비용계산서

Model letter 5 보험계약 신청

Gentlemen : SS

We have been instructed by our friends, American Import Corp. of New York to make an insurance contract with American Underwriters Inc., Seoul on the following goods which are going to forward to New York by the S.S. "Nam Hae", leaving Busan on or about September 5:

1-20 20 cases Sundries.
New York

Please effect insurance for US$6,500 on ICC(B) at the best possible rate and send us the policy in triplicate together with the bill for the charges.

Please let us also have your quotations for cotton towels in cases to Singapore on ICC(C) terms. The goods will be suitably packed for export and go by A_1 Steamer.

Yours truly,

Notes

- policy in triplicate 보험증권 3통
- the bill for the charges 비용청구서
- by A_1 Steamer = by the first-class steamer 일류 기선으로

Model letter 6 보험계약 완료통지

Gentlemen :

In compliance with your instruction of July 8, we have effected insurance with the Global Marine Insurance Company for US$2,500 on 5 cases of Cotton Goods, to be shipped from this port to New York per S.S. "Oriental" on ICC(C). terms at $2\frac{1}{2}$% including non-delivery and theft/pilferage risks, which is the lowest rate of premium we can procure at present.

Enclosed is the policy and we shall be obliged by your remitting us the amount of the annexed account at an early date.

Yours truly,

Notes

- in compliance with~ ~에 따라
- including non-delivery and theft/pilferage risks 불착 및 도난보험 특약으로, 즉 T&P.N.D. Clauses(Theft and Pilferage, Non-Delivery Clauses) 특약의 W.A. 조건으로 부보 하였다는 뜻
- obliged by your remitting us 송금해 주시면 대단히 고맙겠습니다
- annexed account 첨부한 계산서

Model letter 7 지시대로 부보 했음을 통지

Gentlemen :

Thank you for your fax of October 10 referring to Marine insurance for your Order No. 753.

In compliance with your instructions, we have effected insurance against War and S.R.C.C Risks with the Tokil Marine & Fire Insurance Co., Ltd. for U.S. $24,500 on fifty(50) cases of M.T.B. Parts.

Therefore all shipments are to be covered on ICC(A) Clause including War and S.R.C.C Risks for 110% of invoice value.

Please note that our C.I.P. prices are quoted on the basis of ICC(A) only. So we could effect insurance against War and S.R.C.C Risks by your account as per Sales Notes No. 401.

Your orders have been arranged for shipment by a UA Freight Cargo to Detroit. Upon receiving the freight number we will send you the shipping advice by fax.

Best Regards,

Notes

- in compliance with ~에 따라
- S.R.C.C Strikes, Riots, and Civil Commotions 동맹파업, 소요 및 내란
- shipping advice 선적통지

Model letter 8 보험금 지불요구

Dear Sirs,

Re : Your B/L No. BUSP-1010

In reference to the above, we regret to inform you that the shipment arrived at Hongkong on 15th August in a damaged condition.

The result of the joint survey completed by the marine surveyor, Messrs. Cornes & Co., Ltd., shows 10,000 feet of the steel pipe to be rusted.

We enclose herewith 4 debit notes for total of USD 87,000 and shall be much obliged if you send us your cheque for the said amount in settlement of our claim at your earliest convenience.

Necessary document copies of invoice and Bill of Lading are enclosed.

We will appreciate your kind attention to this matter soon.

Faithfully yours,

Notes

- in a damaged condition 손상된 상태로
- joint survey 선사, 수하인, 보험자 등 이해 관련자들이 합동으로 시행하는 감정
- in settlement of ~의 지급으로
- debit note 차변표(借邊票)

① THE MARINE INSURANCE CO., LTD
MARINE CARGO INSURANCE POLICY

<table>
<tr><td colspan="3">② **Assured** KOREA TRADING CO., LTD.</td></tr>
<tr><td colspan="2">③ Policy No. HOT 52642</td><td>**3-1 Ref. No.** L/C NO. KKY521534</td></tr>
<tr><td colspan="2">④ *Claims, if any, payable at/in* NEW YORK, NY</td><td rowspan="3">3-2 Amount insured hereunder
US$80,130.-
(SAY EUGHTY THOUNSAND ONE HUNDRED AND THIRTY ONLY)</td></tr>
<tr><td colspan="2">⑤ *Survey should be approved by* TOPLOS & HARDING INC. NEW YORK, NY</td></tr>
<tr><td>⑥ Local Vessel or Conveyance</td><td>⑦ From(interior port or place of loading)</td></tr>
<tr><td>⑧ Ship or Vessel TITANIC</td><td>⑨ Sailing on or about MARCH 29, 20XX</td><td rowspan="3">3-3 conditions and warranties

ICC(A)</td></tr>
<tr><td>⑩ at and from BUSAN, KOREA</td><td>11 transshipped at</td></tr>
<tr><td>12 arrived at NEW YORK, NY</td><td>13 thence to</td></tr>
<tr><td colspan="3">KIA
LEATHER GARMENT
C/T NO. 1-200
MADE IN KOREA

200 CARTONS OF LEATHER GARMENTS.

14 Subject-matter Insured
□ Subject to the following Clauses as per back hereof
□ Institute Cargo Clauses specified above
□ Institute replacement Clauses(applying to machinery)
□ On-Deck Clause
□ Marks and Numbers as per Invoice No. specified above</td></tr>
<tr><td colspan="2">**15 Place and Date signed in** SEOUL, KOREA. MARCH 22. 20XX</td><td>**16 Numbers of Policies issued**
ORIGINAL 2, COPY 3</td></tr>
</table>

⑳ IMPORTANT

PROCEDURE IN THE EVENT OF LOSS OR DAMAGE FOR WHICH UNDERWRITERS BE LIABLE

It is the duty of the Assured and their Agent, in all cases, to take such measures as may be reasonable for the purpose of averting or minimizing a loss and to ensure that all rights against Carriers, Bailees or other third parties are properly preserved and exercised. In particular, the Assured or their Agents are required;

1. To claim immediately on the Carriers, Port Authorities or other Bailees for any missing packages.
2. In no circumstances, except under written protest, to give clean receipts where goods are in doubtful condition.
3. When delivery is made by Container, to ensure that the Container and its seals are examined immediately by their responsible official. If the Container is delivered damaged or with seals broken or missing or with seals other than as stated in the shipping documents, to clause the delivery receipt accordingly and retain all defective or irregular seals for subsequent identification.
4. To apply immediately for survey by Carriers' or other Bailees' Representative if any loss or damage be apparent and claim on the carriers or other Bailees for any actual loss or damage found at such survey.
5. To give notice in writing to the Carriers or other Bailees within 3 days of delivery if the loss or damage found at such survey.

NOTE : The Consignees or their Agent are recommended to make themselves familiar with the regulation of the Port Authorities at the port of discharge.

INSTRUCTION FOR SURVEY

In the event of loss or damage which may involve a claim under this insurance, immediate notice of such loss or damage should be given to and a Survey Report obtained from this Company's Office or Agents specified in this Policy or Certificate.

DOCUMENTATION OF CLAIMS

To enable claims to be dealt with promptly, the Assured or their Agents are advised to submit all available supporting documents without delay, including when applicable;

1. Original policy or certificate of insurance.
2. Original or Certified copy of shipping invoices, together with shipping specification and/or weight notes.
3. Original or certified copy of Bill of Lading and/or other contract of carriage.
4. Survey report or other documentary evidence to show the extent of the loss or damage.
5. Landing account and weight notes at port of discharge and final destination.
6. Correspondence exchanged with the Carriers and other Parties regarding their liability for the loss or damage.

In the event of loss or damage arising under this policy, no claims will be admitted unless a survey has been held with the approval of this company's office or Agents specified in this policy.

18 CONDITION

Notwithstanding anything contained herein or attached to the contrary, this insurance is understood and agreed to be subject to English law and practice only as to liability for and settlement of any and all claims.

This insurance does not cover any loss or damage to the property which at the time of the happening of such loss or damages is insured by or would but for the existence of this Policy be insured by any fire or other insurance policy or policies except in respect of any excess beyond the amount which would have been payable under the fire or other insurance policy or policies had this insurance not been effected.

We, THE MARINE INSURANCE CO.., LTD. hereby agree, in consideration of the payment to us by or on behalf of the assured of the premium as arranged, to insure against loss damage liability or expense to the extent and in the manner herein provided.

In wittiness whereof, K the Undersigned of THE MARINE INSURANCE CO., LTD. on the said Company have subscribed My Name in the place specified as above to the policies, the issued numbers thereof being specified as above, of the same tenor and date, one of which being accomplished, the others to be void, as of the date specified as above

For THE MARINE INSURANCE CO., LTD.

17 AUTHORIZED SIGNATORY

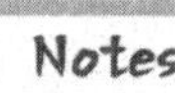 Notes

1. 보험회사(보험자)
2. 피보험자(Assured) 또는 보험계약자 : CIF에서 피보험자에 대한 별도의 약정이나 지시가 없으면 수출자가 자신을 피보험자로 하여 발급받은 후, 환어음 매입 시 백지배서에 의해 양도하면 됨
3. 보험증권 번호(Policy No,) : 보험회사가 피보험자에게 보험증권을 교부할 때 부여하는 일련번호
   3-1 참조번호(Ref. No.) : 보험회사가 업무상 참조하기 위한 번호로서 통상 수출의 경우에는 L/C 또는 E/L의 번호를 수입의 경우에는 상업송장 또는 I/L의 번호를 기재함
   3-2 보험금액(Amount insured hereunder) 보험계약자가 부보한 금액, 보험사고가 발생하였을 때, 보험회사가 손해보상액 즉 보험금(Loss or Claim Paid)으로 지급하는 최고한도액, 보험금액은 보험가액(CIF)에 희망이익 10%를 가산한 110%가 되는 것이 보통
   3-3 보험조건(conditions and warranties) 매매계약에서 합의한 보험조건을 기재, 추가 보험조건도 기재
4. 보험금 지급지(Claims, if any, payable at/in) : 일반적으로 수출의 경우에는 화물의 최종목적항이 기재됨
5. 손해사고 통지서(Survey should be approved by) : 피보험화물에 손해가 발생하였을 때 지체없이 통지해야 할 곳인데, 수출의 경우에는 최종목적항에 있는 보험회사의 대리점 또는 Llyod's Agent의 상호 및 주소가 명시됨

6-7. 국내운송용구 및 출하지(Local Vessel or Conveyance/ From(interior port or place of loading) : 화물의 출하지와 선적지가 다른 경우에 출하지로부터 선적지까지의 운송화물에 대한 부보 시 기재하게 되는데, Local Vessel or Conveyance은 국내운송용구이며, From(interior port or place of loading)는 출하항 또는 출하지임

8. 선박명(Ship or Vessel) :
9. 출항일(Sailing on or about) : 적재선박이 선적항을 출항하는 연월일 또는 예정 연월일을 기재, 선하증권의 일자와 일치하여야 함
10. 선적항
11. 환적항
12. 양륙항
13. 최종목적지와 운송용구(thence to) : 최종목적지가 내륙지에 있어 양륙항과 목적지가 다른 경우, 운송약관에 따라 양륙항에서 최종목적지까지의 운송화물에 대하여 부보할 때, 최종목적지와 운송용구를 기재함. 예를 들어 양륙항이 Seattle이고 최종목적지가 Detroit인데 철도화차를 이용하여 운송한다면 thence to Detroit by rail과 같이 기재하고 운송용구가 불명한 때에는 Land conveyance 또는 any conveyance라고 기재함
14. 피보험화물의 명세(Subject-matter Insured) : 화물의 품명, 수량, 화인 등을 신용장이나 선화증권의 기재 내용대로 기재
15. 보험증권의 발행지와 발행일(Place and Date signed in) : 발행일은 선화증권 발행일보다 이전이어야 함
16. 보험증권의 발행매수(Numbers of Policies issued) : 보통 2통이 발급되며, 그중 1통에

의해 보상되면 나머지 1통은 무효가 됨

17. 보험회사의 서명 : 해상증권은 보험자 또는 보험자의 대리인에 의하여 서명되어야 함

18. 본문약관 : 신 보험증권 신양식의 본문약관은 구 약식의 본문약관보다 아주 간결하게 되어 있음, 그 내용은 준거법조항, 타보험조항, 약인조항, 선서조항으로 되어 있음
Notwithstanding anything contained herein or attached to the contrary, this insurance is understood and agreed to be subject to English law and practice only as to liability for and settlement of any and all claims.
이 증권의 내용에도 불구하고 또는 첨부물에도 불구하고, 이 보험은 모든 배상청구의 책임과 조정에 대해서만은 영국의 법과 관습을 준수한다는 것으로 이해되는 것으로 합의된다. 타보험조항(이득금지조항)이란 재물보험에서 하나의 손해에 대하여 보상책임을 같이하는 보험자가 둘 이상 있는 경우에 보험자 간에 분담여부 및 보상방법을 사전에 약정해 놓은 약관조항을 말한다, 이를 통해 둘 이상의 보험계약으로 피보험자가 이중이득을 얻는 것을 방지하고 보험자 간에 손해분담을 공평하게 하려는 목적이 있다.

19. 난외약관 : 구 약관에 있던 이탤릭체 약관에 대체된 것으로서 Important Clause(중요사항 약관)이라고 하는데 클레임 발생시에 피보험자가 취해야 할 각종 조치 및 절차 등을 일괄 규정하고 있다.
PROCEDURE IN THE EVENT OF LOSS OR DAMAGE FOR WHICH UNDERWRITERS BE LIABLE INSTRUCTION FOR SURVEY DOCUMENTATION OF CLAIMS

단어 및 어휘연구 ••• **상대방의 회신을 기다리는 경우**

- We are looking forward to hearing from you in this matter.
- Since time is running short, we would appreciate your immediate reply.
- We highly appreciate your courtesy in advising this matter to our attention.
- We hope to receive your favor at an early date.
- We await the favor of your early reply.
- A prompt reply would greatly oblige us.
- Your detailed reply will have our utmost attention.
- For further information, please refer to us.

Useful Expressions

1. Please effect insurance on W.A. including War Risk.
   전쟁위험 포함 W.A 조건으로 부보하십시오.

2. Will you please arrange to take out a WA 3% insurance for us on the following consignment of cement ?
   다음의 시멘트 적송품에 대하여 분손 3% 보험에 부보 할 준비를 하시겠습니까?

3. Please quote your rate for a FPA open policy for $25,000 to cover shipments of steel bar and steel sheet from Manchester to Korean ports.
   맨체스타에서 한국항구에까지 철대와 철판 선적 품을 부보하기 위해 25,000불의 분손부 담보조건의 요율을 제시해 주십시오.

4. Please effect insurance for U.S.$240.000 on the goods with F.P.A. term including War Risks, Theft, Pilferage and Non-delivery.
   그 물품에 대해 전쟁, 도난, 발하, 불착위험을 포함하여 분손 부담보조건 240,000불로 부보하여 주십시오.

5. We wish you to effect an open cover for FPA., on the cargo for $ 100,000.
   적하에 대하여 보험금액 100,000불을 분손부담보조건으로 예정보험에 부보 하여 주십시오

6. We would like to insure the goods for 110% of the invoice value.
   그 물품에 대해 송장가액의 110%로 부보하고 싶습니다.

7. Will you please say whether you can issue an all-risks policy on these shipments?
   이 선적품에 대한 전 위험담보 보험 증권을 발행하실 수 있는지 말씀해 주시겠습니까?

8. As soon as I am in possession of any further particulars as to freight, I shall not fail to give you the necessary information for your guidance in effecting insurance.
운임에 대하여 더욱 상세한 것을 알게 된 즉시 부보에 참고가 될 수 있도록 필요한 정보를 틀림없이 알려 드리겠습니다.

9. Oblige us with the lowest quotations for USD4,000 salt and general cargo, per m.s. "Thames," Hong Kong to London.
홍콩에서 런던까지 모터선 테임즈호에 적재된 소금 및 일반화물 4천달러에 대한 최저율을 알려주십시오.

10. Please quote for USD10,000, form Inchon to Australia, cotton goods, in tin or zinc lined cases.
인천에서 호주까지의 주석 또는 아연내강 상자에 내장된 10,000 달러 상당의 면제품에 대한 보험률을 통지해 주십시오.

11. The rate quoted is satisfactory. Please send cover note by return and have policy hurried forward.
통지하신 율로 만족하므로 즉시 승낙서를 보내주십시오. 그리고 보험증권도 빨리 보내주십시오.

12. Please open insurance on the cargo for USD10,0—00, m. s. "Arirang" from Inchon to Manila.
모터선 아리랑호 적재 화물에 대하여 인천에서 마닐라까지 10,000달러정의 보험을 붙여주십시오.

13. Please close insurance on the goods per m. s. "Arirang", form Busan to Manila, for USD10,000.
모터선 아리랑호 적재화물에 대해 부산에서 마닐라까지 금액 10,000달러정의 보험을 붙여주십시오.

필수암기 UCP 주요 조문 (3)

Article 4 Credits v. Contracts

a. A credit by its nature is a separate transaction from the sale or other contract on which it may be based. Banks are in no way concerned with or bound by such contract, even if any reference whatsoever to it is included in the credit. Consequently, the undertaking of a bank to honour, to negotiate or to fulfil any other obligation under the credit is not subject to claims or defences by the applicant resulting from its relationships with the issuing bank or the beneficiary. A beneficiary can in no case avail itself of the contractual relationships existing between banks or between the applicant and the issuing bank.

b. An issuing bank should discourage any attempt by the applicant to include, as an integral part of the credit, copies of the underlying contract, proforma invoice and the like.

Article 5 Documents v. Goods, Services or Performance

Banks deal with documents and not with goods, services or performance to which the documents may relate.

Article 6 Availability, Expiry Date and Place for Presentation

a. A credit must state the bank with which it is available or whether it is available with any bank. A credit available with a nominated bank is also available with the issuing bank.

b. A credit must state whether it is available by sight payment, deferred payment, acceptance or negotiation.

c. A credit must not be issued available by a draft drawn on the applicant.

Article 10 Amendments

a. Except as otherwise provided by article 38, a credit can neither be amended nor cancelled without the agreement of the issuing bank, the confirming bank, if any, and the beneficiary.

e. Partial acceptance of an amendment is not allowed and will be deemed to be notification of rejection of the amendment.

f. A provision in an amendment to the effect that the amendment shall enter into force unless rejected by the beneficiary within a certain time shall be disregarded.

- to be continued p.232 -

제10장

선적과 결제서류

I 무역화물운송

1 무역운송의 기초개념

(1) 무역운송의 의의

상품을 선적할 단계에 이르면 그 상품의 운송에 적절한 운송방법을 선택하여 운송계약을 체결하게 된다. 운송방법으로는 육상운송, 해상운송, 해상운송 및 복합운송이 있으며, 운송계약의 종류로는 개품운송계약과 용선운송계약이 있다.

개품운송(affreightment in general ship)이란 운송인이 불특정 다수 화주로부터 소량 화물의 운송을 위탁받아 이들 화물을 혼재(consolidation)하여 운송하는 것을 말하며, 일반적으로 정기선(liner)의 화물운송에서 이용된다. 용선운송(carriage by charter party)이란 특정 항해구간이나 특정기간 동안에 대하여 선복의 전부 또는 일부를 일정조건하에 임대차하여 운송하는 것을 말하며, 부정기선(tramper)으로 운송되는 것이 보통이다.

용선방식에는 선박 전부를 용선하는 전부용선(whole charter)과 일부용선(partial charter)이 있으며, 일정기간을 빌리는 기간용선(time charter)과 특정한 항해만을 위해 빌리는 항해용선(voyage charter, trip charter), 그리고 선원과 선구는 용선자가 수배하고 선체만을 빌리는 나용선(bareboat charter)이 있다.

(2) 정기선의 운임

정기선의 운임은 기본적으로 기본운임(basic rate)과 화물의 형상, 항만사정, 화물의 특수성, 항해 여건 등에 따라 부과되는 할증료(surcharge) 및 기타 추가요금(additional charge) 등으로 구성된다.

할증료에는 중량할증료(heavy life surcharge), 장척할증료(bulky/lengthy surcharge), 체선할증료(congestion surcharge) 및 도착항선택할증료(optional surcharge)가 있으며, 이 밖에도 통화할증료(CAF, currency adjustment factor), 유류할증료(BAF, bunker adjustment factor) 등이 있다.

부대비용으로는 부두사용료(wharfage), 터미널화물처리비(THC, terminal handling charge), CFS charge(stuffing, lashing, securing), 컨네이너세(container tax), 서류발급비(documentation fee), 도착지화물인도비용(DDC, destination delivery charge), 체선료(demmurage), 지체료(detention) 등이 있다.

운임 산정의 기준이 된 톤수를 운임톤(revenue ton, freight ton)이라하며, 운임톤에는 중량을 기준(weight basis)으로 하는 중량톤(weight tonnage)과 부피를 기준(measurement basis)으로 산출한 용적톤(measurement ton)이 있다. 이 두 가지 방식 중에서 많은 운임이 산출되는 톤수를 운임톤으로 하여 운임을 산정하는 것이 보통이다. 또한, 고가품인 경우에는 상품가격에 2~5% 정도를 할증하여 결정하는 종가단위(ad volorem) 방식이 이용되며, 컨테이너 내장 화물의 경우에는 컨테이너 대당으로 운임을 산정하는 Box rate가 적용된다.

2 수출화물의 선적절차

(1) 개품운송계약의 체결

송하인이나 그 대리인이 선박회사 또는 그 대리점에 선복요청서(S/R, shipping request)를 제출하고 운송인(선박회사)이 이것을 승낙 또는 인수하고 송하인에게 운송계약예약서(booking note)를 교부함으로써 운송계약이 체결된다.

(2) 선적지시

해상운송계약이 체결되면 선박회사는 계약된 화물을 선박에 적재하여 목적지까지 운송할 것을 본선 선장에게 지시하게 되는데 이것을 선적지시서(shipping order; S/O)라고 한다.

(3) 선박회사의 화물인수

운송인이 송하인으로부터 화물을 인수하는 방법으로는 첫째, 송하인이 직접 본선까지 화물을 반입하여 본선에 인도하면, 본선의 선장이 선적지시서에 따라 화물을 본선에 인수하는 방법이다. 둘째로는 운송인(선박회사 또는 대리인)이 특정 수하장소(지정된 장소 또는 부두창고 등)에서 화물을 인수하는 방법이 있다.

(4) 화물의 검량

검척인(measurer)과 검량인(weighter)은 부두에 반입된 화물에 대한 검척·검량을 실시하고 용적중량표(measurement & weight list)를 작성하는데 이것은 운임산정을 위한 자료로 사용된다.

(5) 화물의 검수

세관으로부터 수출신고필증을 교부 받은 화물은 검수인(tally man)에 의한 검수를 받게 된다. 검수인은 본선의 선측 또는 선상에서 선박회사 소속의 검수인과 함께 입회하여 선적지시서와 대조하여 화물의 개수와 화물의 포장상태에 대한 이상 유무를 검수하고 화물을 본선에 인도한다. 이때 검수인은 검수 결과를 기재한 검수표(tally sheet)를 작성하여 화물과 함께 본선에 인도하게 되는데, 만약에 검수 결과 화물의 개수나 외관 상태에 이상이 발견되었을 때는 그 하자 내용을 비고란에 기재하게 된다.

(6) 본선적재

화물이 본선에 반입되면 선박운항 책임자인 일등항해사(chief mate)는 선장을 대리하여 선적지시서와 대조하면서 화물을 수취한 다음 선창(hold) 내에 적부 시킨다. 이때에 본선에서 화물을 수취하였다는 증거로서 본선수취증(mate's receipt; M/R)을 발급한다.

만약에 선적지시서에 기재된 사항과 실제로 적부 된 화물이 일치하지 않을 때에는 M/R의 Remarks 칸에 그 내용이 기재된다. 이러한 기재가 있는 M/R을 고장수취증(foul receipt)이라고 하며, 기재가 없는 것을 무고장수취증(clean receipt)이라고 한다. 고장수취증이 발급된 경우에는 그 하자내용이 그대로 선하증권 면에 기재되는 고장부선하증권(foul B/L or dirty B/L)이 발급된다.

고장부선하증권을 담보로 하여 화환어음을 발행하는 경우에는 은행에서 각종의 불리한 조건을 제시한다. 그러므로 화주는 선박회사와 교섭하여 파손화물보상장(Letter of Indemnity; L/I)을 제공하고 무고장 본선수취증을 교부받아 무고장선하증권(clean B/L)을 발급받기도 한다.

한편, 운송인이 화물을 본선에서 인수하지 않고 부두에서 인수한 때에는 M/R 대신에 부두수취증(dock receipt, D/R)이 발급되며, 이때는 송하인은 D/R을 선박회사 본사에 제시하고 선하증권을 발급받게 된다.

(7) 선하증권의 발행

화물선적이 완료되어 본선수취증을 교부받은 화주는 이것을 선박회사에 제출하여 선하증권의 발급을 신청하게 되는데 운임선지급인 때에는 운임을 지급하고 운임후지급인 때에는 일정한 보증서와의 교환으로 선하증권을 발급받게 된다.

(8) 선적통지

수출업자는 선적이 완료되는 즉시 상대방 수입업자에게 무사히 선적이 이루어졌다는 선적통지를 하여야 한다. 선적이 완료되었음을 통지함으로써 수출업자의 화물 인도 책임은 끝나게 된다.

[무역결제서류의 구성]

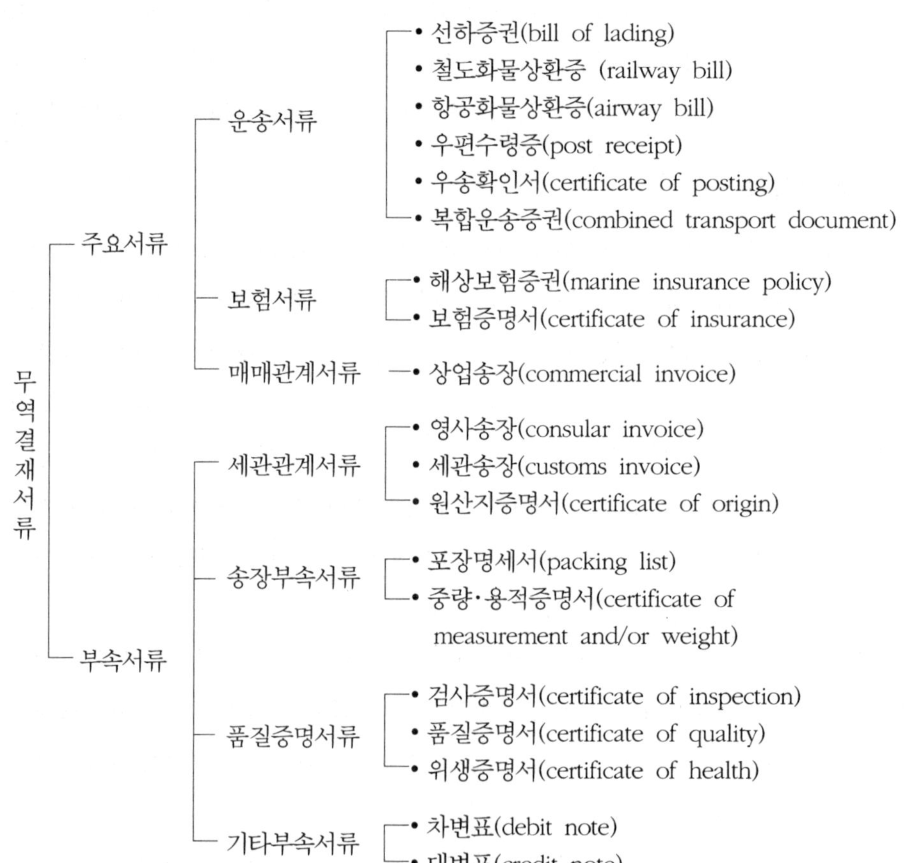

Ⅱ 선적관련 서식 및 통신문

1 선적관련 서류

Model form 1 선복신청서

<table>
<tr><td colspan="6" align="center">SHIPPING REQUEST</td></tr>
<tr><td colspan="3">Shipper
GILDONG TRADING CO., LTD.
159 SAMSUNG-DONG, KANGNAM-KU
SEOUL, KOREA</td><td colspan="3" rowspan="2"></td></tr>
<tr><td colspan="3">Consignee
TO ORDER OF BANK OF AMERICA NEW YORK</td></tr>
<tr><td colspan="3">Notify Party
MONARCH PRODUCTS CO., LTD.
5200 ANTHONY WAYNE DR.
DETROIT MICHIGAN 48203 U. S. A.</td><td colspan="2">S/O NO.</td><td>B/L NO.</td></tr>
<tr><td colspan="2">Vessel
KOREAN DREAMS</td><td colspan="2">Voyage No.
345E</td><td colspan="2">Shipment expiring date on L/C
DEC. 15, 20--</td></tr>
<tr><td colspan="2">Port of loading
BUSAN, KOREA</td><td colspan="2">Port of Discharge
NEW YORK, USA</td><td colspan="2">Final destination
NEW YORK, USA</td></tr>
<tr><td colspan="2">B/L to be issued at</td><td colspan="4">Bill of Lading required : ordinal 3   Copy : 2</td></tr>
<tr><td>Marks and Numbers</td><td>No. & Kind of Pkgs.</td><td colspan="2">Description of Goods</td><td>Gross weight</td><td>Measurement</td></tr>
<tr><td>AA
C/T NO. 1-2
MADE IN KOREA
L/ NO. 99989</td><td>20CTS</td><td colspan="2"><u>LADIES LEATHER GARMENTS</u>
MODEL : SIMON 500 : 200PCS
"L/C No. 99989"
"FREIGHT COLLECT"</td><td>600KGS</td><td>20CBM</td></tr>
<tr><td>Freight & Charges</td><td>Revenue tons</td><td>Rate</td><td>Per</td><td>Prepaid</td><td>Collect</td></tr>
<tr><td></td><td></td><td></td><td></td><td></td><td></td></tr>
<tr><td colspan="3" rowspan="2">Accepted ______________________
KOREA SHIPPING CORPORATION
By : ______________________
Shipping Division
Seoul : 397- 8900
557-0046~8
Busan : 245-4956~7
CY: 245- 9909</td><td colspan="3">Pleasure arrange to ship cargoes as described above
Applicant
add. : C. P. O. Box 8888, Seoul, Korea
Name : Gildong Trading Co. Ltd.</td></tr>
<tr><td colspan="3">Forwarder at the port of loading
Add. : (Tel)
Name :</td></tr>
</table>

<table>
<tr><td colspan="6" align="center">SHIPPING ORDERS</td></tr>
<tr><td colspan="3">Shipper
GILDONG TRADING CO., LTD.
159 SAMSUNG-DONG, KANGNAM-KU
SEOUL, KOREA</td><td colspan="3">Date of Issue
DEC. 10, 20--</td></tr>
<tr><td colspan="3">Consignee
TO ORDER OF BANK OF AMERICA
NEW YORK</td><td colspan="3"></td></tr>
<tr><td colspan="3">Notify Party
MONARCH PRODUCTS CO., LTD.
5200 ANTHONY WAYNE DR.
DETROIT MICHIGAN 48203 U. S. A.</td><td colspan="2">S/O NO.</td><td>B/L NO.</td></tr>
<tr><td>Vessel
KOREAN DREAMS</td><td colspan="2">Voyage No.
345E</td><td colspan="3">Shipment expiring date on L/C
DEC. 15, 20--</td></tr>
<tr><td>Port of loading
BUSAN, KOREA</td><td colspan="2">Port of Discharge
NEW YORK, USA</td><td colspan="3">Final destination
NEW YORK, USA</td></tr>
<tr><td colspan="6">The undermentioned cargo in apparent good order and condition unless otherwise noted below.</td></tr>
<tr><td>Marks and Numbers</td><td>No. & Kind of Pkgs.</td><td>Description of Goods</td><td>Gross weight</td><td colspan="2">Measurement</td></tr>
<tr><td>AA
C/T NO. 1-2
MADE IN KOREA
L/ NO. 99989</td><td>20CTS

MODEL :</td><td><u>LADIES LEATHER GARMENTS</u>

SIMON 500 : 200PCS
"L/C No. 99989"
"FREIGHT COLLECT"</td><td>

600KGS</td><td colspan="2">

20CBM</td></tr>
<tr><td colspan="6">Remarks :</td></tr>
<tr><td colspan="3">This receipt is given subject to all directions of our principal's Bill of Lading
RECEIVED ON BOARD

By : ______________________
No. of Pakgs. ______________________
Stowed in Hatch No. ______________________
Data : ______________________</td><td colspan="3">Please receive on board the above mentioned goods.

(회사명)

By ______________________</td></tr>
</table>

Model form 3 본선수취증

MATE'S RECEIPT

Shipper GILDONG TRADING CO., LTD. 159 SAMSUNG-DONG, KANGNAM-KU SEOUL, KOREA	Date of Issue DEC. 10, 20--	
Consignee TO ORDER OF BANK OF AMERICA NEW YORK		
Notify Party MONARCH PRODUCTS CO., LTD. 5200 ANTHONY WAYNE DR. DETROIT MICHIGAN 48203 U. S. A.	S/O NO.	B/L NO.

Vessel	Voyage No.	Shipment expiring date on L/C
KOREAN DREAMS	345E	DEC. 15, 20--
Port of loading	**Port of Discharge**	**Final destination**
BUSAN, KOREA	NEW YORK, USA	NEW YORK, USA

The under mentioned cargo in apparent good order and condition unless otherwise noted below.

Marks and Numbers	No. & Kind of Pkgs.	Description of Goods	Gross weight	Measurement
AA C/T NO. 1-2 MADE IN KOREA L/ NO. 99989	20CTS	LADIES' LEATHER GARMENTS MODEL : SIMON 500 : 200PCS "L/C No. 99989" "FREIGHT COLLECT"	600KGS	20CBM

Remarks :

This receipt is given subject to all directions of our principal's Bill of Lading
RECEIVED ON BOARD
By : ______________________ (회사명)
No. of Pakgs. ______________________
Stowed in Hatch No. ______________
Date : ______________________ By ______________________

LETTER OF INDEMNITY

DEC. 20, 20--

S. S. / M. V. " " Voy. No. Sailed

Dear Sirs,

In consideration of your handing us clean Bill of Lading for our shipment by the above vessel as descried below, the mate's receipt at which bears the following clause :

We hereby undertake and agree to pay on demand any claim that may thus arise on the said shipment and/or the cost of any consequent reconditioning and generally to indemnity yourselves and/or agents and/or the owners of the said vessel against all consequences that may arise from your action.

Further, should any claim arise in respect of this goods, we hereby authorize you and/or owners of the vessel to disclose this Letter of Indemnity to the underwriters concerned.

Yours faithfully,

Bs/L. No.

Marks & Nos.	No. of Pkgs.	Description	Destination

<table>
<tr><td colspan="3">①Shipper
DAEHAN CO., LTD
C.P.O. BOX 999
SEOUL, KOREA</td><td colspan="4" rowspan="4">K.S. LINE
Korea Shipping Corporation
COMBINED TRANSPORT BILL OF LADING
RECEIVED in good apparent good order and condition except as otherwise noted the number of Containers or other package or units enumerated below for transportation from the place of delivery subject to the terms hereof. One of the original Bills of Lading must be surrendered duly endorsed in exchange for the Goods of delivery Order. On Presentation of this document (duly endorsed) to the Carrier by or on behalf of the Holder, the rights and liabilities arising in accordance with the terms hereof shall (without prejudice to any rule of common law or statute rendering them binding on the Merchant) become binding in all respects between the Carrier and the Holders as though the contract evidenced hereby had been made between them.
IN WITNESS whereof the number of origin Bills of Lading stated below have been signed, one of which being accomplished, the other(s) to be void.</td></tr>
<tr><td colspan="3">②Consignee
TO THE ORDER OF BANK OF AMERICA</td></tr>
<tr><td colspan="3">③Notify Party
AMERICAN DRAGON INC.
500 FIFTY AVENUE NEW YORK, N.Y. 10118 U. S. A.</td></tr>
<tr><td>④Pre-Carriage by</td><td colspan="2">⑤Place of Receipt
Busan CY</td></tr>
<tr><td>⑥Ocean Vessel Voy. No.
OCEAN PEACE, E365</td><td colspan="2">⑦Port of Loading
Busan, KOREA</td><td colspan="4">⑪B/L No.</td></tr>
<tr><td>⑧Port of Discharge
NEWYORK, USA</td><td colspan="2">⑨Place of Delivery
NEWYORK CY</td><td colspan="4">⑩Final destination(for the Merchants reference)</td></tr>
<tr><td>⑫Container No.
DEDA
NEWYORK
C/T. 1-20
MADE IN
KOREA</td><td>Seal No
Marks & Nos.
KSSU1693
3/598763
FCL/FCL</td><td>No. of Container P'kgs.
200CTS</td><td>Kind of package
Description of Goods
1,000PCS OF MEN'S LEATHER GARMENT
"FREIGHT PREPAID"</td><td>Gross Weight
2,000KG</td><td colspan="2">Measurement
40CBM</td></tr>
<tr><td colspan="7">⑬Total Number of Containers or Package (in words)</td></tr>
<tr><td>⑭Freight & Charges</td><td>Revenue Tons</td><td>Rate</td><td>Per</td><td>Prepaid</td><td colspan="2">Collect</td></tr>
<tr><td colspan="2">⑮Freight Prepaid at</td><td colspan="2">Freight Payable at</td><td colspan="3">Place of Issue</td></tr>
<tr><td colspan="2">⑯Total Prepaid at</td><td colspan="2">No. of Original B/L</td><td colspan="3">Date of Issue</td></tr>
<tr><td colspan="3">⑰Laden on Board the Vessel
Date
By</td><td colspan="4">⑱KOREA SHIPPING CORPORATION
By
as Agents for the Master</td></tr>
</table>

Notes

① Shipper(송하인) 송하인의 성명/상호 및 주소를 기재
② Consignee(수하인) 일반적으로 T/T, D/P, D/A 방식에서는 수입상의 상호 및 주소가 기재되는 기명식이 이용되며, 신용장 방식에서는 "to order", "to order of shipper", "to order of issuing bank" 등으로 기재되는 지시식이 주로 사용된다. Invoice 상의 Consignee와 일치하여야 한다.
③ Notify party(적하통지처) 목적지에 화물이 도착하였음을 통지해 주어야 하는 자의 성명/상호 및 주소가 기재된다. 통상 수입업자 또는 수입업자가 지정하는 대리인이 기재된다.
④ Pre-carriage by(전 단계 운송인) 화물 인수지점에서 본선 선적항까지 운송을 담당한 운송인을 기재한다.
⑤ Place of receipt 운송인이 송하인으로부터 화물을 수취하는 장소를 기재한다.
⑥ Ocean vessel(선박명) 화물을 수송하는 선박명을 기재한다. Voyage No.(항해번호) 운송선박의 운송횟수를 선박회사가 임의로 정한 일련번호가 기재된다. 출항·회항을 구별하기 위해서 East(E), West(W), South(S), North(N) 등이 표기된다.
⑦ Port of loading(선적항) 화물을 선적하는 항구명 및 국명이 표시된다.
⑧ Port of discharge(양륙항) 화물의 양륙항 및 국명이 기재된다.
⑨ Place of delivery(인도장소) 운송인의 책임하에 화물을 운송하여 수하인에게 인도하여 주는 장소를 기재한다.
⑩ Final destination(최종목적지) 화물의 최종도착 목적지를 표시한다. 복합운송이 아닌 경우에는 기재되지 않는 것이 보통이다.
⑪ B/L No.(선하증권 번호) 선적항과 도착항의 두 문자를 이용하여 일련번호를 부여하는 방식이 이용되기도 한다. 예컨대 "Busan-Osaka"인 경우에는 "BO-00251" 등으로 기재된다.
⑫ Container no.(컨테이너 번호) 화물이 적입된 컨테이너의 번호가 기재된다.
  • Seal no.(봉인번호) 화물이 적재된 컨테이너 봉인번호가 기재된다. marks & No (화인 및 포장 일련번호를 기재한다.
  • No. & kind of containers or pkgs 운송인이 인수한 화물의 수량을 표기한다. 컨테이너 적입화물인 경우에는 컨테이너의 종류와 수량이 표기된다. (예컨대 1X 40'CNTR)
  • Kind of package, description of goods 포장명세 및 상품내용을 기재되며, 선하증권번호도 같이 기재되는 것이 보통이다.
  • Gross weight(총중량) 포장의 무게가 포함된 총중량을 기재한다. 포장명세서나 상업송장과 일치하지 않는 경우에는 Remark를 부기하여야 한다.
  • Measurement(용적톤) 포장의 부피를 기재한다.
⑬ Total Number of Containers or Package (in words) 상품의 수량 또는 컨테이너의 개수를 영문으로 표기하여 명백히 나타낸다. "In words"는 선하증권 발행자가 직접 상품을 확진하지 못하고 발행하므로 단지 수량이 틀림이 없을 것이라는 추측의 의미로 삽입된 단어이다.
⑭ Freight and charge 상품의 운송에 따른 운임 및 제반비용의 명세를 기재한다. freight, CAF, BAF, CFS charge, Wharfage 등이 기재된다.

- Revenue tons(운임톤) : 중량톤과 용적톤 중에서 운임이 높게 계산되는 톤을 택하여 표시한다.
- Rate(운임율) : 운임톤당(per revenue ton) 운임단가 및 각종 수수료율이 기재된다.
- Per : 용적단위 또는 중량단위로 표시하고, Full container인 경우에는 Van 단위로 표시된다.
- Prepaid(선지급) : 선불운임의 금액을 표기한다.
- Collect(후지급) : 후불운임의 금액을 표기한다.

⑮ Freight prepaid at CIF 조건인 경우 운임이 지불되는 장소를 표시한다. 화물이 부산에서 선적되더라도 운임이 서울에서 지불되는 경우에는 "Seoul"이 기재된다.

- Freight payable at FOB 조건인 경우 수하인이 운임을 지불할 장소가 기재된다.
- Place of issue 선하증권의 발행지는 운송인이 선하증권을 서명하여 하주에게 교부한 곳이며, 선화증권의 발행장소가 기재된다.

⑯ Total prepaid in 선적지 통화기준 선불운임 및 제요금의 합계, 즉 외화표시 운임에 환율을 곱하여 선적지통화 운임액을 산출하고 여기에 제요금을 합하여 총액을 기재한다.

- No. of original G/L 선하증권 원반의 발행통수를 기재한다. 선하증권면에는 "Original". "Duplicate", "Triplicate" 등이 표시되며, 은행과의 거래 가능여부를 "Negotiable" 또는 "Non-negotiable" 등이 표시되기도 한다,.
- Date of issue 선하증권의 발행일자가 기재된다. 수취선하증권은 화물전량이 반입된 날, 선적선하증권에는 화물전량이 선적된 일자를 기재한다.

⑰ On board date 화물의 선적일자가 기재된다. 통상 발행일자와 일치되며, 발행일자가 선적일자보다 늦을 수는 있지만 빠를 경우에는 선하증권 선발행이 되므로 매입을 거절당하게 된다.

⑱ Carrier Name 선하증권 발행권자의 상호 및 서명자의 이름이 기재된다. 선하증권 발행권자는 은행에 서명(sign)을 등록하고 있다.

- By : 선하증권 발행권자의 서명이 표기된다.

COMMERCIAL INVOICE

<table>
<tr><td colspan="2">Shipper/Export KRBCKTRA1117SEO
Gil Dong Trading Co., Ltd.
159 Samsung- Dong, Kangnam-Ku</td><td colspan="3">No. & date of invoice

9905 BK 1007 MAY 20, 20--</td></tr>
<tr><td colspan="2">For account & risk of Messrs.
Monarch Products Co., Ltd.
5200 Anthony Wayne Dr.
Detroit Michigan 48203 U. S. A.</td><td colspan="3">No. & date of L/C
Monarch Products Co., Ltd.
5200 Anthony Wayne Dr.
Detroit Michigan 48203 U. S. A.</td></tr>
<tr><td colspan="2">Notify party

SAME AS ABOVE</td><td colspan="3">L/C issuing bank
CITI BANK, NEW YORK</td></tr>
<tr><td>Port of loading

Busan KOREA</td><td>Final Destination

DETROIT U. S. A.</td><td colspan="3" rowspan="2">Remarks :</td></tr>
<tr><td>Carrier</td><td>Sailing on or about</td></tr>
<tr><td>Marks and numbers of Pkgs.</td><td>Description of goods</td><td>Quantity/unit</td><td>Unit price</td><td>Amount</td></tr>
</table>

P. O. Box :
Cable address :
Telex code L:
Telephone No. :

Signed by ____________________

Model form 7 보험증권

① THE MARINE INSURANCE CO., LTD MARINE CARGO INSURANCE POLICY		
② Assured		
③ Policy No.		⑭ Ref. No.
④ *Claims, if any, payable at/in*		⑮ Amount insured hereunder
⑤ *Survey should be approved by*		⑯ Conditions and warranties
⑥ Local Vessel or Conveyance	⑦ From(interior port or place of loading)	
⑧ Ship or Vessel	⑨ Sailing on or about	
⑩ at and from	⑪ transshipped at	
⑫ arrived at	⑬ thence to	
⑰ Subject-matter Insured	Subject to the following Clauses as per back hereof Institute Cargo Clauses specified above Institute replacement Clauses(applying to machinery) On-Deck Clause Marks and Numbers as per Invoice No. specified above	
⑱ Place and Date signed in		⑲ Numbers of Policies issued

⑳ IMPORTANT

PROCEDURE IN THE EVENT OF LOSS OR DAMAGE FOR WHICH UNDERWRITERS BE LIABLE

It is the duty of the Assured and their Agent, in all cases, to take such measures as may be reasonable for the purpose of averting or minimizing a loss and to ensure that all rights against Carriers, Bailees or other third parties are properly preserved and exercised. In particular, the Assured or their Agents are required;

1. To claim immediately on the Carriers, Port Authorities or other Bailees for any missing packages.
2. In no circumstances, except under written protest, to give clean receipts where goods are in doubtful condition.
3. When delivery is made by Container, to ensure that the Container and its seals are examined immediately by their responsible official. If the Container is delivered damaged or with seals broken or missing or with seals other than as stated in the shipping documents, to clause the delivery receipt accordingly and retain all defective or irregular seals for subsequent identification.
4. To apply immediately for survey by Carriers' or other Bailees' Representative if any loss or damage be apparent and claim on the carriers or other Bailees for any actual loss or damage found at such survey.
5. To give notice in writing to the Carriers or other Bailees within 3 days of delivery if the loss or damage found at such survey.

Notes : The Consignees or their Agent are recommended to make themselves familiar with the regulation of the Port Authorities at the port of discharge.

INSTRUCTION FOR SURVEY

In the event of loss or damage which may involve a claim under this insurance, immediate notice of such loss or damage should be given to and a Survey Report obtained from this Company's Office or Agents specified in this Policy or Certificate.

DOCUMENTATION OF CLAIMS

To enable claims to be dealt with promptly, the Assured or their Agents are advised to submit all available supporting documents without delay, including when applicable;

1. Original policy or certificate of insurance.
2. Original or Certified copy of shipping invoices, together with shipping specification and/or weight Notes.
3. Original or certified copy of Bill of Lading and/or other contract of carriage.
4. Survey report or other documentary evidence to show the extent of the loss or damage.
5. Landing account and weight Notes at port of discharge and final destination.
6. Correspondence exchanged with the Carriers and other Parties regarding their liability for the loss or damage.

In the event of loss or damage arising under this policy, no claims will be admitted unless a survey has been held with the approval of this company's office or Agents specified in this policy.

㉑ CONDITION

Notwithstanding anything contained herein or attached to the contrary, this insurance is understood and agreed to be subject to English law and practice only as to liability for and settlement of any and all claims.

This insurance does not cover any loss or damage to the property which at the time of the happening of such loss or damages is insured by or would but for the existence of this Policy be insured by any fire or other insurance policy or policies except in respect of any excess beyond the amount which would have been payable under the fire or other insurance policy or policies had this insurance not been effected.

We, THE MARINE INSURANCE CO., LTD. hereby agree, in consideration of the payment to us by or on behalf of the assured of the premium as arranged, to insure against loss damage liability or expense to the extent and in the manner herein provided.

In wittiness whereof, K the Undersigned of THE MARINE INSURANCE CO., LTD. on the said Company have subscribed My Name in the place specified as above to the policies, the issued numbers thereof being specified as above, of the same tenor and date, one of which being accomplished, the others to be void, as of the date specified as above

For THE MARINE INSURANCE CO., LTD.

㉒ AUTHORIZED SIGNATORY

<table>
<tr><td colspan="5">PACKING LIST</td></tr>
<tr><td colspan="3">Shipper/Export</td><td colspan="2">No. & date of invoice</td></tr>
<tr><td colspan="3">For account & risk of Messrs.</td><td colspan="2">No. & date of L/C</td></tr>
<tr><td colspan="3">Notify parry</td><td colspan="2">L/C issuing bank</td></tr>
<tr><td>Port of loading</td><td colspan="2">Final Destination</td><td colspan="2" rowspan="2">Remarks :</td></tr>
<tr><td>Carrier</td><td colspan="2">Sailing on or about</td></tr>
<tr><td>Marks and numbers of Pkgs.</td><td>Description of goods</td><td>Quantity/unit</td><td>Unit price</td><td>Amount</td></tr>
<tr><td colspan="5">P. O. Box :
Cable address :
Telex code L:
Telephone No. :
Signed by ____________________</td></tr>
</table>

Model form 9 원산지증명서

CERTIFICATE OF ORIGIN

<table>
<tr><td colspan="2">Goods consigned from(Exporter's name, address, country)</td><td colspan="2" rowspan="2">CERTIFICATE OF ORIGIN
(Combined declaration and certificate)
issued by
KOREA CHAMBER OF COMMERCE AND INDUSTRY
Seoul, Republic of Korea</td></tr>
<tr><td colspan="2">Goods consigned to(Consignee's name, address, country)</td></tr>
<tr><td colspan="2">Notify parties</td><td colspan="2" rowspan="3">For official use</td></tr>
<tr><td>Port of loading</td><td>Port of discharge</td></tr>
<tr><td>Carrier</td><td>Date of shipment</td></tr>
<tr><td>Marks & number of package</td><td>Numbers and kind of packages; description of goods</td><td>Gross weight or other quantity</td><td>Number and date of invoice</td></tr>
<tr><td colspan="2">Invoice price:</td><td colspan="2">No & date of Export License:</td></tr>
<tr><td colspan="2">Declaration by the exporter

The undersigned hereby declares that the above details and statements are correct; that all the goods were produced in the Republic of Korea

Place and Date
Signature:</td><td colspan="2">Certification

We hereby certify that the goods specified above have been duly attested as being of Korean origin.

Signature:

Managing Director
korea Chamber of Commerce and Industry</td></tr>
<tr><td colspan="2">Signature of authorized signatory</td><td>7. Date of issue</td><td>8. Reference Np.</td></tr>
</table>

Model form 10 원산지증명서(GSP)

GENERALIZED SYSTEM OF PREFERENCES

CERTIFICATE OF ORIGIN(GSP)

<table>
<tr><td colspan="3">Goods consigned from (Exporter's Business Name, Address Country)</td><td colspan="3" rowspan="2">Reference No.

GENERALIZED SYSTEM OF PREFERENCES
CERTIFICATE OF ORIGIN
(Combined declaration and certificate)
FORM A
Issued in . .**REPUBLIC OF KOREA** . . .
(country)

See notes overleap</td></tr>
<tr><td colspan="3">Goods consigned to(Consignee's Name, Address, Country)</td></tr>
<tr><td colspan="3">Means of transport and route (as far as Known)</td><td colspan="3">For official use</td></tr>
<tr><td>Item number</td><td>Marks and Number of Packages</td><td>Number and kind of packages; description of goods

SPECIMEN</td><td>Origin criterion (see notes overleap)</td><td>Gross weight or other quantity</td><td>Number and date of invoices</td></tr>
<tr><td colspan="3">**Certification**
It is hereby certified, on the basis of control carried out, that the declaration by the exporter is correct.

. . . .
Place and date, signature and stamp of certifying authority</td><td colspan="3">**Declaration by the exporter**
The undersigned hereby declares that the above details and statements are correct; that all the goods were produce in . . . . . **REPUBLIC OF KOREA**. . . . . . .
(country)
and that they comply with the origin requirements specified for those goods in the Generalized System of Preferences for goods exported to
. . . .
(importing country)
. . . .
Place and date, signature of authorized signatory</td></tr>
</table>

PACIFIC BUYING AND MARKETING SERVICE LTD.

22nd Floor, Kukje Center, 191 Hankang-Ro 2-ka,
Yongsan-ku, Seoul 140. Korea Tel : 797-8721
Tlx : PBMSKBS K 23136/k25975
Fax : 798-0532 Mail Yongsan P.O. Box 68

INSPECTION CERTIFICATE

DATE NOV. 20, 20--

Account	:	JUNIOR PORTRAIT LTD.
Vendor	:	DONG SIN ENTERPRISE CO., LTD
Order	:	2056
Item	:	LADIES P.U. JACKET
Style No	:	6070
Quantity	:	235 PCS
Total F.O.B.	:	US2,867
Ship Date	:	NOV. 30, 20--
Carrier	:	KE 098
B/L No./AWB No.	:	WAC-935 129/180-8449 3242

This is to certify that the merchandise pertaining to the above order has been inspected by Pacific Buying and Marketing Service Ltd. and is approved for shipment. This inspection, however, is primarily a service rendered to both the buyer and the seller and does not relieve the seller of his responsibility to fully comply with the terms and conditions of this order. And to certify that all above merchandise is in good order and that sufficient quota available for import and export purposes. This shipment contains a proper and useable size and color assortment.

Pacific Buying and Marketing Service Ltd.
LON G. GARWOOD
(GENERAL MANAGER)

2 선적관련 통신문

Model letter 1 조속한 제조독촉

Dear sirs,

ANA 357 for Our Customers

Further to your fax of June 29, our customers are very much surprised to know your manufacturing schedule. We feel we should have been advised about such important information much earlier.

The following customers are scheduled to place an order for ANA 357 for the July-August shipment.

Customers	Quantity	Shipment
A Co.	2. 4M/T	Beg. Sept.
B Co.	20. 0M/T	Prompt
C Co.	18. 6M/T	Beg. Oct.
D Co.	1. 2M/T	End Sept

If you manufacture the products in the 2nd half of September, we cannot receive the product until the first weeks of November at the earliest.

According to your suggestion, our customers recently decided to replace the ANA 357 more frequently than previously due to the polymer problem.

The average operation period is 6-12 months. This means that five months of lead time is too long to replace the product safely.

They are very nervous about the situation, and the quantity mentioned above includes their safety stock.

Consequently, we strongly hope you will manufacture a minimum 30-35 M/T of ANA 357 during July specially for them. They are forced to undertake some dangerous operations, and in case of an emergency, nobody is able to deal with the problem.

Your kind understanding and prompt decision would be much appreciated.

Best regards,

Notes

- polymer 중합체(重合體)
- lead time 기획에서 제품화까지의 시간
- MT = Metric Ton
- nervous 초조한

회신

Your fax of July 5 and July 7

I am sorry for the delay, but yesterday I was in Salindres on account of the production schedule.

I should be grateful if you could consider the following possibilities :

We still have in stock 10,500 kg of ANA 357, which is not listed in the specifications but was explained in my fax of June 29th:

- 3,500 kg have a LOI at 1,000℃=8.8%
- 7,000 kg have density of 962 kg/m

We hope that this perhaps will suffice for your emergency needs.

Unfortunately, we cannot start production in July because our schedule is very tight. However, we have succeeded in postponing some other production until late September, which means that we can start ANA 357 production early in September when we re-open the production lines.

We will therefore be able to ship new products by mid-September instead of the beginning of October.

We are very sorry that we are unable to do more than this.

Best regards,

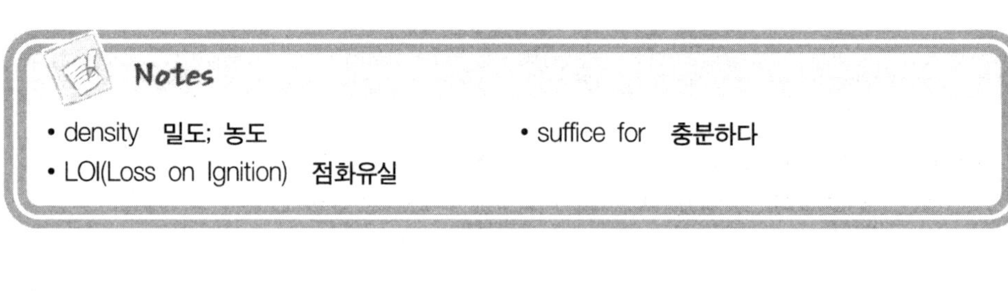

Notes

- density 밀도; 농도
- suffice for 충분하다
- LOI(Loss on Ignition) 점화유실

Model letter 3 선복예약

Dear Sirs,

We are obliged for the arrangements you promised us by telephone this morning to reserve space for two tons on the s/s "Arirang" which is expected to sail from Busan on the 12th March.

The goods are 20 cases of our Cotton Goods destined to New York, which will be warehoused by the 15th March by our shipping agents, HanJin Shipping Co., Ltd.

We learn that some advance in freight rate is inevitable due to the shortage of freight space with the approach of seasonal active transaction, but we are grateful for your doing best to give us your special rate down to $35.00 per ton.

Should there happen any change in the shipping schedule, please let us know of it without delay,

Yours faithfully,

Notes

- be obliged for ~에 감사하다
- arrangement 협정, 타협, 준비
- destined to ~행
- warehouse 입고하다
- shipping agent 선박대리점
- some advance in freight rate 운임율의 약간의 인상
- be grateful for ~에 감사하다
- your doing best to give us your special rate down to $35.00 per ton 톤당 35달러 이하의 특별 할인을 당사에 해 주신 귀사의 최선의 노력

Model letter 4 선적통지

Gentlemen :

We are pleased to inform you that your Order No. AM-258 of 2500 units of Model PB-180 have been shipped on board the M/S Arirang which is scheduled to leave Busan, Korea on January 23, and is due to arrive at San francisco on March 15.

You will find enclosed copies of the transport documents covering your order as follows:

Commercial Invoice	1
Bill of Lading	1
Marine Insurance Policy	1
Packing List	1
Certificate of Origin	1

Please note that we have drawn a draft on your bank at 30 d/s for the invoice amount, under Letter of Credit M-8747072 through the Korea Exchange Bank, Busan. We ask you to accept it upon presentation.

We trust that the goods will reach you in good condition and give you full satisfaction. We look forward to receiving your repeat orders in the near future.

Yours very truly,

Notes

- M/S motor ship
- Commercial Invoice 상업송장
- Certificate of Origin 원산지 증명서
- be due to ~할 예정이다
- Bill of Lading 선하증권
- repeat orders 반복주문

Model letter 5 선적 지연통지

Dear Sirs,

We regret to have to inform you that, as we cabled you on the 26th October, a terrible typhoon struck this part of the country on the 24th, and the S.S. "Jupita", which was scheduled to leave here on the 26th by which your orders were to be shipped, suffered serious damage while at anchor at this port.

The sailing of the said vessel was consequently cancelled, making it impossible for us to ship the goods within the validity of the letter of credit which expires on the 31st October.

Under the circumstance we hope you will agree to extend the credit till 30th November as we asked you by cable.

Owing to this disastrous calamity there is a considerable congestion of cargoes, and we find it quite difficult to secure space.

But as the goods are ready for shipment, we will do everything in our power to forward them at the earliest possible moment.

We again regret the delay in shipment, which, however, was beyond our control.

Yours faithfully,

Notes

- a terrible typhoon struck 심한 태풍이 강타하다
- within the validity of the letter of credit which expires on the 31st October 10월 31일 자로 만료되는 신용장 유효기일 내에
- there is a considerable congestion of cargoes, and we find it quite difficult to secure space 화물이 밀집되어 여 석을 구하기가 무척 힘들다
- goods are ready for shipment 제품의 선적준비가 다 되어있는 상태이다
- do everything in our power to 힘닿는 데까지 최선을 다 하다
- though it was beyond our control 비록 어쩔 수 없는 일이었지만

Model letter 6 선적연기 및 L/C 조건 변경요청

Gentlemen :

We regret to say that we are unable to effect shipment in full of your order No. AG506 for 1500 cases of Model 356-02 since there has been some trouble with the machine control system of our factory.

1000 out of the 1500 cases you ordered are to be shipped by the end of this month as arranged. As to the rest, we have to ask for postponement of shipment till July 15, and those 500 cases will be sent by the first available air freight leaving Inchon, at our expense.

Because of this, we have to ask you to amend the Letter of Credit to reflect this change.

We regret the inconvenience this matter is causing you and hope that you will understand our situation.

We look forward to hearing from you soon.

Sincerely yours,

Useful Expressions

1. As cabled on 8th February, the S.S. "Wilson" has left this port carrying the goods for Order No. 185.
   2월 8일 자 당사가 타전한 바와 같이 귀사 주문 제 185호의 물품을 적재한 "윌슨"호는 이 항구를 출발하였습니다.

2. We ask that all the goods are well packed so as to avoid damage in transit.
   모든 물품은 수송 도중에 파손되지 않도록 튼튼하게 포장해 줄 것을 요구합니다.

3. We are confident that the goods will reach you in perfect condition and will meet your expectations.
   당사는 그 물품이 양호한 상태로 도착되고 귀사의 기대에 부응할 것이라고 확신합니다.

4. The goods can be shipped freight collect.
   그 물품은 운임후급으로 선적될 수 있습니다.

5. The vessel is due at Busan on or about April 5.
   그 선박은 4월 5일경에 부산에 도착할 예정입니다.

6. We will inform you immediately by fax once we book the space for your consignment.
   귀사의 적송품을 실을 선복을 예약하면 팩스로 즉시 알려 드리겠습니다.

7. Please accept our apologies for the delay in shipment.
   선적지연에 대한 사과를 받아 주십시오.

8. We will inform you of the name of the vessel by fax a few days before shipment.
   선적전 며칠 내에 팩스로 선박명을 알려드리겠습니다.

9. Transport document should be made out to order. When you are preparing for transport documents, please send them after you check the B/L whether it is made out to order of shipper.
운송서류는 지시 식으로 작성되어야 합니다. 귀사가 운송서류를 준비하실 때에는 선하증권이 송하인의 지시인에게 작성되어 있는가를 체크한 후에 보내 주십시오.

10. We are enclosing a copy of certificate of origin about the previous shipment, which you requested.
귀사가 요청했던 전 선적 품에 대한 원산지증명서 사본을 동봉합니다.

11. Enclosed are transport documents for 3,600 cartons of fancy goods shipped by s.s. Arirang.
아리랑 호에 선적한 장물 3,600상자에 대한 운송서류가 동봉되어 있습니다.

12. Thank you for your advice of shipment and the bill of lading for the consignment shipped by Manhattan.
맨하탄 호에 선적한 적송품의 선적통지와 선하증권에 대해 감사합니다.

13. Please ship as soon as possible seventy bales of goat skins, kept in your warehouse, to Messrs. White & Co. in London, and send me the Bill of Lading.
귀 창고에 보관중인 산양모피 70표를 지급으로 런던시 화이트 상사 앞으로 출하하시기 바랍니다. 선하증권은 당사앞으로 보내주십시오.

14. As directed in your letter of March 5, we have forwarded to you by fast freight, via Chicago, Milwaukee and St. Paul Railways, the goods, the invoice of which is inclosed.
3월 5일자 서신에 지시하신 바와 같이 이 물품은 시카고, 밀워키, 세인트 폴 철도 경유 급행편으로 발송하였습니다. 동 물품에 대한 송장을 송부합니다.

필수암기 UCP 주요 조문 (4)

Article 13 Bank-to-Bank Reimbursement Arrangements

b. If a credit does not state that reimbursement is subject to the ICC rules for bank-to-bank reimbursements, the following apply:

i) An issuing bank must provide a reimbursing bank with a reimbursement authorization that conforms with the availability stated in the credit. The reimbursement authorization should not be subject to an expiry date.

ii) A claiming bank shall not be required to supply a reimbursing bank with a certificate of compliance with the terms and conditions of the credit.

iii) An issuing bank will be responsible for any loss of interest, together with any expenses incurred, if reimbursement is not provided on first demand by a reimbursing bank in accordance with the terms and conditions of the credit.

iv) A reimbursing bank"s charges are for the account of the issuing bank

Article 14 Standard for Examination of Documents

b. A nominated bank acting on its nomination, a confirming bank, if any, and the issuing bank shall each have a maximum of five banking days following the day of presentation to determine if a presentation is complying. This period is not curtailed or otherwise affected by the occurrence on or after the date of presentation of any expiry date or last day for presentation.

c. A presentation including one or more original transport documents subject to article 19, 20, 21, 22, 23, 24 or 25 must be made by or on behalf of the beneficiary not later than 21 calendar days after the date of shipment as described in these rules, but in any event not later than the expiry date of the credit.

Article 17 Original Documents and Copies

c. Unless a document indicates otherwise, a bank will also accept a document as original if it:

i) appears to be written, typed, perforated or stamped by the document issuer's hand; or

ii) appears to be on the document issuer's original stationary; or

iii) states that it is original, unless the statement appears not to apply to the document presented.

d. If a credit requires presentation of copies of documents, presentation of either originals or copies is permitted.

Article 26 "On Deck", "Shipper's Load and Count", Said by Shipper to Contain" and Charges Additional to Freight

a. A transport document must indicate that the goods are or will be loaded on deck. A clause on a transport document stating that the goods may be loaded on deck is acceptable.

- end -

제11장

환어음 및 대금회수

I 환어음

1 환어음의 의의

환어음(draft, bill of exchange)이란 채권자인 어음발행인이 채무자인 지급인에 대하여 그 채권금액을 지명인 또는 소지인에게 일정한 시일 및 장소에서 지급할 것을 무조건 위탁하는 일종의 지급 지시서이다.

신용장에 의한 무역대금 결제에서는 수출상이 환어음을 발행하여 채권을 추심하는 발행인(drawer)이 되며, 수입지의 개설은행이 환어음의 지급인drawee)이 된다. 또한, 발행인으로부터 어음을 매입하거나 추심을 위탁받은 외국환 은행이 최초로 수취인(payee)이 된다. 그 수취인이 배서하여 어음채권을 양도할 때는 배서인(endorser)이 양도인(transfer)이 되고 피배서인(endorsee)이 양수인(transferee)이 된다.

2 환어음의 종류

(1) 화환어음과 무담보어음

화환어음(documentary bill of exchange)은 환어음에 운송서류가 첨부된 것이며, 무담보어음(clean bill of exchange)은 운송서류가 첨부되지 않은 어음이다.

(2) 일람출급어음과 기한부어음

일람출급어음(sight draft, demand draft)은 제시되는 즉시 지급되어야 하는 어음이며, 기한부어음(usance draft, time draft)은 발행 또는 제시 후 일정 기간이 지나서 지급되는 어음을 말하는데, 기한부어음은 다음과 같이 구별할 수 있다.

① 일람 후 정기불(after sight)

어음이 수입자에게 제시되고 난 후 일정 기간 후 즉 30일이나 60일 후에 지급되는 것으로 "30 days after sight (30d/s)" "60 days after sight (60d/s)"로 표시된다.

② 일부 후 정기불(after date)

어음이 발행되고 난 후 일정 기일이 경과 후 지급되는 어음으로 "30 days after date (30d/d)" "60 days after date (60d/d)"로 표시된다.

(3) 상환청구가능어음과 상환청구불능어음

환어음에 대한 지급거절이 있을 때 환어음을 매입한 선의의 소지인(bona fide holder)이 어음발행인에게 대금의 상환을 청구할 수 있는 어음을 상환청구가능(with recourse)어음이라 하고, 청구할 수 없는 어음을 상환청구불능(without recourse)어음이라 한다.

우리나라에서는 환어음법상 모든 환어음은 상환청구가 가능하게 되어 있어 외국에서 발행된 상환청구불능어음도 우리나라에서는 그 효력을 발휘하지 못하게 되어 있다.

[예시] BILL OF EXCHANGE

① No.______ ② BILL OF EXCHANGE ③ *Seoul, Korea, December 20, 200-*

④ For *US$7,366.74*

⑤ AT 90 DAYS SIGHT OF THIS FIRST BILL OF EXCHANGE(SECOND OF THE SAME TENOR AND DATE. BEING UNPAID) PAY TO ⑥ *THE HANA BANK OF KOREA, LTD.*, OR ORDER THE SUM OF

⑦ SAY US$ DOLLARS SEVEN THOUSAND THREE HUNDRED AND SIX CENTS SEVENTY FOUR ONLY

VALUE RECEIVED AND CHARGE THE SAME TO ACCOUNT OF *⑧ TOKYO TRADING CO.*

⑨ DRAWN UNDER *THE CITI BANK*

⑩ L/C NO. *12345* ⑪ DATED *MAY 20, 1999*

⑫ TO *THE CITI BANK, NEW YORK, N. Y.*

⑬ *KOREAN EXPORT CO.*

(Signed)

Presidents

 **Notes**

① No.(환어음 번호) : 특별한 의미는 없으며, 후일 업무에 참조하기 위해 편의상 부여한 번호가 기재된다.
② Tiltle(표제) : 환어음의 표시
③ Place and date of issue(환어음의 발행지 및 일자) : 환어음을 발행한 도시명 및 국가와 발행일자가 기재된다.
④ Amount(금액) : 환어음의 액면가가 기재된다. 상업송장 금액과 일치하여야 한다.
⑤ 지급만기일의 표시(결제조건) : 어음 문언상의 at ~ sight of의 at~ 다음에 기재되는 것이 만기일(tenor)의 표시가 된다.
⑥ 수취인(payee) : pat to 다음에 기재된다. 환어음 금액을 지급을 받는 자로서 발행인이 될 수도 있고 발행인지 지정한 제3자가 될 수도 있다. 매입은행이 기재되는 것이 보통이다.
⑦ 문자금액 : 어음금액을 아라비아 숫자가 아닌 문자로 기재한다. 아라비아 숫자의 금액과 다를 경우에는 문자금액이 기준이 된다.
⑧ Charge to account of ~ : 발행인이 지급인에게 지시하는 내용으로서, 당해 환어음이 지급인에 의해 결제되면 그 자금은 Account of ~ 이하에 기재된 자로부터 차기하라는 의미이다. 따라서 Account of 뒤에는 신용장상의 Accountee가 기재된다.
⑨ Drawn under ~ 뒤에는 신용장 발행은행이 기재된다.
⑩ L/C No. : 신용장 번호가 기재된다.
⑪ Dated : 신용장 발행일자가 기재된다.
⑫ 지급인과 지급지 : 지급지는 신용장에 별도 명시가 없는 한 도시명의 표시만으로도 충분하다. 지급인은 신용장의 발행은행이나 발행의뢰인 또는 제3의 은행이 될 수도 있다.
⑬ 발행인의 기명·날인 : 환어음을 발행하는 자의 성명, 상호 및 서명이 표시된다.

3 환어음의 발행 및 매입

(1) 발행 부수

환어음은 우송 중의 분실 또는 연착에 대비하여 제1권(first bill of exchange)과 제2권(second bill of exchange)의 2통을 한 조로 하는 조 어음(set bill)으로 발행한다. 제1권 환어음에는 운송서류 원본(original)을 각 한 통씩 첨부하고 제2권에는 부본(duplicate)을 첨부하여 각각 다른 항공편으로 수입지의 지급은행 앞으로 송부한다. 이때 환어음의 이중지급을 방지하기 위하여 제1권에는 "second of the same tenor and date being unpaid"(동일어음기간 및 발행일의 제2권의 환어음이 미지급된 경우에 한함)이라고 인쇄되어 있고, 제2권에는 "first of the same tenor and unpaid"(동일어음기간 및 발행일의 제1권의 환어음이 미지급된 경우에 한함)이라고 기재함으로써 둘 중 어느 것이 먼저 지급되면 나머지 것은 무효가 되도록 하고 있는데, 이러한 문언을 파훼문구(unpaid phrase)라고 한다.

(2) 환어음의 매입

환어음과 신용장 조건에 일치하는 운송서류를 외국환은행(매입은행)에 제시하고 매입해 줄 것을 신청하면 매입은행은 검토한 후 하자가 없으면 이를 매입한다. 매입금액 중 화환어음을 수입지에 있는 지급은행에 송부하기 위한 우편료 그리고 수출상이 이미 대출받은 수출금융이 있으면 이를 차감하고 잔액을 수출상에게 지급한다.

(3) D/A 및 D/P 어음의 매입

D/A 또는 D/P 어음은 신용장 방식과는 달리 환어음의 매입에 대한 은행의 보증이 없으므로, 환어음을 제시받은 외국환은행은 환어음을 매입하는 대신 이를 추심(collection)하게 된다. 따라서 환어음은 수입상을 지급인으로 하여 발행된다.

환어음의 지급인으로부터 대금이 회수될 때까지 환어음의 대금을 지급하지 않거나 지급인의 지급통지가 있을 때까지 어음금액의 일부를 증거금(margin money)으로서 유보하게 된다. 그러나 실무에서는 환어음 발행인의 신용이 확실한 경우 또는 충분한 담보를 제공하거나 수출어음보증에 부보된 때에는 추심 전에 대금을 융자해 주기도 하는데, 이는 은행의 여신행위에 속하므로 신용장 거래에서의 매입행위와는 본질적인 차이가 있다.

4 수입대금의 결제

(1) 환어음의 결제

화환어음을 매입한 외국환은행은 이를 수입지 은행으로 송부하고 수입지의 은행은 이를 수입상에게 제시한다. 수입상은 환어음대금을 결제하거나 환어음을 인수함으로써 선하증권 등의 운송서류를 인도받게 된다. 신용장발행 당시 현금으로 수입보증금(margin money)을 개설은행에 적립하고 있다면 이 보증금이 수입대금의 결제에 충당된다.

무신용장 방식에서는 환어음의 지급인은 수입상이 된다. D/P조건(일람출급어음)인 경우는 추심은행(collecting bank)이 수입상에게 어음을 제시하면 수입상은 어음금액과 지시일까지의 이자를 지급하고 부속된 운송서류를 입수한다.

D/A조건(기한부어음)인 경우는 수입상이 추심은행으로부터 제시된 환어음을 인수(accept)하고 운송서류를 입수한다. 그 후 수입상은 어음만기일이 도래하면 원금과 이자를 그때의 환율로 환산하여 자국화로 추심은행에 지급한다.

(2) 수입화물의 선취보증

수입화물선취보증제도란 수입화물은 이미 도착하였으나 선하증권이 도착하지 않아서 화물의 인수가 불가능할 때 수입상과 발행은행이 연대 보증한 보증서를 선박회사에 제출하고 수입화물을 인도받는 제도이다.

수출지로부터 수입지까지의 항해일수가 비교적 짧거나 항공운송인 경우에는 수입화물이 운송서류보다 먼저 도착할 수가 있다. 또한, 우편의 지연이나 수익자의 운송서류제출의 지연 또는 지급, 인수, 매입 절차의 지연 등으로 관계 운송서류가 늦게 도착하는 경우가 있다.

이럴 때 만약 운송서류가 도착할 때까지 화물의 인도를 청구할 수 없다고 하면 수입상은 뜻밖의 손실을 보게 되고 금융기관이나 선박회사의 입장에서도 바람직하지 못하다. 이러한 불리·불편을 해결하기 위하여 수입상과 발행은행이 연대보증 하여 수입화물선취보증서(Letter of Guarantee; L/G)를 제출하고 수입화물을 인도받기도 한다.

(3) 수입화물의 대도

수입상에게 운송서류를 대여하여 수입어음대금 결제 이전에 화물을 처분할 수 있도록 하는 동시에 한편으로 개설은행은 그 담보권을 상실하지 않도록 하는 제도가 輸入貨物의 貸渡(trust receipt; T/R)이다.

이 제도의 이용으로 수입상은 수입환어음대금의 결제 이전이라도 화물을 처분할 수 있고 은행도 자기 소유하에 있는 수입화물에 대한 소유권을 유보한 상태로 수입상에게 대도하여 그 화물을 적기에 처분케 함으로써 그 판매대금으로 약정기일에 수입대금을 결제받을 수 있게 된다.

수입화물의 대도 방법으로는 수입상품을 판매하기 위한 대도와 수입상품의 창고입고를 위한 대도의 두 가지가 있다. 전자의 경우는 기한부어음거래와 같은 이익을 즉시 향유할 수 있는 데 반하여 후자의 경우는 관계화물을 은행이 지정하는 특정 창고에 입고시킨 후, 은행명의의 창고증권으로 대체하여 놓고 이를 판매하기 위하여 출고할 때마다 일일이 은행의 허가를 받아야 한다.

Ⅱ 대금회수 관련 통신문

Model letter 1 대금청구서 송부

Dear Mr. :

We have been expecting to hear from you with a remittance against our invoices of 2nd October and 3rd November both of them long overdue, 뭉 are surprised at being without your news in the matter, in spite of having sent you our statements regularly every month.

For these accounts, we are enclosing our Debit Note No. 1234 for USD10,000.

We hope you will kindly settle them as soon as possible.

Sincerely,

DEBIT NOTE

The Samsung Trading Co., Ltd.,
No. KY-333 Seoul, 1st December, 20--
To Messrs. ABC Co., Ltd

PARTICULARS	AMOUNT
Dr. to Tennis Ball of 2nd October Tennis Shoes of 3rd November	USD 6,000.00 USD 4,000.00
TOTAL :	USD 10,000.00

Samsung Trading Co. Ltd.
Park CheulSu
Park Chuel-Su
Export Manager

Notes

- We have been excepting of ~하기를 기다리고 있다.
- remittance against invoice 송장금액에 해당하는 송금
- long overdue 만기일이 지난 지 오래된
- statement 계산서
- for these accounts 이 계산을 위하여
- debit note 차변표(소액채권 통지서)
- we hope you will kindly ~ ~해 주시기 바랍니다.

Model letter 2 결제대금 수표 송금

Dear Mr. :

We have received your letter of 1st December enclosing you Debit Note No. KY-333. We are very sorry not to have paid your accounts earlier by an oversight.

Ub settlement of these accounts, we enclose a cheque for USD10,000 covering your invoices up to 3rd November.

We shall be obliged if you will send us a receipt by return of post,

Sincerely,

ENGLAND EXCHANGE BANK

EEB 12345 New York, 15th December, 20--

Pay against this check
to the order of Park Cheul-Su

US DOLLARS FIVE THOUSAND FIFTY HUNDRED ONLY

To KOREA EXCHANGE BANK
SEOUL, KOREA

ENGLAND EXCHANGE BANK
LONDON, ENGLAND

Henry Herman
Herry Herman
Manager

Notes

- We are sorry not to ~하지 못해 죄송스럽게 생각하다.
- by an oversight 잘못하여, 실수로
- in settlement of (account, draft) (계정, 어음 등) 지급하기 위하여, 결제를 위하여
- covering ~에 대한 (결제를 위한)
- by return of post 회신 편에, 지급회신으로,
- pay against ~에 대해 지급하다.
- to the order of ~의 지시에 따라

Model letter 3 결제대금 영수증 동봉

Dear Mr. :

We wish to acknowledge receipt of your letter of 2nd December together with a cheque for USD10,000 covering our Debit Note No. KY-333

We have duly credited this amount to your account, and enclose our receipt for this.

We thank you for the past favor and solicit for your further commands.

Sincerely,

RECEIPT

EEB 12345 — 20th November, 20--

Received of Messrs. ABC Co. Ltd., New York
the sum of

US DOLLARS FIVE THOUSAND FIFTY HUNDRED ONLY

in settlements of our accounts up to 3rd November, 20__

HANKOOK TRADING Co. LTD.
Herry Herman
Herry Herman
Manager

USD5,500.00

Notes

- acknowledge receipt of ~을 받았음을 알리다.
- together with ~와 함께 온, ~이 동봉된
- credit (amount) to one's account (금액을) ~의 계정 대변에 기입, 정리하다.
  (cf. debit (amount) to one's account (금액을) ~의 계정 차변에 기입, 정리하다.)
- past favor 지난번에 베풀어주신 호의
- solicit (ask, request) ~ for (to do) ~에게 ~을 할 것을 요청하다.
- in settlement of (계정, 계산)을 결제하기 위해, ~에 대한 대금결제를 위하여

Model letter 4 대금지급독촉

Dear Mr. :

The latest statement of your account payable has been forwarded to the Collection Department for immediate settlement of your balance overdue $53,993.20.

We have made special arrangement for the heavy-duty truck-trailer to pick up the complete system of machining center at your premises.

As it may snow heavily next week, we request you keep your doorway clear for easy access to the location.

Sincerely,

Notes

- pick up 정돈하다; 집어 올리다
- machining center 복합공작기계(여러 공정을 한 번에 할 수 있는 수치제어 공작기계)
- drastic 대담한; 강렬한

Model letter 5 송금통지

Gentlemen :

Order No. 115241

We are pleased to advise you that on May 1 we remitted US$2500 through KLS Bank of Boston to your account with Sumiwa Bank, Shinbashi in payment of the order No. 115241 for the samples we bought from you.

As we have remitted you by telegraphic transfer, you may have been advised of the remittance by this time. For your reference we enclose a copy of the application for the remittance.

The samples will be sent to our prospective customers who will try them for some time, and will let us have their comments afterwards. Upon receipt of their evaluation, we will contact you again.

Should their reaction be favorable, we expect to place a trial order of several dozen primarily for the customers who like your samples.

Yours faithfully,

Notes

- remit 송금하다
- remittance 송금
- advice ~of ~에게 ~을 통지하다
- place a trial order 시험주문을 하다

Model letter 6 대금결제기한이 지났음을 알림

Dear Mr. :

When as account runs a little past due, we find that most of our customers appreciate a brief note from us, reminding them of the fact, so that they may remedy the delinquency.

The statement enclosed shows a balance overdue, according to our records.

Unless you have some special reason for holding up payment, your check in an early mail will be appreciated very much.

Yours very truly,

Notes

- overdue 기한이 지난
- hold up 지연시키다
- delinquency 태만, 비행

Model letter 7 지급기한 연장 요청

Dear Ms. Finnegan :

I am happy to confirm that, as we discussed by phone earlier today, we have agreed to your request for a 60-day extension to pay the $1065.60 due on your account.

We understand that you are currently having problems with your own collections--and we can certainly sympathize with you on this point.

We are pleased to hear that these conditions are temporary and that you feel certain you will be able to meet the extended payment deadline of November

15. We agree that you will settle your account in full on or before that date.

We want to emphasize that this extension constitutes an exception to our usual credit terms. We are granting it because MDC has been a good and valued customer for many years, and we want to do whatever we reasonably can to maintain that good relationship.

However, you should not expect that we will be able to grant additional extensions in the future.

We thank you for your cooperation, and we wish you well.

Very sincerely
Albert Terranova
Credit Manager

Notes

- sympathize with ~에 동정하다
- temporary 일시적인
- to constitute 구성하다, ~을 만들다

Model letter 8 신용거래 (외상)거절

Dear Ms. Allen:

Thank you very much for the order you placed with us last week. We appreciate your patronage, and we hope we can continue to serve you in the future.

We have carefully considered your application for 120-day credit terms. We are sorry to say that, on the basis of the financial information we have seen so far, we are not able to approve your request.

However, if there is any added financial information you could send us that would allow us to reconsider this decision, we would be happy to do so.

In the meantime, we will be happy to fill this order on a cash basis, with our customary 3% cash discount.

Sincerely,

Thomas Polani
Office Manager
TP/gbb

Notes

- patronage **애호**
- cash discount **현금할인** (open account나 D/A 방식으로 거래하고 있다가 D/P나 L/C 방식으로 전환함으로써 수출자가 제공해주는 할인, Our terms of payment are 5% off the invoice amount at 60 days after sight, but we can make you a special cash discount of 10% (당사의 결제조건은 일람 후 60일 지급으로 송장금액의 5% 할인입니다만 귀사에 10%의 특별현금할인을 해 드릴 수 있습니다.)

Model letter 9 어음처리오류에 대한 사과

Dear Mr Akai :

With considerable embarrassment in answering your letter of September 10 as to the payment of your draft No. 785, I am compelled to admit that the item in point was very poorly dealt with here.

Upon looking into the matter, we have realized that the unfortunate mistakes you indicated stemed from the fact that the draft for USD 1,000 was overlooked by a person dealing with the particular item.

We have cautioned the person in charge to follow the special arrangement made between our two institution and reminded all others within our department to that effect, taking precautions against such unfortunate incidents arising in the future.

We sincerely apologize to you for this mishandling and regret very much the trouble and annoyance your valued clients and your bank have been put to regarding this matter.

Sincerely yours,

CC : The Sanwa Bank, Seoul Br.

Notes

- I am compelled to admit 인정하지 않을 수 없다
- the item in point was very poorly dealt with here 본건은 저희가 너무 소홀히 다루었다
- caution the person in charge 담당직원에게 주의를 시키다
- take precautions against such unfortunate incidents arising in the future 장차 불행한 사례가 발생하지 않도록 조치하다

Model letter 10 어음기간 연장요구

Gentlemen :

We hope this letter may find you well as usual. We are happy to note that there has been a continuous growth or business volumes between you and us. With Christmas season in sight, we expect a slightly better business climate ahead of us.

As you are well aware our business has been done on an L/C at sight basis. You are also well aware that we accepted the sight of the draft on condition that the usance would be reviewed after lapse of one year of when the volume of business has grown to the amount we initially agreed upon, whichever comes earlier.

We would like you to consider an extension of the draft up to 60 days after sight, which will be applied for contracts to be signed from the first day of January.

We are confident that the volume of business has grown satisfactorily enough to justify such financial favor. The extended usance will convenience us a lot.

Your kind attention to our request will be much appreciated, and we look forward to a favorable reply in this regard.

Faithfully yours,

Notes

- on an L/C at sight basis 일람출급 신용장조건으로
- lapse (시간)경과
- justify 정당화하다

Model letter 11 L/C조건을 D/A D/P조건으로 변경교섭

Gentlemen :

Several years have passed since we started doing business with you, and we are happy to note during the years volume of business has grown to the degree where we now see you as one of the most important overseas accounts.

As agreed, we have been doing business strictly on an L/C basis. We believe, however, we have arrived at the stage where we can ask you to consider allowing us to do business without L/C, say, for businesses not exceeding one hundred thousand dollars.

We find it mutually advisable to think of eliminating financial charges that we are forced to pay each time to open an L/C. We are sure that the new terms of payment will contribute much to the business volumes and eventually to your profits as well.

Frankly speaking, we prefer D/A terms but D/P terms are also negotiable.

We, management of Metro Manila Corp., would ask you to take up this request at your earliest convenience and let us hear from you accordingly.

To help you judge our up-dated financial status, we enclose our recent audited financial statements. Your kind consideration will be much appreciated.

Faithfully yours,

Notes

- to say 이를테면
- contribute to 기여하다; 공헌하다
- take up this request 이 요청을 취급하다
- audited financial statements 감사받은 재무제표

Model letter 12 입금 착오액 추가입금요청

Gentlemen :

This is in reference to the payment order by Gukmin Bank, Tokyo Br. dated November 8 and your credit advice of November 23 a copy each of which is attached.

Their payment order indicates that you credited our account no. 544-7-28358 for US$ 65,226.70. However, we find that our account was credited with the amount of USD 40.00 less than the correct amount i.e., USD 65,266.70 in your credit advice.

We would appreciate your investigating that item and refunding the discrepant

USD 40 to your account.

We look forward to your earliest possible response to this matter.

Sincerely yours,

Notes

- payment order 지불지시서
- credit advice 입금통지서
- credit ~with ~을 대변기입하다 *we credited you with $1,000.
- discrepant 차이있는

Model letter 13 수수료 환급요청

Gentlemen :

Please be advised that our letter of credit stipulates that all banking charges including payment commissions should be collected from the beneficiary.

We, however, regret to note that you reimbursed yourself from our account with The Chase Manhattan Bank, N.Y. for the draft amount plus the payment commission.

Therefore, you are kindly requested to examine the terms of our relevant credit letter and refund a total of said US$2,196.92 to our account with The Chase Manhattan Bank, New York account No. 001-1-544582 under advice to us.

For your convenient reference, relevant advices available are herewith enclosed. Other advices are missing which we have not received so far.

For the missing advices, please refer to advice tickets in your possession from The Chase Manhattan Bank (our L/C No.M03031-NS-206-00018).

Your prompt attention to this matter would be highly appreciated.

We look forward to your earliest possible reply.

Very truly yours,

Notes

- all banking charges 은행의 모든 수수료
- payment commission 지급수수료
- beneficiary 수익자
- reimburse yourself from our account 저희 구좌에 상환청구를 하다
- to refund 갚다, 상환하다
- advice 통지

Useful Expressions

1. Please endorse the draft in blank.
   어음에 백지배서 하십시오.

2. The draft matures on July 31.
   그 어음은 7월 31일에 만기가 됩니다.

3. Please credit us with the difference.
   차액은 폐사의 대변에 기입해 주십시오.

4. Other conditions being equal, we do prefer D/A terms to D/P terms since the former allows us to get transport documents by signing a time bill, with which we can deliver the cargo.
   기타의 조건이 동일하다면 폐사는 지급도 보다는 인수 도를 선호합니다. 인수도는 적하를 인도할 수 있는 기한부어음에 서명함으로써 운송서류를 획득할 수 있도록 해주기 때문입니다.

5. We want you to understand that the promissory note is not internationally used, though it is one of the most commonest means of settling debts in Korea..
   약속어음은 한국에서 채무를 결재하는 가장 보편적인 수단 중의 하나이지만 국제적으로 사용되지 않는다는 것을 이해해 주시기를 바랍니다.

6. We would like to stress that the draft at sight is far less convenient than that at 60 days after sight.
   일람출급어음은 일람 후 60일불 어음보다 훨씬 덜 편리하다는 것을 강조하고 싶습니다.

7. The greatest merit of the draft at 60 days after sight is that the bill enables importers to dispense with otherwise necessary import financing

including submission of a Trust Receipt.
일람 후 60일불 환어음의 최대 장점은 그 어음이 수입업자로 하여금 T/R(서류대도)의 제출을 포함하여 별도의 필요한 수입 금융을 면제하도록 해 줄 수 있다는 것이다.

8. Importers have to issue a promissory note to a local bank as security for a Trust Receipt.
수입업자는 현지 은행에 대도(T/R)의 차용증서로서 약속어음을 발행해야 한다.

9. We advise you that we have drawn on you this day for USD10,000, at 3m/d, to the order of yourself, which we commend to your kind protection.
귀하를 지급인으로 하는 일부후 3개월불 금액 10,000달러정의 환어음을 금일 귀하 앞으로 발행하였으니 인수하시기 바랍니다.

10. We have valued upon you through the Hanil Bank at two months after sight for the net amount of USD10,000, to which please accord your due protection.
일금 10,000달러정 상다의 환어음을 한일은행을 통하여 일람후 2개월불로 하여 귀하 앞으로 발행하였습니다. 이를 지체 없이 인수하시기 바랍니다.

11. We are favored with your esteemed letter of the first inst,, enclosing USD10,000 in a bill at sixty days' sight, on George Bury & Co., which, having been duly honoured, will appear to your credit at maturity.
조지·베리상사 앞 일람후 60일불 일금10,000달러정의 어음을 봉봉한 금월 1일자 서신을 틀림없이 인수하였으므로 만기일에 귀하계정에 차기하겠습니다.

12. We have just accepted your draft for USD10,000, with which we have debited your account.
일금 10,000달러정에 대한 귀하의 환어음은 정히 인수하였습니다. 이 금액은 귀계정에 차기하였습니다.

제12장

무역클레임

I 무역클레임

1 무역클레임의 의의

클레임(claim)이란 일반적으로 구상 또는 손해보상청구라는 의미로 매매당사자의 일방이 매매계약의 내용을 충실히 이행하지 않음으로 인하여 손해를 입은 당사자가 상대방에 대하여 손해배상을 청구하는 것을 말한다.

무역상의 클레임의 문제는 손해화물에 관한 클레임(claim on damaged cargo)과 무역거래상의 클레임(business claim)으로 분류된다. 전자는 운송 중의 사고에 의하여 화물에 손해가 생겼을 때 손해배상을 청구하는 것을 의미하고, 후자는 매매계약상의 위반행위에 의한 손해에 관하여 당사자 간에 일어나는 상사분쟁의 구상을 의미한다. 그러나 일반적으로 클레임이라 할 때에는 후자를 가리키며, 양자를 구별하기 위하여 이것을 무역클레임이라 한다.

무역클레임은 매매당사자 가운데 피해자(claimant)가 가해자(claimee or respondent)에게 제기하게 되는 데 일반적으로 Claimant는 매수인이 되고 Claimee는 매도인이 되는 경우가 많다.

일단 클레임이 제기되면 신속한 해결을 위하여 쌍방의 공동노력과 상호간 어느 정도의 양보가 필요하다.

무역클레임에서의 청구내용은, 첫째, 금전배상을 청구하는 것으로 손해배상금, 해약 변상금 또는 가격인상 또는 인하를 요구하는 경우와 둘째, 금전 이외의 방법으로 손해배상을 청구하는 것으로 계약의 해제, 화물의 반환, 부족분의 추가송부 등을 요구하고 있는 경우 그리고 위의 두 가지 내용의 병행을 요구하는 경우 등이 있다.

2 무역클레임의 종류

(1) 마켓클레임

계약당사자의 일방이 상대방의 사소한 결점을 구실삼아 고의적으로 제기하는 클레임을 말한다. 예를 들면 상품 시가가 하락하거나 시황이 좋지 않을 때, 이에 따른 경제적 손실을 만회하기 위해 매수인이 매도인의 사소한 하자를 이유로 클레임을 제기하기도 하는데 대부분의 마켓클레임은 매수인에 의해서 제기되는 것이 보통이다.

(2) 상품에 관한 클레임

① 품질불량 : 클레임의 대부분은 이에 속한다. 견본에 의한 매매의 경우 발생할 가능성이 많다.

② 품질상이, 불량품 혼입, 변질 및 변색, 규격상위 등의 품질에 대한 클레임 등이 있다.

③ 수량상이, 중량상이 등 수량과 관련된 클레임 등이 있다.

(3) 선적에 관한 클레임

선적지연, 선적불이행, 환적 등의 선적에 대한 클레임 등이 있다.

(4) 포장 및 하인에 관한 클레임

불량포장, 부정포장, 포장결함, 불완전포장 등의 포장에 관한 것과 하인누락, 하인의 혼합 등이 있다.

3 무역클레임의 해결방법

무역클레임의 해결방법에는 청구권의 포기(waiver of claim)방법과 화해(amicable settlement)의 방법과 같은 당사자 간의 해결방법이 있고 알선(intercession), 조정(conciliation 또는 mediation), 중재(arbitration), 소송(litigation) 등과 같은 제3자에 의한 해결방법이 있다.

(1) 청구권 포기와 화해

청구권 포기(waiver of claim)란 클레임을 청구할 수 있는 자가 클레임 금액이 미미하거나 미래의 원만한 거래를 위해 스스로 클레임 청구를 포기하는 것을 말한다. 화해(amicable settlement)란 당사자 간의 자주적인 교섭으로 원만하게 해결하는 것을 말한다.

(2) 알선

알선(intercession, recommendation)이란 공정한 제3자적인 기관이 당사자 일방 또는 쌍방의 의뢰가 있을 때 사건에 개입하여 해결을 위한 조언을 하는 것을 말한다. 상업회의소(chamber of commerce) 등의 주로 이용된다. 알선은 강제성이 없으므로 쌍방의 협력이 있어야 실효를 거둘 수 있다.

(3) 조정

조정(conciliation)이란 양 당사자가 공정한 제3자를 조정인(conciliator, meditator)으로 선임하고, 조정인이 제시하는 해결안에 대하여 합의함으로써 클레임을 해결하는 것을 말한다. 일방이 조정을 신청하여도 상대방이 응하지 않으면 조정이 개시될 수 없으며, 조정인이 제시한 조정안은 쌍방 모두가 승복하여야 효력이 발생한다.

(4) 중재

중재(arbitration)란 양 당사자가 공정한 제3자를 중재인(arbitrator)으로 선임하고 이 중재인의 판정에 복종함으로써 클레임을 해결하는 방법을 말한다. 중재로 해결할 것을 양 당사자 모두 합의해야 한다는 점에서는 조정과 같으나, 일단 중재로 해결하기로 합의한 후에 내린 중재인의 판정은 당사자가 거부할 수 없고 강제집행력이 있다는 점에서 차이가 있다. 1심에서 최종판정이 내려진다는 점과 뉴욕협약 가입국 사이에서는 상호 강제력이 보장된다는 점에서 소송과는 차이가 있다.

(5) 소송

소송(litigation)이란 당사자의 일방이 상대방에게 강제를 가하기 위하여 국가 기관인 법원에 제소함으로써 국가공권력 발동을 요청하는 것을 말한다. 그러나 무역과 같은 국제거래는 상대방과 법역을 달리하기 때문에 자국의 재판권이 상대국에 미치지 않게 된다. 그러므로 강제력을 보장받기 위하여 는 반드시 상대국의 법원에 제소하여야만 실효를 거둘 수 있다. 그러므로 소송에 의한 해결은 자주 이용되고 있지는 않다.

Ⅱ 클레임관련 통신문

Model letter 1 상이한 모델의 선적에 대한 클레임 제기

Gentlemen :

We have just received the shipments covering our Purchase Order No. 100 for Cassette Radio and are pleased to inform you of safe arrival by s.s. Arirang-ho.

But regretfully we are bound to say that some of the goods are different from the model on which we have ordered.

When we opened the cases delivered to us, we found Case No. 5/20 and 8/20 were packed wrong in type.

According to the Purchase Order, we ordered 200 sets of KM-300 packed in wooden case containing 10 sets each. But unpacking the said cases, we were surprised to fine KM-400.

We have no wish to embarrass you, for we think there must have been a mistake in executing our orders, and all we would ask is that you will give prompt attention to this matter and provide us with a prompt solution.

Yours faithfully,

Notes

- are bound to ~하지 않을 수 없는, ~할 책임이(의무가) 있는
- packed in wooden case containing 10 sets each 나무상자에 각각 10대씩 포장하여
- unpacking the said cases 해당(전술한) 상자를 풀어 보았을 때,
- we think there must have been an error in ~을 함에 있어서 실수가 있었음이 틀림이 없다고 생각한다.
- as we would ask is that 당사가 요구하는 것은 ~뿐이다. ~만 해주시기 바랍니다.

Model letter 2 클레임 제기에 대한 답변

Dear,

We are very sorry to learn from you letter of April 10 that we have shipped different models against your order.

Upon tracing our records, we have discovered that, owing to a rush of orders, employees of our warehouse made an error to pack Model KM-400 instead of KM-300 as pointed out in your letter.

We are very sorry for this carelessness on our part and in order to settle the matter amicably, we decided to suggest two alternatives as belows :

One : We would ask you to accept KM-400 at an allowance of 30% off the invoice price though the price of KM-300 is lower by 20% than that of KM-400

Two : We will send you the right goods at any earliest vessel with a special discount of 5 percent subject to all of KM-400 to be returned at our own expense.

We will do our best in executing any alternative which you may choose. But if you don't mind, we prefer the first one rather than the second, since redispatching KM-300 and returning KM-400 is a matter of troublesome work.

We apologize again for the inconvenience we have caused and shall appreciate your courtesy in accepting our proposal.

We are looking forward to receiving your favorable reply.

Sincerely,

Notes

- upon tracing our records 당사의 기록을 추적해보니
- as pointed out in your letter 귀사의 서한에서 지적하신 바와 같이
- carelessness 부주의, 소홀
- off the invoice price 송장가격에서 할인한 가격으로
- prefer ~ rather than 차라리 ~을 택하다.
- troublesome 귀찮은 일, 골치 아픈 일

Model letter 3 불평에 대한 해결노력

Dear Mr. Haverty :

Your complaint regarding your receipt of unordered merchandise has been forwarded to me. I am looking into the situation and hope to resolve it quickly. I will certainly be sharing with you the results of my investigation when it is finished.

I assure you that we are taking this matter seriously. You are a valuable customer, and your dissatisfaction is an indication of the need for improvement on our part.

It is possible that I may be contacting you for further information to help me resolve this matter. In the meantime, thank you for your patience.

Sincerely,

Notes

- resolve 해결하다
- in the meantime 한편
- patience 인내

Model letter 4 품질검사 후 배상결정 제의

Dear Sirs :

We regret to learn from your letter of March 10 that you are not satisfied with the textiles supplied to your order No. 200

As the complaints for color are apt to be influenced by aesthetic sense, it is very difficult to adjust a divergence of opinion. We trust that you may understand, as a specialist of textile, owing to the technical limitations, a slight shade of color is unavoidable.

Moreover, we must remind you of the article 7 in Agreement on General Terms and Conditions that the Sellers shall supply the Buyers with the materials which are identified to be equal to the sample : we understand this article means not "just same as samples" but "about to be equal".

After careful investigation of the cuttings you sent to us, we could not find any differences in color with regard to the cutting Nos. 11, 12, 13 and 16, which are indisputable. And about cutting Nos. 14 and 15, it seems possible that some mistakes have been made in our selection of the materials.

For a close examination, we have decided to arrange for Mr. Park to call on you to compare the supplied materials with the samples. As he is a staff member and expert in technical fields, we believe that we will be able to extract a desirable result.

As we quite understand your difficulties as a trader dealing in fashion-conscious commodities like these, you can most certainly rely on us to replace the materials if there is any serious mistake in executing your order.

And if it proves to be insufficient to some extent, we are prepared to allow you a special discount in accordance with the inspection result.

However, we are very sorry for the inconvenience you have suffered.

Faithfully yours,

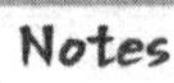

Notes

- aesthetic sense 미적 감각
- adjust a divergence of opinion 견해 차이를 조정하다.
- a slight shade of color 색상의 경미한 차이
- identified to be equal to 동일한 것으로 인정되는
- Nos. 번호(number)의 복수형
- indisputable 논의의 여지가 없는(incontestable)
- extract 뽑아내다. 발췌하다. 인용하다.
- difficulties 곤란, 역경
- fashion-conscious 유행에 민감한
- the inconvenience you have suffered 귀사께서 겪으신 불편

Model letter 5 회신

Dear Sirs :

We were very surprised to learn from your fax letter of yesterday that the sixty copies of English and Business Correspondence ordered on 25th July have not reached you.

We received your order on the 27th and, as the books were in stock, we passed it to our warehouse the same day. We phoned our warehouse manager this morning and he confirms that the books were collected by DHL on 25th August, for delivery to you.

We very much regret the delayed delivery and the inconvenience it is causing you. We have already taken the matter up with DHL at this end and as soon as we have any information for you we will fax you.

Meanwhile, may we suggest that you make similar enquiries at your end.

• warehouse 창고
• delayed delivery 인도지연
• regret 후회하다

Model letter 6 품질에 대한 불평

Dear Sirs :

After carefully examining the dress materials supplied to our order of 15th April, we must express surprise and disappointment at their quality.

They certainly do not match the samples you sent us. Some of them are so poor that we cannot help feeling there must have been some mistake in making up the order.

The materials are quite unsuited to the needs of our customers and we have no choice but to ask you to take them back and replace them by materials of the quality ordered. If this is not possible, then I am afraid we will have to ask you to cancel our order.

We have no wish to embarrass you and if you can replace the materials we are prepared to allow the stated time for delivery to run from the date you confirm that you can supply the materials we need.

Notes

• examine 검토하다
• match 어울리다. 걸맞다
• embarrass 당황하게 하다
• have no choice but to ~하지 않을 수 없다
• material 재료, 옷감
• can not help ~ing ~하지 않을 수 없다
• replace 대치하다

Model letter 7 회신

Dear Sirs :

We very much regret to learn from your fax letter of 2nd May that you are not satisfied with the dress materials supplied to your order No. 87.

From what you say it seems possible that some mistake has been made in our selection of the materials and we are arranging for our shipping manager to call on you later this week to compare the materials supplied with the samples from which you ordered them.

If it is found that our selection was faulty, then you can most certainly rely on us to replace the materials.

In any case, we are willing to take the materials back and, if we cannot supply what you want, to cancel your order, though we should do this reluctantly since we have no wish to lose your custom.

Notes

- call on 방문하다
- faulty 잘못된
- reluctantly 마음에 내키지 않게
- selection 선정
- rely on 신뢰하다, 의지하다

Model letter 8 배상요청액 지불방법통지

Dear Sirs :

First of all, let us apologize for the poor packings which have caused you such inconvenience.

We accept your claim of USD 670.00 in principle but must ask you to allow us to give sufficient time to reimburse them due to the strict foreign exchange control regulation of Korea.

May we propose to overship the merchandise in the next order by the claim amount? That is to say we ship the goods worth of USD 670.00 more than our contracted amount. Or else, for the next order you can open a letter of credit by deducting USD670.00, and we ship the goods according to the original contract.

In this way, we can reimburse your claim without going through all the red tapes required.

If you agree to our proposal, please cable us to such effect so that we can prepare accordingly.

Apologizing once again for the mistake we made, we are.

Very truly yours,

Notes

- sufficient 충분한
- overship 초과선적하다
- go through 겪다
- red tape 형식주의; 비능률
- to such effect 본 취지로
- goods 물리적 형태의 상품을 말함(통조림 제품, canned goods)

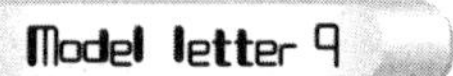

Model letter 9 클레임 신청에 대한 해명과 사과

Dear Sirs,

We have received your claim form Ref. Korea 99,01, and it has been forwarded to our quality control team in our plant in Salindres.

We are sorry concerning this quality failure, which happened in 20-- due to the following reasons:

The origin of the dust, which was noticed in some drums of ADS 2-5, was carefully checked and analyzed by the quality team.

The first action was a careful review of all the plant. It was finally discovered that some powder could accumulate in the curve of a transfer pipe. This accumulation of dust suddenly spills during the packaging operation.

Two countermeasures were decided upon:

1. To re-sieve all the products we had in stock.
2. To put on stream a systematic and periodic cleaning procedure, including an improvement of the dust removal apparatus.

In addition it was decided to improve the basic mechanical properties of ADS 2-5 to avoid any possibility of dust accumulation. We have implemented the most recent innovations of our R. and D. teams, who work in close contact with the industrial division.

A new statistical process control is now on stream. All this was successfully completed by the end of 20-- and we enclose our new data sheets for ADS 2-5 and New ADS 2-5 which show the improvements that have been achieved.

In conclusion, we are grateful for the remarks from our customers that have helped us to find, understand and improve our global quality level.

Please convey our apologies and be sure that the confidence of our customers is the most important factor for us. All our efforts are aimed toward this end.

If you need further information, please let us know.

With our best regards,

- analyze 분석하다
- apparatus 기구, 장치
- innovation 혁신
- spill 엎질러지다, 흘러나오다
- implement 이행하다, 충족하다
- on stream 생산 중에, 가동하여

Model letter 10 클레임조정 거절

Dear Ms. Wrightson :

We are sending back to you under separate cover the filigree tourmaline earrings ordered through the Gem House catalog last month. We are happy to explain the company's policy on returning earrings for pierced ears.

Because we want our customers to be aware that for hygienic reasons-that is, for their own protection- pierced earrings cannot be returned, we include a statement to that effect at the top of each page of our catalogs. We certainly have no intention of surprising our customers with policies hidden in fine print.

Since the Gem House is a mail-order company, our catalog is, in a sense, our sales staff. Because of this, we take a great deal of care with it.

The colors of the gemstones pictured in it represent as accurately as possible the colors of our gems in stock. However, colors are notoriously difficult to reproduce exactly; in addition, they vary slightly from stone to stone.

Because of these factors, it is true that the tourmalines in your earrings do differ somewhat in color from those shown in our catalog.

If you are ordering jewelry to complement a specific garment and the exact shade is important, why not send us a sample of the material? Just a small swatch would be enough to allow a member of our staff to match the color precisely.

I wish it were not necessary to return these earrings to you, but unfortunately our company policy dictates that we must. I'm sure you can understand this necessity, and I hope we can serve you in a less inconvenient way in the future.

Cordially,

Notes

- tourmal / tourmaline 전기석(電氣石)
- pierced ears 꿰뚫은 귀
- fine print 매우 작은 활자체
- swatch 견본
- under separate cover 별봉으로 separately
- hygienic 위생적인, 건강에 좋은
- gemstone 보석의 원석
- company 기업(= firm, house, concern)

[사고의 통지(Notice of Claim)]

3nd December, 20--

Messrs : The Hanabi Navigation Co., Ltd.
Seoul, Korea

Dir Sirs,

Notice of Claim

Please be advised that we have found the shortage and damage in connection with the under-mentioned cargo as follows :

Name of vessel	: M/S "TANAKA MARU" Voy No. 123
Loading port	: Long Beach, California, USA.
Discharging port	: Busan
Arrived at Busan	: 23nd Dec. 20--
B/L number	: KELP-1234
Kind of cargo and quantity	: Milk powder 2,000bags I total
Remarks of Boat Note	: 10 bags slightly cover torn 30 bags slightly wet and stained 50 bags wet and stained

For the above shortage and damage, we reserve the right to file a claim with you when ascertained, You are requested to inform us in writing your option on your investigation into this matter at your early date.

Yours faithfully,

c.c : Shipper
Business Dept.

Han Kook Nam
Han Kook Nam
General Manager
Traffic Department
Seoul Trading Company

[클레임 제기(Final Claim)]

25th December, 20--

Messrs. The WATANABE Shipping Co., Ltd.

Dear Sirs,

Claim for Shortage

Referring to our claim notice dated 25th Nov. 20--, we wish to advise you that we have found, to our surprise, the contents of 4 gunny bags repacked at Busan, saying with running out content from one drum which top was taken there due to Stevedore's rough handling, are entirely of different quality.

The content should be used Faucet and Cock af noted on the invoice which copy was attached herewith for your reference.

And the fact was recognized by a staff of Kwang Dong Warehouse Co., your landing agents who was present at the reweighing time. As the content of 4 bags being the lowest class of Brass Scrap, we are not in a position to accept it as for the substitute of our Goods.

We are therefore, enclosing herewith our Debit Note, claiming for the shortage of one drum, and ask you kindly to settle the claim at your earliest convenience.

Yours faithfully,

ABC General Manager
Seoul Trading Companyt

Encl. Debit Note
Copy Commercial Invoice
Certificate of Weight
B/L, Statement of Account

Useful Expressions

1. The goods we ordered on January 30 have arrived in a damaged conditions.
   당사가 1월 30일에 주문한 상품은 파손된 상태로 도착되었습니다.

2. Upon examinations, we find that all the cases weigh short by from 5 to 12 lbs.
   검량해 보니 각 상자마다 5 내지 12파운드가 부족하다는 것을 알았습니다.

3. There is little doubt that the breakage happened in transit.
   이 파손이 수송 중에 일어났다는 것은 거의 의심할 여지가 없습니다.

4. Unless the goods arrive by the end of this month, we will cancel the Order No. 20.
   그 상품이 이 달 말까지 도착하지 않는 한, 주문 제 20호는 취소하겠습니다.

5. Please replace the broken items as explained on the enclosed list.
   동봉한 일람표대로 파손된 상품을 바꿔 주십시오.

6. We are most anxious to compensate you for the shortage in weight mentioned in your letter of February 4 by offering you an allowance of seven per cent.
   2월 4일자 귀 서한에서 말씀하신 중량의 부족에 대해서는 7%의 가격인하로 보상해 드리겠습니다.

7. We would suggest that this claim should be settled in accordance with the arbitration rules of the International Chamber of Commerce.
   당사는 이 클레임이 국제 상공 회의소의 중재 규정에 의거하여 해결되어야 한다는 것을 제의합니다.

8. We must claim upon you for 40% of the amount.
   그 금액의 40%에 대해 귀사에게 손해배상을 청구해야 되겠습니다.

상대방의 확인을 필요로 하는 경우

- Please confirm the receipt of this order as soon as possible.
- We request you to acknowledge our letter.
- Please let us have your confirmation of this order.
- We trust we shall be able to receive your confirmation soon.
- Your prompt confirmation will have our careful attention.

상대방에게 오퍼 또는 견본 등을 요청하는 경우

- We shall be glad to receive your offer by return mail.
- We request you to send us your quotation.
- Kindly forward us the relevant catalogue and samples.
- Awaiting your further quotation as soon as possible.
- We would be interested in receiving your price list,
- Hoping to receive your best offer based on FOB.
- Your prompt offer will be appreciated.

오퍼 또는 견본 등을 발송하는 경우

- It will be our great pleasure to serve you at any time.
- May we expect your tentative order by return mail?
- In reply to your inquiry of January 5, enclosed you will find an offer sheet for full range of our products,
- We hope that our prices will meet with your approval and induce good result for mutual benefits.
- If you can place an order with us now, we can ship the goods at 5% discounted price.
- We can give you immediate response from our stocks.
- Looking forward to your order confirmation near the future.
- Expecting your volume order within the end of this month.

참고문헌

강호경, 「최신 무역영어」. 도서출판 두남, 1997

김덕권, 「Best 국제무역사」, 한국무역협회 무역아카데미, 2012

김동엽, 최원익, 「국제통상영어」, 신영사, 1998

김복문, 「최신 무역영어」, 법경사, 1996

김상조, 김영근, 이재달, 「무역영어」, 학문사, 1995

김선희, 「무역영어」, 도서출팜 두남, 2011

김원배, 신한동, 「최신 무역영어」, 삼영사, 1998

남풍우, 「무역영어」. 도서출판 두남, 2008.

서대윤, 「Business English」. 법경사, 1996

손태빈, 「신 무역영어」. 도서출판 두남, 1997

시사영어사 편집부, 「실무영어대전」, 시사영어사, 1979

양영환, 오원섭, 「무역영어」, 삼영사, 1998

이호건, 「무역실무영어」, 동성출판사, 1997

한승철, 「무역영어」, 형설출판사, 1996

한주섭, 장흥훈, 고용기, 한재필, 「현대 무역영어」, 도서출판 두남, 2008

저자 약력

■ **유 하 상**

- 원광대학교 경영대학 무역학과(무역학 학사)
- 원광대학교 대학원 무역학과(경영학 석사)
- 원광대학교 대학원 무역학과(경영학 박사)
- 관세청근무
- 서울시교육청교육과정심의위원
- 군산세관/익산세관 이의신청심의위원
- 한국항만경제학회 사무국장/상임이사
- (현) 원광대학교 조교수

〈저서〉

- 무역상무론, 양서각, 1999
- 무역학개론, 두남, 2003
- 무역실무, 양서각, 2005
- Foreign Trade Practive, Hamamm Publishing C., 2006
- 국제통상실무, 삼양미디어, 2007
- 무역창업실무, 서울특별시교육청, 2008
- 무역법규, 서울특별시교육청, 2008
- 무역영어, 두남, 2009
- 국제마케팅, 두남, 2011
- International Trade Management, Dunam, 2011
- 무역실무, 비즈프레스, 2012
- 국제결제론, 두남, 2013
- 국제통상학개론, 무역경영사, 2013

국제통상영어

초　판 1쇄 인쇄 —— 2013년　8월 14일
초　판 1쇄 발행 —— 2013년　8월 20일
지은이 —— 유 하 상
펴낸이 —— 전 두 표
펴낸곳 —— 도서출판 두남
서울시 강동구 성내로6길 34-16 두남빌딩
신 고 : 제25100-1988-9호
TEL : 02) 478-2065, 2066, 2067, 2311
FAX : 02) 478-2068
E-mail : dunam1@unitel.co.kr
http://www.dunam.co.kr

정가 19,000원

ISBN 978-89-6414-436-7　93320